Life in Old Van Diemens Land

Also by Joan Goodrick:
Vandemon's Daughter

Life in Old Van Diemens Land

JOAN GOODRICK

LONDON:
ROBERT HALE LIMITED

ADELAIDE:
RIGBY LIMITED

First published in Great Britain 1978

Copyright © 1978 by Joan Goodrick

Robert Hale Limited
Clerkenwell House
45/47 Clerkenwell Green
London EC1R 0HT, U.K.

ISBN 0 7091 6833 0

To Gregory Paul Goodrick

Contents

		Page
1	The Settlers	1
2	The System	13
3	The Early Governors	26
4	Government Departments and Personalities	41
5	The Aborigines	49
6	The Bushrangers	59
7	'Tassels on a Blind Cord'	68
8	The Factory: Female Prisoners and Emigrants	78
9	Paupers, Pensioners and Political Prisoners	85
10	Butchers, Bakers and Candlestick Makers	96
11	Operations of the Plough and Sickle	105
12	Animals and Native Fauna	115
13	Health Hazards and the Town Creek	123
14	Bridges, Ferries and Highways	134
15	Ships and Whalers	142
16	Regattas and Recreations	151
17	Religion and Education	160
18	Entertainment and Festivals	170
19	The Weather and Natural Phenomena	179
20	Colonial Newspapers, Humour and Poetry	187
21	Acts, Petitions and the Jubilee	201
	Bibliography	211
	Index	212

Acknowledgments

I wish to express my thanks to the officers of the Archives Office, State Library of Tasmania; to the Tasmanian Museum and Art Gallery; and to the Allport Library and Museum of Fine Arts, for their permission to use the material and illustrations in this book. I also thank H. Craw, B. Valentine, G. Stillwell, A. Tulip, and the Hobart Gas Company for their valued assistance.

1

The Settlers

It was Abel Tasman who first sighted Van Diemens Land in 1642, and named it in honour of a Dutch High Magistrate and Governor-General. The French were next to visit this small island in 1772, and the first English landing was made by Captain Tobias Furneaux a year later. On his third and final voyage to the Pacific, Captain Cook touched at Adventure Bay in the *Resolution* on 26 January 1777. Others were to follow in his wake, including Captain William Bligh.

The first settlement was made in the south of the island by Lieutenant Bowen in 1803. This move was motivated more by the fear that the French had intentions of annexing it than by the desire to acquire more land. This colony then became another place of punishment for felons convicted of second and third offences and transported from the sister colony in New South Wales.

The initial camp at Risdon Cove was transferred on 19 February 1804 to a more suitable site at Sullivans Cove which was later to be called Hobart Town. The population was increased in 1808 by the arrival of 554 Norfolk Islanders, men, women and children, of whom only twenty-three were prisoners, although at that period Hobart was a closed port and virtually a gaol on a large scale.

Free immigrants began to arrive in Hobart Town in the year 1816, after the war in Europe had ended. The inducements held out were the promise of free grants of land according to the rank in life and capital of the emigrants, and the lure of white slaves to do the work for them, the slaves of course being the convicts. Aid was also promised until the land could produce crops to supply the settler with his own needs. Once the flow of settlers became a steady stream, the inducements were withheld and no land was given free after 1830.

Life was still very hard for the early settlers who found themselves subjected to the English 'system' enforced by the despotic men in power. Later transports brought out direct to Van Diemens Land cargoes of convicts (referred to in the slang of the day as 'rattlesnake cargoes') in such quantities that the free settlers protested in futile anger. Thus the first people to make up a large proportion of the population were, in the eyes of contemporaries, of a most vicious description, and vice appeared to abound in every quarter.

Apart from the dangers which threatened the lives of the settlers — hostile Aborigines, marauding bushrangers and the like — their main complaints were against the Government. During the first twelve years or so of the colony the few free settlers were forced to bring their grievances under public notice by posting their complaints on the large stump of a gum tree which was not far from where the Hobart Post Office stands today. On one occasion, a free man was in the act of pasting up a notice when he was spotted by the person he was complaining about, who immediately informed the military Commandant. There and then a kind of court martial sat, and in a few minutes a sentence of 300 lashes was pronounced as a verdict, the flogging to be executed to the roll of a drum.

Settlers who arrived after 1816 were also subjected to many indignities, especially the free poor who were not in a position to be able to bribe their way out of any common difficulty. The cause of much of their distress was the long delay in receiving grants of land, which meant that many were forced to wait about in Hobart Town spending their meagre capital on lodgings and food for their families. This resulted in their sinking deeper and deeper into debt so that by the time they finally received their holdings they were without money to sustain them through the first difficult years. The gaols were full of insolvent debtors, and a letter written on their behalf, which was sent to the *Hobart Town Gazette* in 1828, stated that many had been in confinement in the two gaols in the colony from one to two and a half years! Some had their farms and properties taken from them for a quarter of their value, purchased by creditors during their imprisonment.

One hopeful debtor confined in the gaol made this suggestion to his creditor: 'I have been thinking it is a very foolish thing for me to put you to the expense of seven shillings a week. My being so chargeable to you has given me great uneasiness; and God knows what it may cost you in the end. Therefore, what I would propose is this; you shall let me out of prison, and, instead of seven shillings, you shall allow me only one shilling and the other six shillings shall go towards the discharge of the debt.' Quite an ingenious idea, but hardly likely to be acted upon!

With the arrival of the Great Seal in the colony in 1829 it was hoped that the community would benefit, and that for the settlers there would be no further delay to prevent them from receiving their grants of land after waiting for many years. It was pointed out that 'nothing can be more satisfactory to a cultivator of the soil who wishes to realize some property for his family, than to have his title deed in his possession of that estate where he has domiciled himself and upon which he has laid out and expended all his capital and labour'. Many people were afraid that their grants of land were insecure, and as a result were kept in a continual state of suspense.

The unsettled state of titles to landed property throughout the colony was still the subject of anxiety three years later, and the settlers' hopes were dashed even further when it was learned that the long promised grants were not being prepared. The granting of land to absentee owners was another great fault of the colonial Government, with tract after tract of the finest soil belonging to someone in England or India. This was also cause for discontent among the settlers.

However, for the lucky settler who had received his grant without any hold-ups, probably during the governorship of Colonel Sorell, prosperity could come fairly quickly. Those who were at first content 'to make shift with a little house', very likely would have made do with a mode of building introduced to Van Diemens Land about 1823. These were sod huts — warm, durable houses built of rammed earth. As well, so luxuriant was the pasture of the colony and so prolific the sheep that one well-known settler near the Macquarie River, whose sole stock two years earlier had been 100 ewes, had become by some miracle the owner of no fewer than 1500.

Ironically, a man could still be hung for stealing a sheep, despite their great fecundity. The lack of fencing made it very difficult for the farmers to identify their own stock, and in many apparent cases of sheep-stealing there was no intent to commit such a crime. Sheep-stealing (a term later deemed vulgar, with 'speculating in wool' being preferred among the gentlemen traffickers in that line) was still carried on extensively. A settler was robbed of fifty-five sheep in 1825, and suspected that the stolen stock was brought into town in a butchered state. This was afterwards confirmed when he met a cart apparently containing nothing but straw, but with its track 'rendered peculiar' by continual drops of blood. This method was thought to be the one frequently used by smugglers and sheep-stealers.

If the possession of sheep brought riches to some, it also brought tragedy to a great many more; in fact it seemed to exert a strange influence on the minds of many. A farmer who had been reported missing for several days in 1816 returned unexpectedly to his home at Kangaroo Point, then disappeared again, taking with him his whole flock of sheep. From then on his whereabouts remained unknown. Another man, a fettler, hanged himself, leaving his flock of sheep to his daughter. An inquest held on the body of a man who had drowned in a river near his home revealed the fact that he had been recently sheep-stealing, and to escape the hands of justice had drowned himself.

Although the settlers complained of the habit of the authorities of extorting money from them, they realised that the opportunities offering in the colony were far greater than in their homeland.

Nothing can denounce the injustice of the persons who would decry the advantages of this Colony more, than the strong desire which those, who had once been settlers, have to return to its shores. The love of our native country is too apt both to magnify the enjoyments and to smooth away the inconveniences of England, until a second residence contrasts the difference.

The *Hobart Town Gazette* reminded the people of this truth in 1826.

Those who lived in the town were concerned at the number of dilapidated sheds which spoiled the appearance of some of the main streets. Traders had stalls and sheds out on the streets for some metres in front of their houses. There were lolly-pop shops, oyster shops, butchers' stalls, barbers' shops, and a variety of others, to the annoyance of their neighbours, whose view of the street was obstructed. A little civic pride was beginning to take hold of the inhabitants, and they were anxious to see Hobart Town take on the aspect of a small city. They felt it would have made quite a difference to the town if the houses were all built of the fine white stone in the Government paddock. Every centimetre of ground from that area to New Town was taken, and it was rumoured that the paddock was to be given as grants for town allotments, so that the town could be extended on that side, in preference to the Mount Wellington side.

This of course was proved to be wrong, but people were eager for progress.

The following advertisement shows the type of home the respectable and well-to-do members of the community thought suitable to their station:

4

To Be Sold or Let by Private Contract:
A recently erected most substantially built and elegantly finished dwelling-house, in Hobart Town, containing eighteen rooms, two of which are thirty feet by fourteen, with Stable, Coach-house, large Store-room, Garden, and every other convenience required in a first-rate family residence. The premises are situated in the most respectable and healthy part of the city, and command an unrivalled prospect. Terms moderate.

Another newly built dwelling-house in Collins Street, containing a dining-room, parlour and five bedrooms, a kitchen, store-room, scullery etc., was let at a moderate rent of £42 a year, while a dwelling-house and shop in Murray Street was sold by auction in 1850 for £605.

The monotony of the scene in front of the stone buildings in Macquarie Street was enlivened one day by a performance of the almost obsolete ceremony of punishment with the horsewhip, administered on the back and shoulders. The flayer on this occasion was a builder of the firm of Barclay and Kershaw. The victim was the Government Surveyor in the Irrigation Department, lately Clerk of the Works, Colonial Government. Apparently the surveyor, knowing Messrs Barclay and Kershaw as contractors for public works, had got them to accept some of his rent bills which they had to pay, and this was the ruin of those two industrious and clever tradesmen. The horsewhipping was administered in the presence of the Chairman of the Quarter Sessions. Corporal punishment was not only given to the convicts, but to anyone who had transgressed in some way or other, even if he did belong to a Government department.

Unfortunately, the settlers had few ways of settling their grievances, other than loudly complaining through the press. Their heavy taxes kept them at the mercy of the authorities. In June 1831, because one or two of the banks discontinued their usual discounts, the sudden lack of money was felt by all, and it was feared that unless the increasing capital then in the Treasurer's chest was put into circulation every farthing would be drained into that grand vortex.

The money market became daily more and more alarming, although compared with their poor countrymen back in England the settlers were living in clover! Well-executed forgeries of bank notes were in circulation by 1832, which meant the public had to be careful of being defrauded of what little money it had. As well, all hopes of the colony becoming rich and prosperous were blighted by ruinous importations.

The *Colonial Times* published a letter from a settler, who although born in London, suspected that he was not entitled to call himself an Englishman, as he possessed 'none of the advantages of a British subject, although disadvantages were too heavily heaped upon the devoted heads of the poor Settlers'. They were taxed three times more than they had any right to be, and the money was spent just as Colonel Arthur and a few more pleased, without even asking the consent of one single individual who contributed it. The Governor was accused of behaving in opposition to an Act of Parliament, and the fact that the Legislative Council had not been called for the past four years seemed to prove that the Home Government was more content with Colonel Arthur's management of the affairs of the colony than with the Legislative Council constantly troubling it with efforts to reduce the excessive taxation.

The Home Government was throwing the whole expense of the Colonial Government upon the colonists themselves — not only the civil, but the military establishments alike were to have costs defrayed out of the colonial revenue. One small grain of comfort in 1834 was that the best English bills were at three per cent discount, and that a deathblow was shortly expected to be struck at the usury system which had been so damaging to all except the usurers themselves. Highly influential and wealthy individuals in England, learning the real state of the colonies, established a banking company on a magnificent scale.

However, affairs grew worse instead of better, and in April 1835, the *Times* announced:

> The crisis has at length arrived, there are no means now left for our merchants to remit for their goods imported from England! Treasury bills there are none. Private Bills there are none! Produce none to export! Our situation is desperate. It behoves the merchants forthwith to call a meeting of the mercantile interest, for the purpose of shewing their English creditors the true state of the Colony, and the total impossibility of remitting for the debts owing.

Soon ruin would overwhelm the greater part of the colonies if such a dreadful state continued. Credit had received a deathblow, and the colonists could not feed their own population. 'The free people of this Colony are not in a position to say their property is their own; indeed, they possess none — everything is British, and the Government is purely British, not Colonial...No Colony, or rather, no British Colony of modern date, has been in such a dreadful state as is that of this settlement...' proclaimed the *Times*.

By 1836 more than one half of the colonists were insolvent. There was a bank failure at Launceston, with the Tamar Bank suspending payment. As well, everyone was in need of fuel. A large quantity of coal, which was not required for the Public Service, was locked up in the Government coal depot, but it could not be sold, even though the householders were prepared to pay a fair price for it. The authorities were said to be 'without orders' about its disposal, but it was apparent that they were protecting their own interests as usual. The consuming topic was distress, and in an editorial in January 1845 the *Colonial Times* gave this description of the state of the colony:

> Another year has passed and brought with it much of misery and affliction. Many who, at its commencement, were comfortable — nay, happy and affluent — at its close have found themselves engulphed in the general vortex of ruin, which has involved the Colony throughout the whole length and breadth of the land...Our whaling parties have been more successful than of late; our wool is in great demand in England, and even realizes good prices here, while the resources of the Colony are abundant and must be brought out and developed to the eventual benefit of the Colonists.

It was hoped that the Government both in England and in the colony would see the vital importance of applying compulsory labour to public works. This was the opinion of all, despite their political leanings.

The only healthy sign of prosperity was shown at New Norfolk, where not an uninhabited house was to be seen. The basic wage of the labouring class was £15 per annum, with the census for 1847 giving the total population as 70 164. The number of male convicts employed on public works was 3739. The disproportion between the sexes was considerable, being about one female to two males.

'Far better is it to arrive in this Colony as a Prisoner of the Crown, than as a poor Free Settler!' The *Colonial Times* expressed this opinion in 1835, and it was true that free settlers in particular were treated shamefully. Free men were handcuffed and taken to the Police Office merely on suspected offences. In one instance, a tradesman in the town was handcuffed to a prisoner on a false charge of stealing a snuffbox, and paraded through the streets. The *Times* once again emphasised the need for badges to be worn by the prisoners of the Crown so that they could be easily distinguished.

Another man was put in the gaol in a complete state of nakedness.

When the under-gaoler's attention was called to this, a very satisfactory prison discipline explanation was given. It appeared that the man before his trial was a free man, and free men in Hobart Town gaol had to go naked if they could not provide themselves with clothes. The convict, under similar circumstances, was clothed at the expense of the Government!

A poor free man, who could not read or write, was fined £5 for not paying taxes which had been published in the 'Orders and Notices' of the *Gazette*. He had been under the impression that a collector would call to collect the taxes as in England, but no leniency was shown him.

Another factor which acted against the 'lower orders' was the strong class division. The *Colonial Times* tried to define the state of society in Van Diemens Land:

> There are two great or leading distinctions, viz., the free and the prisoner populations, although again, the former are almost as much divided and subdivided among themselves, as these two sets are from each other. In speaking of the free inhabitants of the Colony then, it may be said that the first in point of order, are chiefly those who are in the pay of the Government ... and seem to consider this circumstance a sufficient ground for keeping separate or aloof from the rest of the community, and that it would be degradation to them to associate with any who did not belong to their own order. They are sometimes jeeringly styled the 'aristocracy'. The next or second class are infinitely more numerous, more wealthy and more influential than the others and comprise the respectable free inhabitants who are un-connected with Government — and form a little world of their own ... presenting a lesson in many respects which the aris-tocrats might do well to follow. A third set are free persons of an inferior station — men who form the link between the merchant, banker, or first rate settler, and the mere labourer. These again chiefly confine themselves to their own circle, neither of them amalgamating with the others, more than can be con-veniently avoided. The fourth or last class are the prisoner population, between whom and all others a line of demarcation is drawn, which effectually forms them into a distinct or separate set; being seldom admitted to anything like social intercourse, except among themselves.

A gentleman, who no doubt regarded himself among the upper crust, wrote to the *Colonial Times* in 1829, giving his opinion that the colony could not go forward without a peasantry, as it now resembled a head without a body, 'a monster in nature', and that the formation of a peasantry should be among the 'constant persevering exertions of the Government'.

With convicts assigned to the settlers as servants there was no need for a peasantry, although the colonial-born were later to show a marked aversion to the old English tradition of having the poor work for the betterment of the upper classes.

Those in the colony who did belong to the wealthy class were able to live in a little world of their own, which could ignore the unpleasant facts of being in a penal colony. While felons were swinging on the gibbet the colonists could assemble together to 'enjoy that most pleasing, exhilarating and healthful amusement, the joyous dance'. A dancing school was opened in Hobart Town in 1829 to teach the 'truly elegant and graceful accomplishment of dancing'. According to the *Times*, 'nothing can be more disagreeable than to find a young Gentleman or young Lady entering a room awkwardly; it dims the lustre of all the other requirements, and gives them an appearance of being ill-bred. We should like to see the truly beautiful and sylph-like forms of our fair Tasmanians set off to the best advantage, and capable of adorning a drawing-room'.

Other essential accomplishments were catered for at the Polyglot Academy, where French, Italian and Spanish were taught by Ferrari's Comparative Method, by one of his own pupils. There was also a Professor of Dancing, Monsieur Gilbert, who handled that graceful art, instructing his pupils in all the new quadrilles being practised in the salons of London and Paris — the polka, the schottische, the waltz (in double and triple time) and the celebrated cotillons of Cellarius. He was also happy to give instruction in the French language with the 'true pronunciation'.

Those who wished to acquire a useful accomplishment could attend Mr Smith's Teaching Rooms in New Town Road, where pupils were instructed upon 'his universally admired systems of Writing and Short Hand in Ten Lessons, admirably adapted either to the correspondence of Ladies or the general routine of business'. In fact, all the latest novelties and inventions brought out from England were for the enjoyment of the wealthy class. When the daguerrotype process was introduced into the colony in 1848, Mr Bock, a local artist, was patronised by the social élite, so that 'faithful likenesses could be taken according to this scientific process'. These tin-types would, of course, have been put in the family album.

However, 'the prevailing taste for public amusements' by the inhabitants of Hobart Town was helping to remove the line of demarcation among the classes, just a little. The concerts, races, and the regatta served to bring persons into contact with one another, and in turn gave life or stimulus to the activities of many hard-working people.

There were many instances of the 'class war' which generally occurred where a number of grades were introduced into small societies. The arrival of the *Imogene* was quite an occasion in the world of fashion and gaiety in the colony. The officers of the ship issued cards for an entertainment on board, and as it had been announced that the novelty of private theatricals was to make up part of the *soirée*, it was naturally supposed that nearly everyone who had been invited meant to attend. It was not to be. A short while before the entertainment was to take place, no less a personage than one of the leaders of the upper set asked for the names of some of the people whom she had been invited to meet. On being told, she at once said that many of them were not on her list and it was out of the question that they should be permitted to sit down in her company. The lady was peremptory, and the non-attendance of herself and her associates would have ruined the whole affair — 'indeed the very idea of having a grand party on board His Majesty's ship *Imogene*, and not to have it graced by the female Aristocracy of the place (such as it is) would have been horrible in the extreme', the *Times* added sarcastically. The end of the matter was that the lady struck her pen through several names; those people were told, in terms of regret, that circumstances had occurred which would prevent the officers of the ship having the pleasure of receiving them.

On one occasion, a lady was invited to a ball, given by one of the 'aristocrats', but her husband was not considered sufficiently aristocratic to be admitted among the 'pure merinos', being only a clerk. Such difficulties were always arising upon the issuing of invitations.

The *Colonial Times* delighted in publishing stories of a derogatory nature about the 'pure merinos', and this one obviously alludes to a not very highly esteemed member of the colonial clergy:

We were gratified the other day, at seeing the pope's carriage draw up before the shop of a small pork butcher's, but guess our astonishment when we saw his high mightiness, the pope, descend from the carriage and enter the shop! Curiosity induced us to approach, when we heard the dealer cry out loudly, 'That's my lowest price, Sir.' Then rejoined the other, 'I will not have them. I never in my life gave more than eightpence half-penny a pound.' 'I can't help it,' said the pork butcher. 'I never takes no less from nobody.' Here the speakers said something which was inaudible, and we were just coming away, when we saw the pope coming out of the shop, with (Oh! ye Gods and little fishes!!) — two pounds of pork sausages wrapped up in an old *Trumpeter*. Where is now our aristocracy?

There was probably no part of the world where slander was so prevalent as in the little Tasmanian metropolis. Monopolies were also well established.

'It's all in the family,' said a gentleman to us the other day. 'His brother is coming out, and he is an Undertaker — so there will be the son, the Doctor, to kill the people, the brother the Undertaker to bury them, and the Parson to read the funeral service over them. Oh! what a place for monopoly is this Hobart Town.'

The vocabulary of Van Diemens Land was commented on from the earliest days. The *Hobart Town Courier* mentioned the fact that although the English language was more generally spoken than any other on earth, 'a lamentable want of purity prevails in most of the colonies'. It was stated that 'the original emigrants carried their mother tongue along with them, but the peculiarities of a new country soon loaded it with new terms and new acceptances to old words. The greatest mischief, however, arose from a sort of apathy or slovenliness of speaking on the one part and an affectation of new words and phrases on the other'.

There were two aspects of colonial life which knew no class barriers, and they were death and accident, the common lot of all people. Even the lady of the Chief Justice was thrown from her gig 'in consequence of a stump' and received severe contusions. The women, especially, suffered much through lack of proper medical care. The wife of a settler living in the Lake Plains died in childbirth. The midwife was intoxicated which helped towards the death of the mother. The husband took the death of his wife so much to heart that shortly afterwards he cut his throat, 'whereby in five minutes he became a lifeless corpse alongside his deceased partner; leaving four young orphaned children (including the new-born babe) to lament their loss'.

A number of deaths occurred among the people through eating a species of fish called the toad fish, later discovered to be highly poisonous. The wife of a settler and two children of an overseer died this way, while others had narrow escapes, saved by an emetic.

Despite the high mortality risk to all the inhabitants, there were

11

some who lived to a ripe old age. An old settler, John Walters, died in January 1826, aged 107. He had been present at the battles in the rebellion of 1745, went round the world with Lords Anson and Byron, and served in the great sea fights under Lords Hawke and Rodney, and in various other engagements. In 1831 two of the oldest settlers in the island were carried to the grave. 'Old Blundell died after a few days' illness, his wife who had been lingering and ailing for nearly two years, survived him but two days. The same grave served for this old pair, who had lived together for nearly forty-four years.'

The settlers in the colony were always sensitive about their image as seen by the folks back home in England, who thought that because they were living in a penal settlement they must all be rogues and thieves. Therefore, a gentleman of Hobart Town, who made a speech at a public dinner in 1854, was congratulated by the *Hobarton Guardian* for the tact with which he described the inhabitants who had come from England, Ireland and Scotland.

'This Colony,' said this very enterprising and intelligent gentleman, 'could boast of very valuable importations. They had the frankness of the Englishman, the caution of the Scotchman, and the liberality of the Irishman. Let them endeavour to blend these honorable stocks. Let us use the frankness of the English in dealing with practical matters, the caution of the Scotch; and in cases of distress, and in the cause of education, the hospitality and liberality of the Irish!' It is almost needless to add, that most enthusiastic cheers followed the enunciation of these just sentiments.

The intermingling of the national characteristics of the English, Scots and Irish was to be the common heritage of most of the descendants of those early settlers in Van Diemens Land.

2

The System

That ship must voyage half the world —
The convict far away must go;
His deed was as the darkest night,
And justice frowning in his sight,
Pronounc'd his sentence so!

After the English judge had 'pronounc'd his sentence so', the convict would be banished beyond the seas to serve his time in Van Diemens Land, where he would be subject to laws even harsher than in his homeland. Those that transgressed any further would be re-convicted and put in gaol or made to work in the chain gangs. This meant that the gaol was soon filled to capacity, and it was necessary to find other places of correction. This resulted in the formation of the station for the incorrigibles at Macquarie Harbour in 1822. Another penal establishment was opened in 1825 at Maria Island, on the east coast of the island.

The Maria Island penal settlement was said, by the *Colonial Times* in 1826, to be 'in many respects ill-calculated as a place of secondary punishment, as it was originally intended. Scarcely a week passes without some prisoners...effecting their escape, by passing to the mainland in canoes, built from the bark of the trees'. A number of prisoners were drowned in their attempts to escape. It was rumoured in 1829 that Maria Island was to be evacuated for the purpose of being subdivided into grants. However, it was not until September 1832 that the settlement was finally abandoned. Of Macquarie Harbour, about which many fearful tales have been told, the *Colonial Times* asked after its abandonment in 1833:

'The Government Brig *Tamar* on returning from her last trip to the Settlement of Macquarie Harbour brought up the residue of the civil and military establishment...thus do we find that "earthly hell" after years of labour has been wasted upon it, abandoned ... and what advantage has been the Settlement?' The word 'advantage' could not be related to Macquarie Harbour in any sense, as it was to leave a darker stain on Tasmania's history than any of the infamous deeds of the past.

Port Arthur, the most famous of the penal settlements in Van Diemens Land, was opened in 1830, where, as well as the men already serving their sentences on the island, hardened criminals transported from other colonies were also sent. The original offences which brought the convicts to the colony from Britain were often of a very trivial nature, and an item in the *Times* telling of the arrival of a person under sentence of transportation for seven years, for stealing fruit from a garden, was regarded as astonishing, even in the colony.

A general muster of all the inhabitants, with the exception of the civil and military forces, was conducted annually. The *Gazette* announced in 1826 that the muster was to be discontinued, with the credit given to Lieutenant-Governor Arthur, although 'Muster Day' is referred to many times for twenty years or more after this edict was given.

'Our country friends will perceive with pleasure, that the whole of the prisoners by the *David Lyon* have been assigned to Settlers up the country.' This was stated in 1830, although this practice had been operating since the arrival of the first settlers. A letter to the *Colonial Times* in 1826 stated the opinion that the many cases of ill-behaviour of assigned servants were due to the harsh and rigorous treatment which they often received from their masters. A scanty allowance, clothes, and too much work demanded, 'exacted by the terror of the lash', was the primary cause of men taking to the life of banditti.

A list of absconders appeared regularly in the *Government Gazette*, giving a detailed description of the runaways. The men were often 'pockpitted' and tattooed with a variety of symbols on their arms and fingers. A cotton spinner from Manchester was tattooed with a flowerpot, a woman, mermaids, an anchor and three sets of initials on his arms, besides four lines of poetry, which read:

> And must this body die
> And this mortal frame decay
> And must these active limbs of mine
> Lay mouldering in the clay.

The escapees' appearance was often described as being marred by missing teeth as well as other defects, consistent with malnutrition and lifelong neglect due to poverty. A reward of £2 was offered for their capture.

A prisoner of the Crown was assigned to his wife and had the chance to carry on work to support his family. A neighbouring gentleman employed the prisoner, owing him £50. When the prisoner requested cash payment he was brought before the magistrate of the district who separated him from his wife and family and drove him into the public works in Hobart Town. 'The family may starve, but shall a convict dare insult a gentleman?' asked the teller of this story.

The colony was alive with rumours of how these 'great men' used the prisoners to their own advantage to improve their estates at the expense of the public. It was considered strange that 'while some hundreds of men employed in chain gangs can be employed at the new works at the Arthur Jetty, not one Government hand can be spared for the mercantile interest of Hobart Town, to cleanse the present almost impassable thoroughfare to the Old Wharf'.

Ticket-of-leave men were banned from entering St David's Church, built expressly for their use by British money. Instead, they were marched off to the prisoners' barracks to parade among hardened convicts, those in the chain gang. This situation was remedied a couple of months later. However, the treatment of convicts continued with great injustice.

Is it true that one of the Deep Gully road party was found dead in his hut last week, and that the overseer reported the circumstance to the nearest coroner? ... The Officer arrived to hold inquest on the body on spot, which was found in a rather decomposed state... That trifling circumstance, together with the difficulty of procuring a Jury...the distance to any station at which lunch could be procured...the cold and wet...the utter uselessness of making enquiry on such a 'subject' induced the Coroner to order the body to be at once consigned to its mother earth without a Coroner's Quest...
'And as the rascals bore the body by,
He called them untaught knaves unmannerly,
To bring a slovenly unwholesome corpse,
Betwixt the wind and the nobility.'

A prisoner of the Crown, an assigned servant to a gentleman in Hobart Town, applied for an indulgence — a ticket-of-leave. As his character had remained unblemished for nearly five years he was hopeful that his request would be granted. However, he was told to re-apply in twelve months' time, and if his character continued without a stain, he might hope for a favourable answer. The reason for the rejection was that four and a half years before the prisoner had been charged with being drunk.

In 1831 the system of flogging, practised by many magistrates for very slight offences, was given publicity, to the detriment of the 'masters who have their servants warmed'. Old men were known to have been flogged, sometimes receiving more than the forty-eight lashes allowable.

A public whipping at a cart's tail took place in 1833. The victim had absented himself without leave from the chain gang station. There was no question that the punishment was necessary as far as the man was concerned, but compassion was expressed for those in the neighbourhood where the man was flogged, as they had nothing to do with the crime! The sight of a man writhing in torture under the cat o' nine tails of the public executioner was to the ordinary mind a 'punishment of no trifling nature', and it was hoped that these revolting public exhibitions would take place in private. 'Example is one thing, revolting punishment quite another...'

Although the crime rate seemed to prove otherwise, an official return from the Police Office stated that the number of convicts sent to the colony since 1821 was 16 606, of whom 4833 had not a single offence recorded against them in the colony. This was taken as a sign that the morals of the prisoner population were improving beyond the most 'sanguine expectations'.

Instructions were received from England in 1834 that seventeen of the men who had arrived in the colony from the last prison ship, men sentenced to transportation for life, were to be worked for seven years in irons, and fifteen others were to be treated similarly. Presumably, after seven years they were expected to be serviceable members of society. A member of the hulk chain gang was transported for seven years for stealing a pair of boots from a fellow prisoner. Even among his own kind a prisoner could become an outcast.

For prisoners assigned to service, the temperament of their masters determined whether they became willing workers or not. A man was sentenced to receive twenty-five lashes for refusing good food supplied to him, although assigned servants were later to cause an uproar when they were fed sheep's heads, food considered good, wholesome and nutritious by the authorities.

Some masters, usually government clerks ('pure merinos'), often kept their prisoner servants in livery. An assigned servant, a chubby little boy, appeared at the Police Office in full dress livery, charged with stealing an ounce of tea. 'The anxiety of the master upon this distressing occasion was remarked by everyone present, particularly in taking off the little fellow's laced coat on which the master seemed to set more store than on his servant, for fear it should be soiled at that contaminated and filthy place, the Prisoners' Barracks.'

There were many conflicting reports of the treatment meted out to the prisoners. At the general muster of ticket-of-leave men in 1834, nearly 500 men, considered the very best the island contained, assembled. They were clean, and it was reported that they appeared healthy and content. Obviously they had good masters, or perhaps they were working as free men, thus gaining some independence and self-respect. The following year 200 probationers became free to work on their own account and return to barracks. No complaint was preferred against any of them.

However, they did not live up to this exemplary beginning, and it was being said in 1841 that the probation system would do great harm to the colony. Housebreaking was becoming the vogue, and absconding could never be prevented. The men were allowed to move about town without any control, which did not please the inhabitants. The state of the colony three years later under the probation system had begun to alarm everyone, and there was not one district in the island where people felt themselves safe against bushrangers.

To make matters worse, another large party of Norfolk Island convicts had arrived by the *Duke of Richmond*. They all had what were called 'the tickets of character of that Colony', and at least forty of them were said to be 'very black sheep'. The Sydney Norfolk Islanders all had the reputation of being desperate characters.

The holders of tickets-of-leave had their indulgences suspended for the most trivial offence, and were dealt with severely, forfeiting all claim to any further indulgence until they had served three complete years without trouble. A man and his wife were charged with being out after hours, and with representing themselves as free. They both pleaded guilty to the charge and were each sentenced to one month's hard labour. A rogue and vagabond back in England would not have been punished so severely.

The probationers were given more privileges than those holding tickets-of-leave. A ticket-of-leave man would get a month or two at the mill for being out ten minutes after eight o'clock, while a probationer would receive half that punishment for offences which had sent many a poor wretch to Port Arthur. A probationer who overstepped the mark, however, was still brought before the magistrate very smartly. One man was charged for insolence towards his master and refusing to do his work. Described as 'giving himself airs of a man of some consequence', he was proved to be a 'saucy, insolent, ungrateful fellow', and sentenced to step fourteen days at the treadmill.

In another case two probationers were sentenced to four months' hard labour for circulating malicious rumours about a respectable female, knowing such rumours to be false. Evidently such caddish behaviour was too much for the court reporter, who could not forbear adding to the account: 'The vagabonds ought to have been whipped into the bargain!' He seems to have made a habit of such comments, expressing a personal view again when a ticket-of-leave man had his existing sentence extended for two years for stealing a bullock's tongue from a butcher's shop in Liverpool Street — 'Serve him right, the dainty gentleman!'

General disapproval of the probation system grew stronger with each succeeding year. It was thought to be ineffectual and unwise. Robberies were being committed 'by those petted persons called Passholders, or Probationers'. Probation servants, described as 'free-and-easy gentlemen', were often summarily and severely dealt with by the courts, but by 1846 probationism was the established penal system of the colony.

No change in the system occurred in 1847, much to the people's disappointment, as the usual amount of pilfering and other offences were still as prevalent. A prisoner left a gang of probationers as they were passing along the road between the city and New Town and threatened a young woman with a knife as she was standing beside the clothesline. He walked around her several times with the knife in his hand, while the girl stood in a state of stupid terror, until some companions came and took him away. Another probationer went to the Cornish Mount Hotel, asking for food and drink, inviting five or six other people to join him. Afterwards, when asked to settle the 'shot', he fled. He was later discovered to be a flash pass-holder, well known by the name of 'Boxer', in the hired service of a man who had allowed him to do as he liked.

Still more convicts arrived that year, among them thirty-two men who had been convicted in the Supreme Court of Sydney and then sent to Van Diemens Land in the *Waterlily*. They were escorted by a strong military escort through the streets to the prisoners' barracks. Many of them were in heavy irons. As well as being doubly or trebly convicted, they were now under sentence of transportation, not merely for the term of their natural lives, 'but for two lives — if they had them!'

However, an important announcement was to come in 1848 of

18

a new system hoped to be the deathblow to probationism. The new system, known as the 'free-ticket system' meant that all prisoners from Great Britain were to be landed in the colony as ticket-of-leave men. 'This system is worse than any that as yet preceded it,' was the reaction of the newspapers, and no doubt of the readers as well. The following explanation of the meaning of transportation was given by the *Hobart Town Courier* in 1851:

Few people now understand what transportation means; all that is known is that it does not mean transportation, and that a convict sentenced to it is certain not to be sent beyond the seas for a considerable space of time. The convict is to be worked up into an article for exportation, and for Colonial consumption. For this purpose he is shut up in prison for a time, at the end of which he is supposed to become a different being...

The cessation of transportation was not to come until 1853, when the inhabitants of Van Diemens Land went wild with jubilation.

Whichever system the prisoners and people were forced to suffer under made no difference to the determined efforts many of the convicts made to escape from the colony, whenever an opportunity was offering. In 1820, seven prisoners confined in the stone cells of the gaol, under committal for trial before the Court of Criminal Judicature, broke out by working through a drain and perforating the wall. Constables and troops were sent after them. Again, escaped convicts, who had got away in the brig *Deveron*, were delivered up to a ship in the harbour of Rio de Janeiro in 1825, two years after they had made their escape. In 1831 seven prisoners were charged with conspiracy to piracy while on board their transport. Another prisoner seized a dinghy belonging to Judge Montagu, and paddled himself to the American whaler *Roman*, but was pursued and brought back and sentenced to twelve months at Port Arthur. Another two runaways were found stowed away among the oil casks on board the American whaler *Amethyst*, and were taken into custody by the police in 1839.

A set of criminals attempted to scale the wall of the penitentiary in Bathurst Street, in 1842, but were seen as they neared the top of the wall and were returned to prison. Prisoners of the Crown frequently tried to escape by hiding among ordinary ship travellers. Two were caught on board the *Union* in 1846, one a ticket-of-leave man, and the other a woman who had tried to disguise herself by wearing false hair. On Good Friday of the same year, eight convicts escaped from Port Arthur by stealing a whaleboat.

The stories are numerous. Four prisoners seized the Lord Bishop's yacht in 1849, intending to go to California. They went around the town trying to buy charts of the Pacific and its islands. These are just a few of the known cases.

The practice of flogging human beings like 'brute beasts' was censured by the *Colonial Times* in 1840, as three or four letters had been received concerning the revival of these brutal punishments. For instance, seven men employed by one master were sentenced to receive thirty-six lashes each in the same week, and two other men were also sentenced to a similar punishment. 'We aver that a man once flogged is a spoiled, disabled and a most hardened man,' was the decided opinion of the *Times*.

A young man flogged at the triangles at New Norfolk took seventy-five lashes, although the surgeon wanted to postpone it. With perfect *sang-froid*, the young man answered, 'Oh, no! I can take them now and no mistake.' Later the surgeon asked him what he meant, and he replied: 'Master, I am a seven year's man, and have served nearly all my time; but as I cannot keep a civil tongue in my head, I have scarcely had a sound back since I came here.'

Opinions were divided on the question of the value of hard labour. There were some who said that although most people found it unpleasant to hear the police magistrate sentence a prisoner to hard labour upon the roads, a look at 'these worthies "nut cracking" would quickly cause them to alter their opinion and laugh at the farce'. However, there was little pleasure in seeing shackled men labouring on the roads in all kinds of weather. An old hand at 'nut cracking' gave a few tips to the prisoners employed in breaking stones. 'It is,' he said, 'the mechanical power of the wedge which ought to be applied to the stones. Persons employed in breaking them should bring the hammer over the shoulder smartly down upon the hardest part of the stone. The blow forces the part struck to act the part of a wedge. The soft part of the stone should be avoided, as a great part of the blow is lost. Spitting in the hand, or holding the hammer too firm, is hurtful to a young beginner.'

Despite all the problems of the prisoner population, 421 conditional pardons were gazetted in June 1853.

Another bane of the people's lives were the convict constables. Complaints about them were a constant source of news. A letter from a citizen of Hobart Town to the *Gazette*, had this to say:

Do the constables discharge their duty? For, although we cannot deny that between the hours of eight and nine each evening, they are indeed as busy as bees in all directions, and at every corner yet we can assert as a truth, well and generally known, that from those hours until day-light, you may in vain scream about the streets until your lungs bleed for one of them! Pray is their appointment nullified at night fall? Is the Penitentiary-bell their curfew? Or has the once depraved portion of the inhabitants become so well-regulated, moral, pious and confidential that in sooth night-guardians are superfluous? No, but they prudently decide that a seat before their own blazing hearth is far more healthful and agreeable than a bleak or an aguish walk on the exquisite roads of Hobart; they imitate Gray's ploughman, 'and leave the world to darkness' and those cracksmen who, if you have any more Spanish dollars in your house than you know what to do with, will ease you of them because they know to an instant when the coast is clear! O, by the way, if our worthy Chief Constable would discontinue to let a fierce dog loose in his yard, any inhabitant wanting his assistance, might possibly obtain it. The other night it was wanted, and could not be obtained in consequence of the fears of a bitten leg.

Two other correspondents wanted to know whether free persons were subject to imprisonment if found at late hours in the night walking on the King's highway without a lighted lanthorn. The question involved a serious problem, for if the community were to be protected the enforcement of the law had to be impartial. Obviously there is the silent innuendo that worthy citizens could be mistaken for the despised convicts, which riled people, although the constables also abused the powers given to them. The complaints continued against constables who stopped respectably dressed gentlemen walking after 8 p.m., insolently asking their names.

An elderly woman was taken to one of the watch-houses one night on a small matter. A constable, formerly an executioner, was in charge. Soon after the woman had been placed in his custody an alarm was given. She was found dead, with her throat cut from ear to ear! The constable was discovered to have the knife upon him; his hands all 'embrued with blood'. The coroner's inquest returned a finding of wilful murder, and the man was tried accordingly.

A woman was knocked down by a drunken constable while she was on her way to get a doctor for a woman 'labouring under the accumulated pangs of *accouchement*'. Another constable adopted a novel method of carrying a drunken woman by holding her feet, placing them behind his shoulders, and dragging her along behind him!

However, by 1830 the vigilance of the constabulary of Hobart Town was being highly commended, particularly considering the types of people they dealt with. The streets were quiet and there were comparatively few instances of house robbery. The inhabitants felt that property was now much safer from depredation than it was in England. This did not mean that crime was less prevalent, but it seemed more confined to the lower classes. Three-fourths of the cases heard by the Supreme Court came from this class.

The constables did not stay popular for very long. The people had been harassed by the 'poundings law' for a long time. Cattle were pounded and trespass-money of one shilling per head was charged, besides the regular pound fees. The convict constables were reaping a very profitable harvest by 1832. Although not allowed to possess money, in the course of a few hours they often openly obtained from the public £4 or even £5.

The evils of the Impounding Act were even more oppressive by 1833, and few, including the authorities, could deny that it was arbitrary and unjust. The temptation given to the town constables to get the money easily for a glass of ale by rounding up the odd horse, cow or goat was partially the fault of the Act. It was common practice among certain constables to go to the outskirts of the town and drive any animals they could find into streets merely traced by the Survey Department, unknown to the rest of the world, then take their name to the pound. Although little better than felony, this was justified by the Impounding Act.

With the influx of pauper emigrants and commuted pensioners it became imperative that the number of the police establishments be quickly increased, but no steps were taken. The practice by the constables of annoying respectable people had also increased, and it was almost hazardous for any decent person to go home after dining at a friend's house or taking a glass of wine at a tavern. It was felt strongly that the Act of Council should not apply to individuals who may have been enjoying a friendly glass of wine, and that drunkenness be considered as nearly wholly confined to the lower orders. 'It is the dose and the drinker of the dose "rum", who introduces so much disorderly conduct in our streets and it is not the respectable portion of the community that should labour under the general censure, and be subject to the penalties and inconvenience awarded indiscriminately...' reported the *Colonial Times* in 1834.

The way in which the police of the colony were organised awoke the colonists to the situation in which they were placed, and the whole of the free population demanded the rights and the privileges they should have. A public meeting was called for this purpose. One point that was raised was that cattle- and sheep-stealing was being carried on widely in the New Norfolk district, but it appeared that the constables were too much engaged in 'dancing attendance'

TOP: Port Arthur, Van Diemens Land, in 1846, from a lithograph by John Skinner Prout. BOTTOM: A settler's bush home at Deddington, *c.* 1840. (*Both from the Allport Library*)

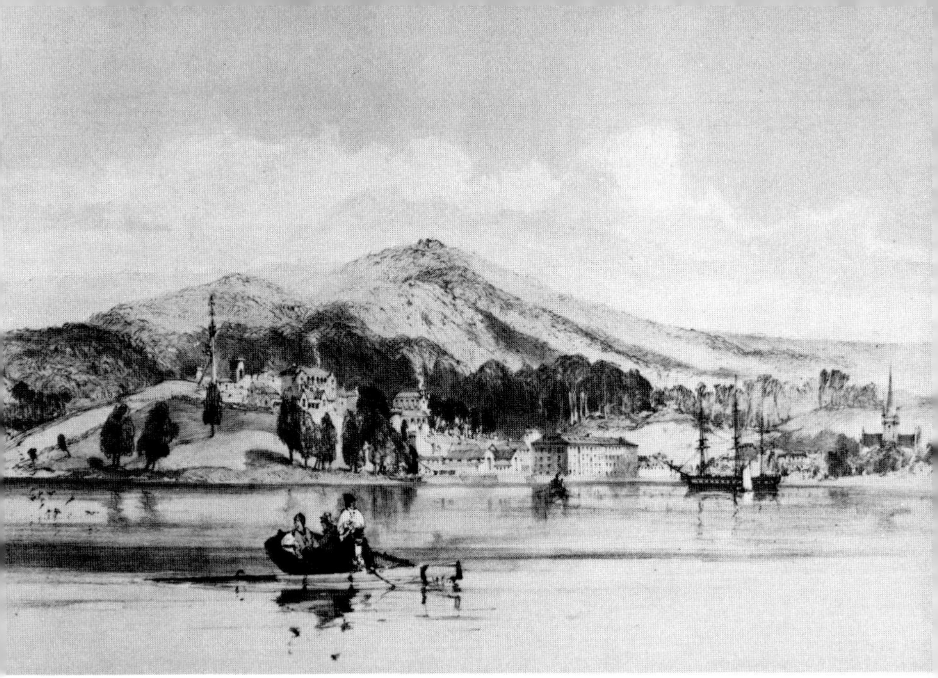

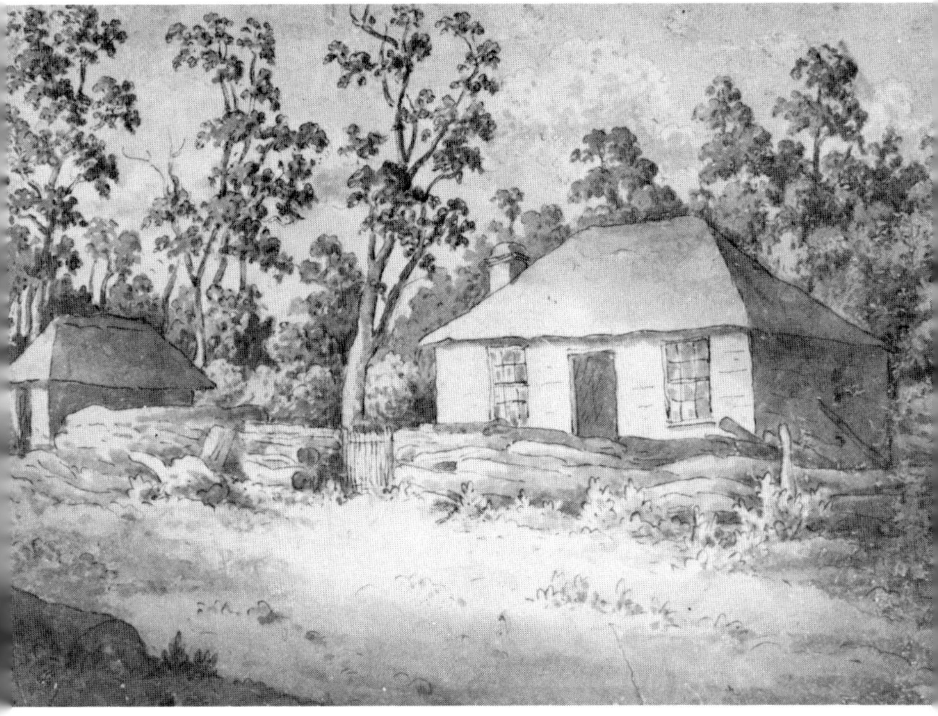

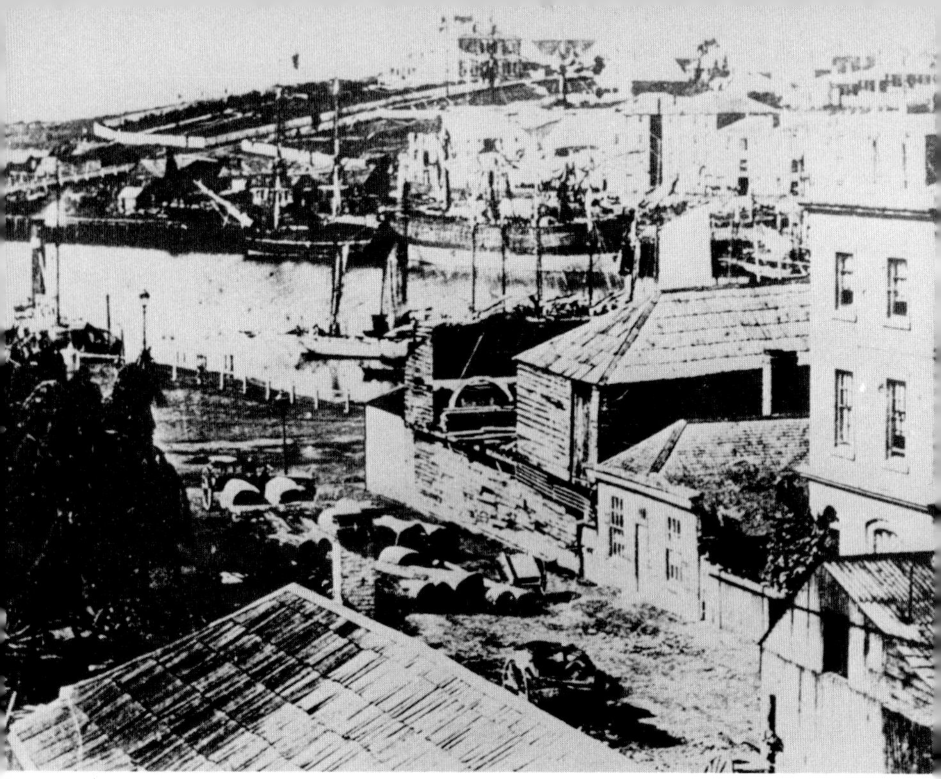

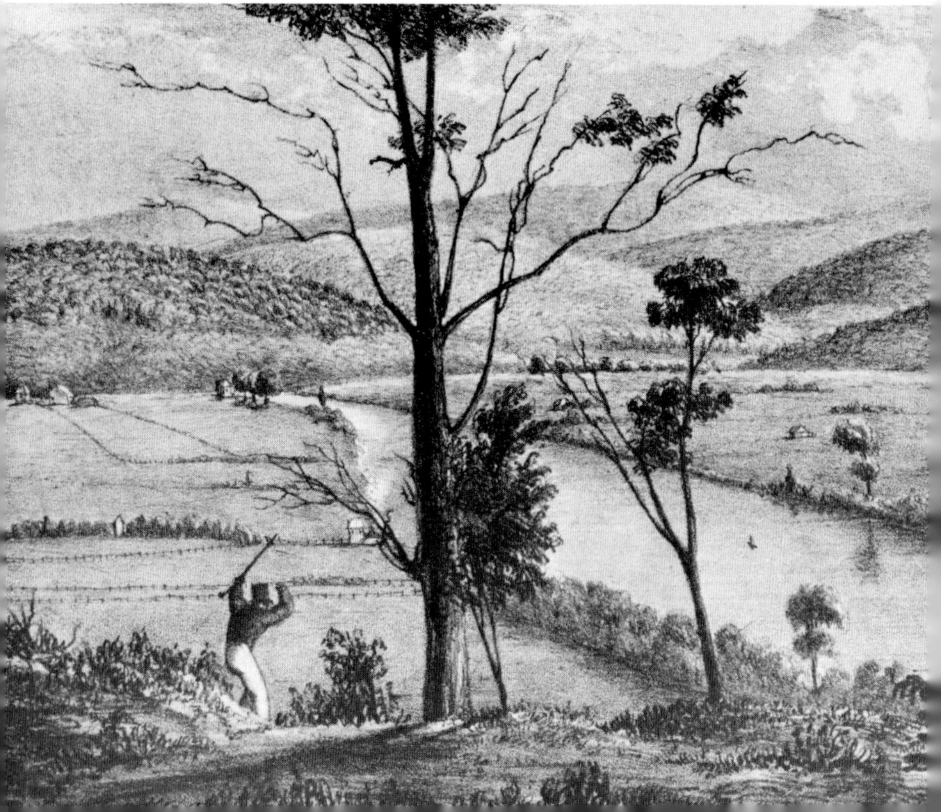

on the great men of the district to pay attention to these thefts.

It was common for constables to provoke people into striking them, as a heavy fine would have to be paid by the guilty party. New constables often joined the force just for the purpose of realising fines. The system of appointing felon police to be the preservers of lives, properties and morals of the free population continued daily to become more unpleasant. Not only were they allowed to enrich themselves by harassing and tyrannising the free, but whatever they chose to do was not only authorised by law, but seemed to be especially protected by the authorities.

Reports came in daily of the indignities the people suffered at the hands of the constables, indignities which did not abate over the years. A correspondent to the *Times* complained in 1840 of the violent manner in which people were kidnapped and taken to the watch-house, asserting that he could enumerate 'more than fifty' whose deaths had been brought on directly or indirectly by the treatment they had received there by the constables.

There was a report current in 1844 that it was His Excellency's intention to provide a corps of fifty mounted police, to be divided into squads stationed in the several police districts, under the command of an active officer, ready to pounce upon evil-doers of every description. This still did not meet with the full approval of the citizens, and the exact amount of the annual expense of the 'gillie-goolie Mounted Police', estimated to be little short of £3000, soon came under notice. What was the use of this 'gala-day' corps? Further, it was considered that it should be stationed in the interior, and not in Hobart Town. Even then the cost should not be supported by the colony.

The agitations of the police, however, appear to have been quite ineffective, for even as late as 1854 misconduct was taking place at the Hobart Town watch-house. A free married woman placed in custody was subjected to insults by a constable, a matter which was to be brought under the notice of the police magistrate for investigation.

The other custodian of the peace and defence of Van Diemens Land was the military, and it appears to have been capable of creating many disturbances also. There was a reference to its activities in 1832 regarding the 'late disturbance between the military and the people', which gave rise to many very serious reflections. 'Is it true,' asked the *Times*, 'that a fracas of no ordinary magnitude took place at the billiard room of the Ship Inn, on Monday night last? What with the battle between the gallant 63rd, and the "whalers", the rows among the "Colonists", the "war" between the Clerk of the "Peace" and Mr Muster Master

Mason, the town appears to be in a pretty considerable state of excitement at present.'

There were amusing sidelights, however. A military gentleman, not held in very high regard, wanted to buy a few more cockades for his servants. He wanted these ornaments so much that he decided that the coachman who drove his one-horse 'chaise' should wear four in his castor (a hat of beaver fur or some substitute), namely, one in front, one behind, and one on each side. His female cook was to wear two, and the housemaid one!

A lack of discipline among the men of the 21st Regiment was evident after a fracas occurred in 1836, while a military outrage in 1840 was described as the most atrocious which had ever disgraced any of the colonies. A riot at Launceston between the military and civilians took place in 1845.

The defence situation in the colony was a problem in 1838. The colony had been established thirty-two years, and yet there was no vessel of war on their coasts. It was thought the Home Government should be induced to offer a little protection to the place, both from sea and from land, seeing that it was a penal settlement. The way things were in Hobart Town, if any pirate or privateer carrying half a dozen guns was to anchor off Government House, the whole colony would be in danger. 'Not a gun is there in the battery (so improperly called) that could discharge a shot, not a man is there to fire a gun, if it were loaded...'

Four years later, thirteen beautiful thirty-two-pound cannons were landed to be mounted on the new fortifications; the frames, carriages and wheels were all of iron, and an excellent quality. There was to be a military increase as well, with the force expected to be of 2000 rank and file members. 'Farewell then to thieving and bushranging in this great gaol, and welcome the guardians of peace and safety, and also the assistance in the consumption of bread and meat,' was the fervent prayer of the inhabitants.

Orders were said to have arrived the following year for the accommodation of two more regiments of soldiers and 12 000 additional prisoners, because of the breaking up of the penitentiary system in England. This was supposed to be good news for the agriculturists, but was dismal tidings for most.

Life in the military was not exhilarating for the lower ranks. A private in the 96th Regiment was subjected to corporal punishment in the presence of the regiment in the barracks square at Launceston; 150 lashes were administered for breaking a window in town and stealing some trifling object. The object of this punishment was to deter and caution others.

There was one soldier whose good fortune was publicised in

the *Times* in 1853. A private soldier, formerly of the 99th Regiment, an Irishman named Loftus, was discharged from that corps about the year 1849. Almost penniless, he went to Victoria, and by 1853 had amassed £42 000, and received a handsome rental of £950 per annum on his properties. This was considered to be the result of industry and perseverance in a 'golden country'.

The people in the colony often keenly felt their lack of protection in the southern hemisphere, with England so far away. A strange vessel entering the harbour could be considered a threat until the signal station proved otherwise. What the people went through can be gauged by this incident, which occurred in 1837:

Much anxiety was occasioned among the inhabitants of this town one day in the early part of the week, in consequence of a vessel being signalized from Russia. No one could comprehend what business a Russian vessel had in the Port of Launceston, and fears were expressed of her amicable intentions, which were much increased upon its being reported that she was a man of war, showing three tiers of guns, and manned by huge men wearing mustachios, and a tuft of hair of marvellous length below the under lip. Rumour had it that the crew were monsters, and had an eye in the middle of their foreheads, and that some of the crew, when bunting the sails on the vessel's coming to, had tails like monkeys. Some had it that the pilot was bastinadoed when the ship was given into his charge, of way of cautioning him to be careful, and that his crew were served out for fresh provisions among the sailors. Various were the rumours, and various the anxieties expressed. Some fancied themselves already breathing the salubrious atmosphere of Siberia — others shrugged their shoulders, and shuddered when they thought about the knout — and the gourmand's stomach became disordered, as he fancied the taste of train oil. The eyes of everyone were directed to the signal staff, and with palpitating hearts, the meaning of each after signal was enquired; when, by and bye, the previous signal 'No. 49 — Vessel arrived is from Russia' was telegraphed: 'A mistake — should be "Vessel arrived is from King George's Sound".'

3

The Early Governors

The first military Governor of Van Diemens Land was Colonel David Collins, who transferred the initial camp from Risdon Cove to a more suitable site at Sullivans Cove, which was later to be called Hobart Town. This was founded on the 19 February 1804. Collins appointed magistrates, who set up a jurisdiction of their own. Criminal trials were conducted on free-and-easy lines, directed in every way against the prisoner, and the penalties inflicted were a combination of the provisions of a military and of a civil court. When dealing with prisoners the magistrates acted very much as they pleased.

Collins died quietly in his chair in 1810, apparently worn out with all the difficulties encountered in the infant settlement. The shortage of food supplies caused the convicts to wander freely through the bush in search of food; a practice which lead to the beginning of the bushranging era.

The next official Governor was Thomas Davey, known as 'Mad Colonel Davey', who took up his appointment in 1813. He was to inherit the legacy of the bushranging menace, but was to plunge the colony into further infamy with his lax control over morals and drunkenness. He was as brutal as the men who served under him, responsible for the flogging of free men, or of anybody bond or free who left their house at night, after the enforcement of the curfew law. The conditions which existed during Davey's time are evident in this public notice which appeared in the first issue of the *Hobart Town Gazette*, 8 June 1816:

Amongst the improvements that are taking place in Hobart

Town, we have to notice a commodious and very useful Wharf has lately been erected on Hunter's Island by the officious attention of Captain Nairn; and if hands could be spared from other Public Works, it would be of great utility to have a Causeway erected from the Island to the Main, a little higher than highwater mark, for the better conveyance of carts, and accommodation of those Persons whose business requires them to frequent the Wharf.

As the Bodies of the Felons that were Gibbeted on Hunter's Island were close to the place where the Wharf is erected, and became Objects of Disgust, especially to the Female Sex, they have been removed (by command of His Honor the Lieutenant Governor) to a Point of Land near Queenborough, which in future will be the Place of Execution.

People travelling between the settlements of Hobart Town and Port Dalrymple were cautioned not to proceed without firearms owing to the hostility of the Aborigines.

Davey mixed freely with convicts; it was also said that 'not one out of ten of his officers was living with his wife but with convict concubines!' On the day that the Governor laid the foundation stone of St David's Church, on 19 February 1817, he proclaimed the day a 'Thanksgiving Day' and a public holiday. He ordered half a pint of rum to be given to each of the soldiers and constables. This rum was served from 'bucket and pannikin', a custom always adopted and recommended, to prevent the men from robbing each other of their due share of rum. Poured into a bucket, all shared alike, and there was no chance to steal any bottles.

On 9 April 1817, Colonel Sorell assumed the reins of government. Although compelled to adhere to the rigid system, he set an example which few of his successors were able to emulate, being very popular and respected by the inhabitants of the colony. From the time of his arrival emigrants from England began to land in great numbers, and received every consideration and assistance from the Governor, so that in a short space of time they were able to take possession of their land and start work on their own property. With their capital still intact they were able to start easily in their new country.

A petition was framed and adopted at a public meeting in Hobart Town to retain the services of Governor Sorell for a fresh term of office after the customary period had elapsed, but it was unsuccessful and he was replaced by Colonel Arthur in 1824. After the presentation of a piece of plate, and an emotional address was given, 'the people followed him en masse to the shore, all eager to manifest their regard to receive a parting glance — the sorrowing countenances around giving how much he was beloved; and thus parted Colonel William Sorell, than whom a more popular ruler never swayed the destinies of British subjects'.

Colonel Sorell lived at Government Cottage at New Norfolk for a short while after the arrival of his successor, one who would have been fully aware of the adulation given to his predecessor, but who apparently made no effort to follow in those footsteps.

Colonel George Arthur and his family reached the colony in May 1824. To celebrate his arrival a general illumination took place in Hobart Town in the evening. By February 1825 murmurings against his past life were being spread around Hobart Town, which were ultimately to result in the printer of the *Hobart Town Gazette* being found guilty of publishing three libels upon the Government, and later there were two 'scandalous and malicious' libels in the *Colonial Times*.

The *Colonial Times*, however, still continued its attacks upon the administration of Governor Arthur and in May 1831 ran a long editorial on the injustices which the colonists were expected to tolerate:

The fact that has been reported and reported...now stands revealed to the world in its full truth, that Colonel Arthur has no power to lay out our surplus money in public improvements... After having drawn from our pockets very large sums, they are not to be spent for our own benefit or advantage, but for the purpose of strengthening our local Government in the estimation of their friends and patrons at home — the English Ministry. We now find that our surplus revenue is to be applied towards defraying the expense of the convicts who are sent hither from the Mother Country; and thus whilst the inhabitants of such a place as Hobart Town are to continue to run the chance of all diseases, by being compelled to drink the poisonous stream that runs through our town rivulet, and which is in a most unwholesome state at least six months in every year, we are to be taxed at a rate per head, in proportion to our free population, unknown even in England, for the two-fold purpose of feeding and paying an immense tribe of do-nothings, and their first-cousins do-littles, who are sent here by the English Ministry because they have claims they cannot disregard, fearing, lest they might lose their own patrons or supporters in the persons of some distant connexion of these worthies; and secondly it now seems, of maintaining the rogues and vagabonds of the Mother Country! The subject is far too important in all its different bearings to be properly discussed in our present number...

Our entire condition as Colonists becomes involved in the question for once admitting the principle, where is the line to be drawn? We may expect to have the Military, who are quartered here, palmed upon us for their pay — maintenance; nor even have we any right to suppose that the evil would stop here. The great mischief has been, that Colonel Arthur in strengthening himself has weakened the Colonists. His having so changed the face of affairs here, as instead of a deficient income, to have a considerable surplus, which he considered himself bound to ask the Home Government what he should do with, is no doubt, in their estimation, a great feather in his cap, and for which he will be highly rewarded. (He should never have suffered the revenue to run ahead of the expenditure, but have kept the two nearly a balance.) But what is the consequence upon us, who have to pay the piper? In the first place we are grievously taxed, being out of all proportion to our sister Colonists in New South Wales; and, in the next, the proceeds are to be applied to purposes, in every respect, the most objectionable; whilst, at the same moment, works of a public nature that are imperatively called for, and for which we are willing to pay, are withheld from us, because our Government has no power to authorise them... Truly, fellow Colonists, we are in an enviable plight! Although we must admit, in a great measure, it is the effect of our own supineness when the enemy first made his lodgement. We took the yoke of heavy taxes too easily, and behold how we are rewarded for our weakness! The fable of the horse that sought the protection of man is not inapplicable in its moral to our present condition — 'Once wear the bit and bridle, and reflection comes too late!'

One of Colonel Arthur's first acts on reaching Hobart Town was to appoint his nephew, Captain Montagu, to the position of Colonial Secretary. 'Warming-Pan' Montagu, as the settlers called him in derision, who was only too willing to take over other duties that would return a profit, soon became as hated and feared as his uncle.

Previous complaints to the Home Government with regard to the shocking conditions in the colony under Governor Arthur's administration were over-ruled as they were not made through the proper channels; the inhabitants' cries for justice went unanswered. Still, they evidently kept on trying, as is shown by this item in the *Colonial Times*, 18 January 1832:

If report says true, the *Eliza* will leave our shores with no ordinary cargo, having in addition to the outward and visible signs of freight, passengers etc. which are reported in our Customs-house, returns of the week, various papers, documents... connected with some of the goings on in this Colony, which will at least open the eyes of our great men at home, to the real character and pretensions of their most obsequious servants — our great men here...

Every public action Colonel Arthur made usually produced disparaging reactions from the people, and very rarely did he receive a favourable write-up from the press. On one subject, however, he did gain approval from all concerned; it was pointed out that the Lieutenant-Governor had shown himself independent of dis-approving religious influence and had ordered that twenty-five women who were confined in the factory, and who had received eligible offers of marriage, should be allowed to accept these.

By the end of 1832 his popularity had not increased in any way; in fact it was even worse. The *Colonial Times* was of the opinion that 'the public interests cannot be more seriously injured than in the case where as much as possible is taken from the people and as little as possible is returned to them', while the *Courier* held the view that the Governor should 'make roads and save the Colony'.

An instance of the low esteem in which he was held by the people can be estimated from this small news item: 'The Governor is off on Thursday next — yes, reader, off, but not as you may perhaps hope, for he is only off to Launceston — worse luck say you!'

It was being said in 1834 that Colonel Arthur's occupation was more that of a clerk or book-keeper than that of a Governor, and the complicated machinery of his pen-and-ink Government made so much work that he was unaware of the 'glaring absurdities' going on around him. This in turn kept everything respecting the Government in complete secrecy, so that the people never knew what would next appear before them. This assumption can easily be seen to have some basis by the fact that the requisition in the *Government Gazette* for best quality quills amounted to 36 000 in 1832!

At one stage it was rumoured that the successor to Colonel Arthur was known in the colony, and that Major-General Sir William Carroll was to replace him. This, of course, was later proved incorrect.

The papers were full of criticisms. The most important feature in Colonel Arthur's prison discipline was unproductive labour, with 900 men employed at Port Arthur in work which was not known to the general public, and many in other seemingly futile activities. In August 1835 this editorial appeared in the *Colonial Times:*

His Excellency's flattering account of the prosperity of the Colony has at length produced positive instructions to charge the whole of the police expenditure on the Colonial fund. This is a secret and a troublesome one for his Excellency. How does the folly of crying out prosperity appear? We have neither bread nor meat to feed ourselves with, and here comes a claim for £22 000 annually!... If the Colony is to pay for the police, we trust there will be no more convicts sent out. Nine-tenths of the police (and every Government Department) is employed in convict affairs, and the Home Government has no right to expect a young Colony to pay her felons as Police Officers.

In January 1836 a public meeting was called by the colonists for the purpose of framing a petition to His Majesty to remove Colonel Arthur from the colony. By May there was some 'hopeful intelligence' that the Governor had been positively recalled, and that official notice had come by the *Elphinstone* prison ship that week. Then at last came the long-awaited announcement on 31 May of the Governor's recall: 'It was with the utmost satisfaction that the inhabitants of Hobart Town welcomed the happy intelligence publicly made known on Wednesday last that Colonel Arthur is forthwith to be removed from this Government...REJOICE, FOR THE DAY OF RETRIBUTION HAS ARRIVED.'

The people had to curb their elation, however, until the actual departure took place. First of all the money had to be raised for the customary piece of plate to be presented to the Governor. The subscription was described as being 'neither voluntary, nor... a subscription of the people', as few individuals dared refuse to give something under threat of intimidation. The police were accused of getting up 'the thing', so there was little choice but to co-operate. Many of the subscribers later refused to make good their promises all the same.

Premature celebrations could not be entirely checked, and the inhabitants still managed to give vent to their feelings. The *Colonial Times* joined with them in this enthusiastic report:

The *Hypocrite* was performed at the Theatre — this piece was well selected for such an occasion, and *More Blunders Than One*, was the afterpiece. As to the rejoicings of the people, never was anything like it witnessed in this quarter of the world. The whole town was illuminated with fireworks from six o'clock till twelve ... the streets literally covered with paper, betokening the millions of fire-works discharged ... fifty soldiers remained under arms in the Barrack yard during the whole of the night;

it would appear that Colonel Arthur was personally afraid of the ebulition of public feeling... In spite of all intimidation, in spite of felon power and brute force, the people would have their way, and they put in defiance the engines of intimidation. The next jubilee will be a most splendid one, for people who have not dared to come forward will not then be afraid.

Felon constables were recommended to shelter themselves in houses during the next jubilee — the first night of Colonel Arthur's absence, when he would no longer be in power — otherwise they would be treated as they deserved. During the first jubilation a young man bought some Chinese crackers, lighted a bundle and then threw it into a box of rockets. However, a bucket or two of water was at hand, and the premises were saved.

Even after such outbursts the Governor was still set on extracting the last penny from the colony, and it was said that there was 'sad havock among the possums in the Jerusalem district'. This was because the Governor had 'turned up' all his men and sent them into the bush with powder and shot to kill the possums. The slaughter was great, and Colonel Arthur was expected to realise some few hundreds of pounds in the fur trade.

As he departed, the ex-Governor was hooted aboard his ship. He was reported to have returned to the town that night, remaining until 4 a.m.; he then went back to the ship to leave Van Diemens Land, to the people's great relief, for ever!

The constables assaulted many people who saw the Governor's departure, putting the finishing touch to his infamous reign.

The *Cornwall Chronicle* greeted the arrival of Sir John Franklin with this verse, which neatly summed up the unenviable task awaiting the new Governor:

> *Come, come, Sir John, the wind will soon be o'er,*
> *The hail and rain will shortly cease to pour;*
> *Follow with us, and rather brave the storm,*
> *Then take the road that leads you to reform.*
>
> *Ah no, I've sailed the Arctic Regions twice,*
> *Where every Element seemed to join together;*
> *I've been hem'd in with mountains formed of ice,*
> *And wanting food and clothes, to brave the weather.*
>
> *But ne'er till now, has danger reared its head,*
> *To thus repel me with its hideous form;*
> *Let me return, much rather I'd be dead,*
> *Than take a road that leads to such a storm.*

Sir John Franklin arrived at Hobart Town in January 1837 in the *Fairlee* and insisted on landing with all due honours. Thousands of people assembled on the New Wharf to meet him with loud shouts of welcome, in contrast to the yells and shouts Colonel Arthur received when he left the Friday before. At 12 a.m. the new Governor was accorded military honours. Later every house in Elizabeth Street and Campbell Street was illuminated, 'and the numerous cottages, interspersed on the side of the several hills, displayed lights in honor of the occasion'. It was remarked that 'some Government Officers, that is the aristocracy of Colonel Arthur's making, did not of course condescend to join with the people on this occasion'. Fireworks were let off before sunset to midnight, and the mob gave Sir John three hearty cheers on his entering Government House. Even if he had given one half of his fortune, Governor Arthur could not have obtained such hearty cheers.

The following month His Excellency paid a visit to New Norfolk where everyone welcomed him. By April the novelty of having a new Governor had worn off, and the *Colonial Times* remarked that 'little or no improvement had taken place in the pecuniary state of affairs or social fellowship'. It was only three months since his arrival but apparently little was to be expected.

Disenchantment soon followed, and more and more criticism of the new régime was reported in the newspapers. Sir John and Lady Jane Franklin also upset the upper class residents with their social arrangements. Marked distinctions were made when invitations were issued to a series of balls at Government House, to be held on four distinct nights. Some people received invitations for the whole series, while others only received a 'singular invitation', with the fortunate holding the others in contempt. The Franklins were not reputed to be lavish with their hospitality, the kitchen chimney and the flues of Government House being rarely seen to be billowing with smoke. 'The chimney had caught cold, and the flues the influenza, and the news of the death of Royalty is not likely to heal the complaint,' was the reason put forth by a correspondent.

Lady Franklin was also under fire for her interference in her husband's affairs. An allusion to this at the time suggested that as Queen Victoria was on the throne it could be unequivocally and unhesitantly asserted that the island and dependencies of Van Diemens Land were ruled by a Governor under petticoat government. It was also being said openly that the Governor sanctioned 'that most gross and corrupt of all jobs, the monopolizing of Government printing'.

The Governor, his indefatigable wife and suite, set off in January

1838 for an annual tour of the interior, as well as going to Flinders Island. His reception at New Norfolk was not so warm this time, the imagined benefits the people had anticipated from him not having been realised. Other than fixing upon Turriff Lodge as his country seat it was alleged he had done nothing for the township of New Norfolk.

The news that Colonel Sir George Arthur, now Governor of Upper Canada, was committing horrible barbarities there and hanging without mercy, did not deter the editor of the *Colonial Times* from saying he was 'not sorry' at an unofficial report of Sir John's resignation.

Apparently the present Governor's ineptness was just as unacceptable to the people as Colonel Arthur's brutalities.

A grand ball and supper at Government House in honour of Her Majesty's birthday was treated in a very sarcastic manner. 'The supper excellent — all cold and in the best style. . .the dancing most sprightly. The Ballroom lit with 33! Sinumbra Lamps. Belle to beau pleasantries.' Dancing was suspended at twelve o'clock, when a bell rang for supper, with everybody eagerly scampering off to the supper room. About one hundred young ladies sat down to the table and a cold collation. 'As great a failure for these last twenty years,' was the final comment. At a later occasion, when a similar function was held, a sample of the supper provided for about forty persons was given as 'a shoulder of mutton, a saddle of mutton, cray fish, a pair of fowls, with a few tarts and jellies, and some excellent sour wine'.

The vice-regal couple were having adverse remarks made on all their activities, whether social or official. Sir John was lampooned for his 'vice-regal masonry' in relation to the two foundation stones which he had laid for the proposed college at New Norfolk and the new Government House at Pavilion Point. On both occasions the coins deposited under the stones had been stolen, which led to another verse being written in the *Colonial Times*, set to the air of *Those Evening Bells:*

> The wicked press — the naughty press,
> It tells some tales of me I guess;
> And tho' it does not call me fool,
> It says, indeed, poor is my rule.
>
> I wish again, upon my soul,
> That I, once more, were at the Pole;
> For tho' alas! I then had cares,
> I there ate up the grumbling bears.

The College stone, in vain, I laid;
With coins and cash, by John Bull paid,
And tho' some rascals stole the same,
(With Latin bad) yet mine's the fame.

The Palace stone I also stuck,
In bed of sand — (how hard my luck);
Some knowing hand, to paper sent
A tale, to show my true intent.

Much longer here I shall not stay,
Tho' pickings good have I, and pray;
A hint I've got, that I leave you
Ye grin, ye rogues! but I look blue!

As well as a farm on the Huon, Lady Franklin had another at Kangaroo Bottom, and it was hinted that she had not wanted for assigned servants, sawyers or Government mechanics to improve her property. Concern, however, had been felt for the Governor and his party in May 1842 when they were on an expedition to the rugged west coast of the island and were thought missing. About a week later they arrived safely in Hobart Town after enduring some 'little privations' at Macquarie Harbour during the 'last gales' in the shape of short allowances of bread and meat.

Rumours of Sir John's recall still persisted, and in October 1842 they seemed quite certain. The Governor's 'consistent morality' was another source of discontent, and in his zeal he ordered that no ship should sail from the port on Sunday. He also forbade 'horse-racing, theatrical amusement, and latterly boat racing, except, we suppose, by teetotallers... (and also His Excellency's carriages and family rolling along the streets for recreation on the same day?)'.

It was further reported that after a visit to Launceston Sir John and Lady Franklin, accompanied by some half-a-dozen people and the band of the 96th Regiment, were 'drummed out of town'. On their arrival home, 'the cortège passed through in solemn silence'. Lady Franklin had provided against such want of personal respect and ordered a Guard of Honour to receive her. 'No noisy rogues threw up their caps and cried, "God bless them".'

Apparently to compensate for their fall in esteem more cards than ever were issued for the Government ball held shortly after-wards. People who had previously been looked upon with contempt were now honoured with an invitation. All the Government clerks were expected to attend, along with many people who could not resist the summons and who could suffer the insult of being so long overlooked by the Governor. However, several people did return their invitations.

Sir John had made known his intention of leaving for England by the *Eudora* once his successor was announced, but he was persuaded to await his arrival. It would have been considered in incredibly bad taste if he had not done so. Official notification of Sir Eardley Wilmot's appointment had been given in July 1843.

The new Governor, Sir Eardley Wilmot, arrived in August 1843, although the public did not have the opportunity of seeing him for a while. The Governor's ship, the *Cressy*, had overshot the port and came to anchor in Lagoon Bay, where he took up residence with Mr Bicheno until Government House could be prepared for him. However, by September he was 'fairly enthroned'.

It only took about four months for Sir Eardley's stocks to make a rapid decline, when it was announced that the people were to be taxed 'by way of experiment, by the proposed Act to provide for the Lighting, Paving, and Cleansing the City of Hobart Town', an astounding proposition on the part of the new Governor. There was a hue and cry from one end of the city to the other against so unconstitutional a proceeding, and a public meeting was called to frame a petition against the 'unjust imposition'. The Act was later to be rejected by the Legislative Council.

Mysterious happenings were taking place behind the scenes, for in April came the surprise announcement of the Governor's recall. In an editorial dated 6 October the *Colonial Times* spoke of the matter which was puzzling:

> In renewing the subject of the strange recall of Sir Eardley Wilmot, it is necessary again to look at the reasons assigned by Mr Gladstone for so doing. What are they? They are distinctly and expressly stated to have arisen in no shape whatever from any differences between His Excellency and his Council, but solely and entirely 'because that, from various statements which have been conveyed to Her Majesty's Government from individual communications, it appears sufficient attention has not been paid by Sir Eardley Wilmot to the moral and religious welfare of the convicts...'

The next issue had more to say:

> The more seriously any fair-judging man reflects upon the recent recall, the more he will be convinced of the very ill-treatment which Sir Eardley Wilmot has received.

In a flashback of events for the year 1846, the *Courier* shed a little light on the subject:

The beginning of the year saw Sir Eardley Wilmot in the pomp of power and the confidence of stability. The opposition that resisted his arbitrary measures in Council was apparently crushed...the close of the year saw Sir Eardley Wilmot hurled from his high office...But the blame of indiscretion and folly rests not alone with Sir Eardley Wilmot. Reckless as was His Excellency's career, his measures found advocates and defenders. The *Colonial Times* undertook — and the *Spectator* was avowedly established — to vindicate them...The three leading features by which the year that has closed was characterised, and which we have briefly endeavoured to illustrate in their obvious prominence, are, the attempt to establish a petty despotism — the bold determination to support it — and the ultimate triumph of just and liberal principles...From the character and energy of the present ministry, from the prevailing tendency of public opinion in Britain, and from the measures now under consideration in the Colonial office, we have everything to hope for and nothing to fear.

Another shock was in store for the inhabitants with the announcement that Sir Eardley's medical attendants gave little hope of his recovery from a severe fever. The death of Sir John Eardley Wilmot took place in February 1847, at the residence of his private secretary in Macquarie Street. The cause of death was stated as 'complete exhaustion of the frame — in customary phraseology, a nature of decay'. He was to be buried in the colony, and his remains exhumed later to be sent to England at his request.

The *Colonial Times* remained his champion to the end, and black banners edged the pages of the issue of Friday, 5 February. The newspaper gave a different account of his death:

On Wednesday night, soon after eleven o'clock, Sir Eardley Wilmot was liberated from the mental suffering his assassins occasioned him, by death!...We can now only state this moral assassination — God forgive the miserable wretches who by their execrable slanders worked upon the creature Gladstone to become their executioner.

The late Governor's character was vindicated to some extent by a letter signed by all the inhabitants of Hobart Town and its neighbourhood, contradicting the statement that his recall had

37

been influenced by reports injurious to his moral character.

An Acting-Governor, Mr La Trobe, had arrived in October 1846 and taken over control of the colony until the new Governor, Sir William Denison, had assumed office after Sir Eardley Wilmot's death in 1847.

Sir William began his duties by making his first tour of inspection across the island to Launceston. He seems to have survived the first two years of his term of office without upsetting the inhabitants unduly, but by December 1849 it was being said that he advocated the system of transportation, and was trying by every indirect means to deprive Van Diemens Land of free government.

Lady Denison continued the practice of giving an occasional ball at Government House. A description of such an occasion on New Year's night, 1850, reads:

Lady Denison gave a ball and juvenile entertainment on New Year's night, and the amusement of the evening commenced by distributing presents in the German fashion as last year. Dancing was then commenced by the juveniles and lasted until a pretty late hour. Supper was served at twelve o'clock, and it was past three o'clock when the company retired...The visitors consisted of the principal Government and other officers with their families, and others of the most influential inhabitants... 400 cards were issued, but that number did not attend. The new ball-room was made use of for the first time. It was lighted by three large sconces of seventy-two candles each. Its dimensions are sixty-five feet in length, thirty-five feet in breadth, and twenty feet in height. The rooms contain an orchestra, capable of accommodating thirty musicians; for the first time it was occupied by the quadrille band of H.M. 99th Regiment.

The Governor, however, began the new year by falling out with the Chief Justice, Sir John Pedder. 'William the Doubtless', as he was then dubbed, was censured over his proposal to Sir John Pedder to give place to another whose opinions concurred with Sir William's views of law, which most regarded as being 'ridiculously outrageous'.

Meanwhile, news had been received of the search for a previous Governor, Sir John Franklin, who was missing, believed to be in the northern seas. The late Sir Eardley Wilmot's remains had been exhumed and finally deposited in the vault of a new monument erected by public subscription in the cemetery of St David's Church. The vault was described as the 'finest piece of monumental architecture in these colonies'. No mention was made of returning the

Top: Hobart Town's first official Post Office (1822–1836), which stood on the site of the now demolished Arcadia Hotel in Murray Street (*Tasmanian Museum and Art Gallery*). Bottom: A fine, well-established dwelling in Macquarie Street, Hobart Town, in 1838 (*Allport Library*)

WHITE HART INN · DeGRAVES BEER & ALE

MRS HART

BAR

PARLOUR

remains to England, although the cost of his funeral was defrayed by his family.

Public feeling had turned against Sir William by April 1850, and the *Courier* was writing passionate appeals to the people:

Have the Colonies so abandoned themselves to despair that they will permit it to be said that they have ceased to feel as men? Do they mean that Sir William Denison shall write their condemnation and vindicate all he has said of their sordid spirit — their immorality, their social worthlessness that Lord Grey should stand up and quote his despatches to justify his own despotism? ...Let the Colonists look forward to better times; they will outlive their oppressors; but let them discharge their duty and place on record their detestation.

It was starting to have a familiar ring. Another nail in the Governor's coffin was his persecution of the Irish exiles in 1851, which received wide publicity, not only in Australia, but overseas as well. The effect of Sir William's policy was being felt throughout the colony.

An editorial in February 1853 gave the *Colonial Times'* view of the situation:

The six years are up — and Sir William Denison is trying to obtain some semblance of popular approbation at his recall. But it is in vain... He may vary the position of figures but he will obtain no new ones... Sir William Denison is the best Governor we ever had! So say the thieves, and a statue or public monument is to be set up in the very centre of the St Giles' of this city in celebration of His Excellency's virtues as a ruler and socialist. But what say the respectable settlers of Van Diemen's Land? ... The Government of Sir William Denison has been selfish and disreputable throughout. The natural characteristics of his temper are displayed in rudeness and swearing. The name of the Almighty and the name of the devil are always upon his lips as the common expletive of his talk.

The rumour of the Governor's recall was verified in March, and a little advice given along with it: 'We would recommend His Excellency to act upon the advice given to Dan Tucker and "get out of de way" as quickly as possible.' However, it was some time before the Governor made his departure, and the people were dumbfounded to read in the *Hobarton Mercury*, of 13 September 1854, that 'Sir William Denison for well-governing Van Diemens

Land is now Governor-General of all the Australias and Governor of New South Wales' and was to move to his new post within two months, by the steamer *Monarch*.

Sir Henry Fox Young succeeded Sir William Denison in January 1855. At one period of his government of South Australia he had been 'the best abused' of all Australian Governors, next to Sir William Denison. However, it was felt that the numerous attacks on them would have taught them both a lesson.

All the people were on the *qui vive* on the Saturday morning when the new Governor was expected. The steamer came in sight at eight o'clock, and at nine the private signal was made. . . About eleven o'clock a guard of honour accompanied by the band proceeded to the wharf, attended by crowds of spectators who swelled the number already congregated; the *Antipodes* and *Mary Ann*, with other vessels, were gaily decked with flags, and their rigging was occupied by a great number of persons curious to witness the reception. The Mayor and Corporation were also there to welcome the new Governor on his arrival.

By February the old familiar story seemed to be about to start once more. A remark in the *Hobarton Mercury* said that 'the new Governor's forte appears to be retrenchment (a favourite hobby with all new Governors)'.

4

Government Departments and Personalities

Living under a military Government was not conducive to a happy relationship between the free settlers and the authorities. They had plenty to complain about, and complain they did, loudly and bitterly, in the manner of true Englishmen fighting for their rights. It did very little good at first, but after keeping up the clamour for forty years or more they eventually succeeded in gaining some entitlements.

One of the few pleasures derived from any service under the direction of the Government was the sending and receiving of mail. In the beginning letters from England were the mainstay of the people's morale, and a letterbag was kept at the Post Office for the reception of letters to be sent home by the first ship returning to England. A notice in the *Hobart Town Gazette*, 23 November 1816, advised the inhabitants that the letterbag was open for mail by the brig *Spring*, which was due to sail about 1 March next. Letters were also lying at the Post Office for collection. Long lists of names were published regularly so that the people could pick up letters which often remained unclaimed for long periods. Settlers living in the interior were not always able to come into town every time a ship arrived in port.

The delivery of mail within the colony must have been very sporadic also, as the *Colonial Times* announced in 1832 that a mail cart was about to start running between Launceston and Hobart Town, which they hoped would make the post regular. At the same time a very spirited correspondence was going on in its columns about the conveyance and postage of letters. A couple of correspondents put the position very plainly:

It is 'out of the frying-pan into the fire' for ever with us, when we get rid of one curse another jumps up. When we succeeded in doing away with the Sunday muster, which caused all the convicts to prowl about with their dogs all day, we little thought to see the same system revived, but the new Post Regulations have set them all on the move again, as instead of the postman leaving the papers and letters at the various houses, he takes them all on to the Post Office forsooth, and we must send in every direction after him. Well may it be said, what a folly it is to make laws for the Colony in London, when those in Hobart Town even know so little of the country. The public houses now receive, by permission, all the Settlers' servants, and then to raise a shilling, pilfer every little moveable to pay for their rum, and treat their friends. Not only that, but we lose the services of our men, and then we must take them to a Magistrate, in short it is a bad business altogether.

The second letter is just as succinct:

I have written to Dr Ross, and I now beg to inform you that I can no longer subscribe to your paper, in consequence of the Postman passing my place with his cursed bag locked. He told me, I should follow him to Perth, if I chose; but twenty-eight miles there and back, is no joke, so the letters may remain in the Post Office till doomsday for me.

Chief Justice Pedder honoured the mail cart in 1833 by riding in it on a trip to Launceston. It was hoped that this way of learning of the real condition of the roads would get them better attended to than they were at that time. However, a few months later, when the reduction in postage and despatch were to be considered, there was talk of a new postal system. Whether it was of any benefit to the people or not was doubtful as there was always a new problem forever cropping up. In 1834 the latest complaint was: 'It is a pity that the Post Office will so bother the people by the changing [of] the signal flags at the Battery. No sooner do the Public become well acquainted with the various signals, than alterations take place, which leave them again in total confusion.'

The *Colonial Times*, which had been persecuted by the Government for its efforts to gain a free press, still took every opportunity to ridicule the authorities in its pages:

How pleasing it is to note the little elegancies of great minds! We have heard that the Captain Director of the Post Office writes his officials on tinted paper, and that his table is covered always with as many coloured letters, as the magnanimous director possesses coats. His clerk, the little leviathan with the long name, although the extent of his wardrobe precludes him from exhibiting himself in as great a variety of disguises as his master, nevertheless considers it 'vastly genteel' to affix his signature, a splendid specimen of potholes, to aught but paper as delicate as his own fashionable person.

Among local improvements imperatively necessary in 1843 the Post Office was held to be the first that should be called to the Governor's attention. There had been three repeated robberies of the mail, and in February 1844, after the stolen mail had been found by the police at Antill Ponds, it was forwarded to the Hobart Town Post Office. There were a great number of the letters unopened, 'which by the assiduity of the working officers of the department, were without delay delivered to their respective addresses'. A cheque taken from a letter was later presented at a bank at Hobart Town and cashed on the following day. It was felt that as the robbers were so soon able to turn a cheque into money, they must have had accomplices who found no difficulty in negotiating some of the stolen bills of exchange and other money securities. It was thought that the robbery was not the work of ordinary bushrangers. The mail bags restored to the Post Office had been carefully 'weeded'.

In April, the Launceston mail coach was stopped and robbed by four armed men. Cash and Co. were at large at that particular time, and it was not a mere coincidence that the robberies happened to take place at that period.

In July the inhabitants of New Norfolk forwarded through the Postmaster-General a petition to His Excellency praying that they might be allowed a post office messenger for the township. Post offices in the country towns were established by 1848. In that year a singular notice was posted up at the entrance of a newly erected post office not far from the Richmond racecourse. It read: 'This business of this shop carried on at the store. Whoever cannot read enquire within.'

The letter carriers of Hobart Town appeared for the first time in official costume on 24 May 1853. The colour of the coat was blue, the cuffs and the collar being turned up with red, 'in fact, an exact copy of the uniform formerly worn by Mr Hookey Walker, the twopenny postman of London celebrity'. By then the Post Office was a very busy establishment, and it was said that the sooner the staff was increased the better. Two or three of those on whose shoulders fell the whole of the work had an exhausting time when the mail was delivered from Adelaide, with still more to come.

At the end of June the Launceston postmen appeared in uniform for the first time also. A new postal system came into operation on 1 November, and by May 1854 the Post Office in Hobart Town had been enlarged to cater for all the extra work involved in running a much more efficient postal service for the people.

Other Government departments were constantly being censured, too, and at the end of 1832 the *Colonial Times* brought up facts about the way the accounts of various departments had been withheld. The following month they were reporting: 'It is said Treasury Bills to the amount of £1000 have been traced and found to be in the possession of an individual of high standing in the money market. Doubtlessly the party gave value for the Bills, but rumour says, that they must be given up. If so, the chest will be £1000 gainer, and the individual a loser to the same extent.'

An editorial was written on the 'hidden mysteries of the Registrar's Office', and a number of other matters were investigated as well, so that by the end of January 1833 Government suspensions had become the order of the day.

The management of the Survey Department was another bone of contention. When in February 1834 it was reported that Hobart Town was again to be surveyed, it brought this outburst from the *Times:* 'Only once more! This will make the seventy-sixth time the Town has been surveyed within the last five years. Oh! What a precious nest is that Survey Office!' The satire expended on members of the Government departments by the editor of the *Colonial Times*, who was later to be imprisoned for assisting in saving the life of an innocent man, must have been enjoyed immensely by the people.

A new promenade was made to the Government garden at New Town in 1831, making a delightful walk for those who felt inclined to take a stroll after church on Sunday. 'It seemed the effect of enchantment, or as if Aladdin's lamp had been discovered in these regions,' enthused one pedestrian after a visit to these gardens. However, the people were not allowed to enjoy the treat for long for it soon became known that only the respectable members of the community were permitted to walk there; even then proper application had to be made first, and on no account was any of the fruit to be touched.

In 1832 questions were asked about expenditure on the gardens, which naturally the authorities did not feel disposed to answer:

What again becomes of the immense crops, that are, or ought

to be, grown at New Town? Whose tables are benefited by the productions of the gardens at New Norfolk? or that of George Town at Launceston?... Who is there that will pretend to tell us that the satellites of the greater powers — the friends, hangers-on, dependants, relations of the Head of the Government have a right to share in the good things that result from these establishments?... If it be sold, how are the proceeds disposed of?

The Government garden at New Norfolk also came under fire when it was discovered that at least seven men, besides an overseer, were all paid for by the colony. It was rumoured as well that the garden was shortly to be sold by public auction, and that a certain 'exalted personage' was considering buying it. The rumours in this case were unfounded.

'Oh! What a piece of folly is this cabbage garden,' exclaimed the *Colonial Times*, referring once again to the garden at New Town. This opinion must have been shared by those responsible for its upkeep, for after the departure of Colonel Arthur it became neglected, and by 1838 it was said to be in a deplorable state.

There were other matters of a more exasperating nature to try the patience of the inhabitants; in particular, the number of young men who had come out to 'nob it up' in the colony. In the words of the *Times*, they had been 'bred up as clerks at a desk, upon a paltry salary of fifty or sixty pounds a year...creatures, who have been obliged to clean their own shoes and live upon bread and cheese and onions, lording it over the community in the most arrogant and impertinent manner'.

The most objectionable of these was a young man, recognised by another colonist as 'a scrubby-faced boy, who was clerk in a country house, next to the King's Head chophouse, in the Old Jewry, London'. This was Thomas Mason, the Muster Master, who was later also appointed by Colonel Arthur as the Assistant Police Magistrate in Hobart Town. To appoint a young inexperienced man to such a situation was seen as an extraordinary oversight. Although it was the custom for Government officials to be lampooned in the newspapers, none was so contemptuously ridiculed as this young man. The *Colonial Times* singled him out for special attention.

He was usually referred to scornfully as Mister Muster Master Mason, and of all the criticisms levelled at him there was only one which could be construed as unfair. That was in the matter of his age, as he was only twenty years old. However, time soon took care of that, and on every other count Mister Muster Master Mason fully deserved the reputation he earned as a junior despot.

Is it true that Mr M.M. Mason has sported a new black stock, two and a half inches wider than the former one he was in the habit of wearing? The first made him carry his head much higher than any drum major — the additional breadth will so discompose his chin, as to turn him topsy turvy altogether.

This was the type of chit-chat the *Times* delighted in, although this was only minor needling compared with what followed later. However, at one stage the paper declared that it was so tired of Mister Muster Master Mason that it was about to form a resolution never to mention his name again. But some fresh outrage always compelled it to report the further doings of this young man.

The *Colonial Times* ridiculed him, along with other arrogant Government officials who held much sway in the colony, with such comments as these:

The Lip Whisker, brought lately into fashion, has been attempted by some of our nobility with various success. 'Don Pedro the Second' has succeeded to admiration, having a tuft dangling from the lip equal to any turkey cock. Little Master Sutton will in time be furnished with a lock; but with all the aid of Macassar and Russia oil from Prince's of Hanover Street, Bear's grease, Atkinson's curling fluid, and every other greasy ointment, it has proved a dead failure with Frederick Fitzclarence Fitzpatrick Tunbridge Fitzhardinge and M.M.M.M; neither of them being able to raise even one single hair. How distressing!

A young soldier, who abstracted an ounce or so of tea and sugar from the commissariat of Don Pedro the Second, was tried, found guilty, tied up to the triangles, and punished by the Provost Marshall, as a terror to the recruits. 'The Don' was purported to be the nephew of a baronet. M.M.M.M., as he was often called, ceased to be a figure of fun after the Greenwood affair. Greenwood was a runaway who had absconded from his master and was caught at the New Town racecourse, wounding a convict constable slightly in a struggle during his capture. He was brought before the Assistant Police Magistrate, Mason, who sentenced him, according to Henry Melville, the editor of the *Colonial Times*, with the words: 'You will first receive a hundred lashes, and then be handed over to the Supreme Court [on the capital charge of cutting and maiming], where you will be found guilty, and, I have no doubt, be hung.'

Greenwood went to the gallows with the marks of the lash still unhealed on his back. His sufferings brought a cry of compassion from the people, and from then on Mason became feared as well as hated. The *Times* spared him even less:

> Before the prison ship *Muffat* had fairly anchored, five Government boats, Mr Deputy Assistant Muster Master General Emmett, and four of M.M.M.M's myrmidons put off upon a special mission to select for his personal service, at his villa of 'Greenwood', the most select men of the following descriptions — two valets, one cook, two butlers, one hairdresser, one laundry man, and a lollypop maker, his last confectioner having died last week from the fright he received, asserting at his last moments that the miserable 'Greenwood' had jumped in and out of his window, he verily believes, with his poor master under his arm, dressed in his usual costume of an old blue cotton pocket-handkerchief tied tight round his head.
>
> Some evil-disposed persons are constantly annoying our Assistant Police Magistrate by putting on his door every night printed labels with the name of 'Greenwood' in large letters — nor is this all, for the same parties, it is believed, are in the daily habit of forwarding to him at his office, letters with the important initial O.H.M.S. and the word IMMEDIATE, and when the letters are opened in anxious expectation the printed labels still stare the Assistant Police Magistrate in the face. We have of late seen some placards of witty description posted in various parts of our streets.

Surprise was expressed that Mr Mason did not apply to be removed to some interior police magistracy, where any Government officer could do as he pleased, more especially so, a police magistrate, 'who is lord paramount in the district over which he presides and against whom no charges are heard'.

The stories continued in this vein until Mason became a police magistrate of New Norfolk. He had also been involved in a trial against another magistrate, Mr Lascelles, who had accused him of 'gross and wilful perjury' in the case of Greenwood. A farthing damage was awarded to the plaintiff. In June 1836 the New Norfolk inhabitants demonstrated their feelings when they heard the happy news of the almost certain removal of the police magistrate, Mr Mason. 'On the most conspicuous hills were to be seen bonfires of no ordinary size, and where fire-works or guns were to be had, a constant succession of explosions took place. The *Colonial Times* kept the people informed, then in September announced that Mason had been appointed Commandant at Flinders Island. 'For this relief many thanks,' was its parting shot.

Much to the horror of the people, in 1838 orders arrived from England to re-instate Mr Thomas Mason to the police magistracy of New Norfolk. A final word on Mr Mason — in 1847 the *Courier* mentioned that he was to resume his magisterial duties at New Norfolk, and that Mr Wilmot would fill the police magistrate's chair at Hobart Town, so he obviously did not suffer for his misdeeds.

There was one member of the Government who did not enjoy any special privileges, and that was the town crier. In the early days, a settler complained that though the night-watch was an extremely ancient institution in all civilised and well-regulated communities, the people in the colony did not receive such protection. This was remedied in time, but it seems as if the town crier needed a little protection as well, according to this story of 1832:

One day last week, as our most sonorous town crier was following his avocation, and proceeding to the sale of land at the Battery Point, when on the New Jetty he was suddenly impressed with some of the advantages derived from a military Government. The man, little guessing that the bell and his oration might be a injury to public discipline, jogged forward in his usual way, when suddenly he was levelled to the ground by the sentry guard, and the sergeant immediately ordered him to be taken in custody. The poor man was for some time unconscious of his crime. He was not aware that it was against all decorum to ring the bell and bawl out in the presence of the chain gang.

5

The Aborigines

Ah! White man, why — Oh! why thy childhood's home
Did'st thou abandon, to drive us from ours?
Why, unprovoked, with terrors did'st thou come
To cloud with woe a people's once glad hours?

If these questions had been put to the early settlers of Van Diemens Land, very likely the response would have been one of dumb incomprehension. Lured by false promises by the British Government to start a new life in the colonies, they knew very little of what was to be in store for them once they arrived. The fact that the land belonged to the Aborigines probably never occurred to the average settler, and many would not have known that the island was already inhabited by a native population.

The Aborigines suffered cruelly at the hands of the sealers and escaped convicts long before the influx of settlers, but little was known of their plight outside of the colony. However, by the time the numbers of settlers became increasingly higher, from 1817 onwards, the Aborigines had begun to retaliate and seek their rightful revenge against the white race. Now their hunting-grounds were being taken from them and given to the settlers, and it was then trouble started to come to a head.

Reports that came to hand concerning the Aborigines were all given from the white man's point of view. At first the few items which appeared in the *Hobart Town Gazette* relating to the 'sable inhabitants', treated them rather as a curiosity, and gave brief, interesting accounts of them now and then. A Tasmanian Aboriginal, given the name of George Van Diemen, had been taken to

England by a Mr Kermode. Another, named William Thomas Derwent, had also been sent to England, but died shortly after arrival. This was in 1822.

In August 1823 a delightful story appeared in the *Gazette* about an Aboriginal girl, heroine of a 'singular and unprecedented circumstance which had occurred in the Macquarie District':

> A fine horse, worth 100 guineas, the property of a Gentleman residing in that district, had been missing for several days; when, to the astonishment of many who saw it, the animal was rode at a full gallop down a valley in view of Allenvale house, by a black native girl, with a long tether rope round the horse's neck. A servant was immediately sent on horseback in pursuit of the fair Tasmanian jockey (the first of her race who has perhaps ever before been on a horse at full speed); but owing to her riding the animal so wonderfully fast, the man could not keep up with her, after a pursuit of four days. Mr J.R. has requested us to say that he will give £5 for the recovery of the animal.

This happy, carefree picture soon fades at the appearance of an obituary notice in the *Gazette* in November 1826:

> Mary Dempsy, a black native girl of about sixteen years of age, who has acquired some civilized habits and used to ride off with the horses of the settlers about New Norfolk, died last week in the General Hospital.

As a result of the practice of firing on Aborigines, Lieutenant-Governor Arthur issued a proclamation in July 1824 to the effect that they were now considered under British Government protection. It was also stated that the Governor, through the medium of a very acute Aboriginal who had been reared by a settler family since he was four years old, had hopes for civilising the Aborigines of the island.

From that year onwards, however, sympathy turned away from the Aborigines, and the only news concerning them concentrated on the outrages they committed. It was believed that a Sydney Aboriginal named Musquito was inciting them to violence, and when he was at last captured, severely wounded, in August 1824, many felt that conditions would then improve. This was wishful thinking, for the attacks continued.

By the end of 1826 the papers were full of the 'dreadful murders' committed by the Aborigines, and feelings were running high. On 7 November it was reported that Black Tom and his tribe, 'to the number of 300', had descended upon the farm of Mr George Simpson at Pennyroyal Creek. In a surprise attack on the hut one of the two occupants received a spear through his back while trying to escape, and died in excruciating agony three days later. The other escaped to 'tell the tale of blood'. Another similar attack was made the same week by a 'tribe of these treacherous race of human beings', as they were described, and it was believed that 'the cunning and wiles of the blacks are like those of Satan himself'.

Black Tom and four other natives were caught in December 1826 at Pittwater and gaoled at Sorell Town. Apparently Black Tom was not long there, for he was to meet his death in a skirmish under the western Table Mountain. Once again hopes were raised that the atrocities would cease, but the Aborigines, aided by the ferocious dogs they kept, remained hostile.

In an editorial in November 1826 the *Hobart Town Gazette* commented that 'had they any affinity to the African negro... we might entertain some distant hope of civilizing them'. The pattern continued and fresh attacks kept making the headlines. In September 1829 Mr Batman and his party at Ben Lomond fell in with a tribe of about seventy Aborigines who had no fewer than forty dogs. The dogs' barking warned the tribe, enabling them to make the first attack with their spears.

By February 1830 concern about the Aborigines was so grave that a Government order was issued offering a reward of £5 for the capture of every adult Aboriginal and £2 for a child — delivered alive at any of the police stations. Events were rapidly leading up to the Black War!

Official orders were given in September of the same year asking the community 'to act en masse on the 7th October next for the purpose of capturing those Hostile Tribes of the Natives which are daily committing renewed atrocities upon the settlers...'

Now that decisive action was to be taken, doubts and anxiety were being felt by many people. Perhaps consciences were beginning to prick a little, although there were a great number only too anxious to join the Grand Army. In a cautious editorial the *Colonial Times* had this to say:

That some grand movement is necessary on the part of the inhabitants of this Island to effectually check the outrageous depredations of the Aborigines, we doubt not every Colonist will readily admit; and it having been ultimately considered advisable, that all should... rise in a body to protect the general tranquility of the interior; we, inhabitants of Hobart Town, in this case cannot help considering that we have not experienced of His

Excellency that degree of confidence which we had a right to expect. It has been hinted to us that the Government are desirous of marching into the interior as many of the Military as can be conveniently spared from Hobart Town, in order to assist in the present laudable exertions of bringing this harassing war to a close; but, we say, are the inhabitants of this Town not able, for such a period as the absence of the Military may be required, to undertake the duties of the several guards? Under nearly similar circumstances have they not proved themselves worthy of being so trusted? We are pretty well acquainted with the general feeling of our townsmen, and we say, there are hundreds of the most respectable who would willingly volunteer their services for such a purpose.

Government orders quickly followed one after another, confusing the people and causing them to wonder what course was to be adopted with respect to the Aborigines. Two years before, a proclamation had been issued creating an imaginary division of the colony into two parts, stating that one side of the supposed line was to belong to the English inhabitants, and the other to the Aborigines. If the latter attempted to pass this line, and were seen in the territories reserved for the others, they were to be considered under martial law, and to be treated accordingly. A chain of military and police posts were to be placed along this boundary to aid the settlers in driving back the Aborigines should they attempt to cross it, and the inhabitants alerted to keep themselves armed, along with their servants, in order to clear the country of their 'sable visitors'.

This edict gave the whites licence to hunt, kill and destroy the Aborigines, and was acted upon with great ardour by those unable to understand the true purpose of this proclamation. The result was that any Aboriginal, no matter whether friendly or not, was chased down with savage ferocity, even if he was only seen in the vicinity of a settled district.

An ineffectual move on the part of the Government to counteract these orders only led to more misinterpretations by the brutally inclined, further bewildering the public and adding to the general muddle. The *Colonial Times* spoke out strongly against the 'inconsistent and ill-advised conduct of the Government towards this benighted race', and referred to what it regarded as an 'indelible stain upon the history of the Colony'. It was alluding to the execution for murder of two Aborigines three years earlier, when 'a greater cruelty was never practised'.

As things now are, we ourselves really do not understand, nor have we been able to meet with any who could explain to us, whether the sword or the Bible is meant to be the means of instructing the Aborigines in their relative duty to ourselves. In other words, whether destruction or civilization is to be the order of the day...Are the numerous parties which are soon to scour the interior, to destroy or save these misguided creatures? Whatever may be the intention of the Government, we are fully convinced that most of those who are now preparing for the interior are not aware of the manner in which the Government expect them to act...We will therefore sum up by saying, that whatever may be the result that attends the unanimous endeavour of the Government and Settlers, to bring to a close the distressing scenes so frequent in the interior, one thing is most certain, which is, that every individual in the Island must, directly or indirectly, be benefited by the present operation, causing as it will so large a proportion of enormous sums to be put in circulation, which are now lying idle and useless in the iron chests of the Treasury.

A settler, in a letter to the editor of the *Colonial Times*, put his views forward:

Hacknied and threadbare as this subject of the Aborigines may appear to some, every reflecting man — everyone who has the least consideration for the lives of his family and the safety of his property...must be convinced that never at any one moment since the existence of the Colony have their atrocities assumed a more fearless aspect, never have they so plainly shewn that they are actuated by the principle of revenge. Their attacks on the lives and properties of the inhabitants on the North side of the Island during the last month, reaching to within a very short distance of our Northern Capital, fully confirm the opinion long entertained by many, that to them, as to all savages, revenge is one of the overpowering passions. In spite of the manner you have handled the subject, you will allow His Excellency has incessantly been devising means to subdue these formidable enemies of the Settlers, and few are there among us that do not lament the end has not justified the means. As to those who are 'loud and long' upon the subject, who can shew plainly, as they say, how the several treacherous tribes may all be taken, without its costing the Government more than a mere trifle... who would undertake to capture them on such and such terms... who blame the measures that have been adopted, have they done anything more than talk? I venture to say they have not, and yet those individuals continue unabated in their clamour. Had such communications been forwarded to Colonel Arthur they would have met with every attention...been acknowledged in the manner they deserved, and might have proved most fortunate in their results. It is the duty of every individual, who from long residence in the interior has become acquainted with the habits of Aborigines, to communicate any striking features to the Head of the Government. I say, Sir, it is their interest — it is the interest of every Settler, although perhaps his own dwelling or those of his dependents have not been pillaged, nor his men speared, nor his children immolated — sacrificed at the altar of revenge, by these wretches — humanity, I say, requires the mental and bodily exertion of every Settler in the Colony, so that an effectual stop may be put to their enormities.

What the Aborigines' views were on the subject of their future status evidently nobody ever bothered to find out. One thing is certain, however; after the fiasco of the Black War had ended, if it had been possible to declare the victor of this ludicrous affair, the title would undoubtedly have gone to the Aborigines.

Stories and rumours were being circulated throughout the colony on the progress of the Grand Army. One man heading a party left the body of a black in the spot where he fell on being shot, in order to entice his comrades to the place. He made his party lie in ambush, to destroy all that came within shooting range.

A scout, or picquet, who was about a hundred metres ahead of one of the battalions of the Grand Army, was speared when he was lighting a fire. The man was only slightly wounded, but the Aborigines after throwing more spears came and drew them out themselves and then made off. They were reported as robbing every hut they came to, which they found relatively easy as people fled, most of them being unprotected. All those who could carry arms were off fighting the Aborigines.

A number of ticket-of-leave men who had arrived in town from their whaling stations were put in requisition by the police magistrate to be enlisted and sent to the interior to assist the Grand Army. In a report received on 12 November two girls were said to have been speared by natives, one critically. In a further message the line was reported to be still advancing. Two mobs had been seen the day before, one of about thirty Aborigines, and the other of twelve, both believed to be still behind the lines.

A few days later one Aborigine was landed at the jetty and taken to the gaol. It was believed that this was the only prisoner taken by the parties in pursuit of the Aborigines. And on this note of anticlimax the 'Grand Army' folded its tents and wearily trudged its way home again. This humiliating end to the Black War brought forth a great deal of criticism from all concerned, although the Government acted as if it had achieved a resounding victory. A report that another black expedition was to be begun was quickly vetoed.

By the end of January 1831 the question was being asked: 'What has become of all the Aboriginal tribes?' They appeared at all events to have been frightened by the war. Some people said that it was the season when all the tribes congregated in the western part of the island, and that they would not be heard of for a couple of months, but after that time it was expected their attacks would be even stronger. Tribes had been seen making their way westward at fixed periods, generally going and returning by the same route.

A news item the next month remarked that it was quite amusing how civilised the blacks were becoming under the superintendence of Mr Robinson, the conciliator. Two or three Aborigines were continually parading up and down the streets to show themselves, dressed in long superfine blue coats, for all the world 'looking like gentlemen with no shoes'.

The picture was not quite so benign a few months later when a number of blacks were reported as prowling at the back of Mr Scott's farm on the Macquarie River, and in September of the same year several murders had been committed by hostile Aboriginal tribes near Port Sorell.

In January 1832 twenty-six Aborigines captured by Mr Robinson marched into town, when it was stated:

A more grotesque appearance we have seldom witnessed than the arrival of these natives. At an early hour the inhabitants were expecting them; but it was ten o'clock when we observed a crowd of persons descending the hill... The number of blacks, including the tame mob, amounted to forty, all of whom, with the exception of trowsers that had been presented to them a short distance from town, were arrayed in battle order, each male carrying three spears of twelve to fifteen feet long in the left hand, and only one in the right. As they continued their advance, they shrieked their war song. They then proceeded to Government House and were met by the Lieutenant-Governor, who gave each a loaf of bread. A Band was playing to the astonishment of the natives, who later gave an exhibition of spear throwing.

During the next two years reports came in occasionally of sightings of small bands of Aborigines, but they appeared to have lost their aggressiveness. In 1839 news from the Aboriginal establishment stated that under the instruction of the celebrated Mr Robinson the Aborigines had so improved in the arts of civilised life that they had built piggeries and cured pork of the very best quality, so prime, indeed, that some consignments had already reached Hobart Town. However, three Aborigines still at large had lately shown a decided hostility to the whites, having made an attempt upon the lives of two men near the River Dee.

In 1841 a party of eight or nine Aborigines twice visited the farm of Mr King at Rocky Cape. Everyone had thought that there were none in the island, notwithstanding reports of some having been seen to the westward now and again. No doubt now existed. They were all believed to be of one family. Four or five of these people were afterwards caught and sent to Flinders Island, the rest being last seen in the vicinity of Cape Grim.

Another group of seven Aborigines of Van Diemens Land arrived in the cutter *Vansittart* in 1842 and were placed under the care of Mr Thomson at the gaol before being taken to Flinders Island. They were of the one family, the children being five boys.

Further news of the Aborigines now came mainly from the £2000-a-year Aboriginal establishment at Flinders Island, where it seems that there was not enough water on the island for the use of the establishment, and that fresh water had to be taken from Hobart Town. The complaint was also made that proper attention was not being paid to morals or religion, neither among the whites nor blacks, and that the late Superintendent had not been supported in his attempt to regularise the settlement. It was hinted that he had been thwarted by Sir John Franklin, who wanted a situation for a certain protégé who had been ousted from a previous appointment.

It was rumoured in 1845 that the Government intended to remove the Aboriginal tribes (or what remained of them) to the mainland. It did not meet with public approval as it was felt that these 'interesting people' might yet prove a source of much annoyance to the peaceable settlers. Teamed with runaway probationers, they could cause further misery, and although the settlers had always deprecated the enormous expense of maintaining these 'native lords of the soil', it was still considered better than the chances of their getting loose again.

Two years later it was reported that the projected removal of the remnant of Aborigines from Flinders Island had awakened 'the most humane consideration'. The *Hobart Town Guardian* gave the following account in November 1847:

The remaining portion of the original inhabitants of this Island, who have been so long in exile in Bass's Straits, have at last been returned to their native country, and are now localised at Oyster Cove in D'Entrecastreaux Channel. For some short period after arrival there, these people seemed to entertain fear; but that feeling has now gone off, and they now venture to roam about in diligent search of their favourite food — the kangaroo and opossum. They have succeeded in capturing several of the former animal — and seem quite delighted to have an opportunity of once more enjoying the chase on their native soil. They occasionally visit the houses of the neighbouring settlers, and, as they now understand the English language, remove any unfavourable impression which a recollection of their former atrocities might have raised. We hope that the Mechanic's Institute will procure a grouped drawing of these people, so that our descendants may be able to form correct ideas as to the personal appearance of the original inhabitants of Van Diemen's Land.

Another report of the activities of this declining race appeared in the *Colonial Times* in December 1854. On a pleasure trip in the steamer *Culloden* to Oyster Cove and the channel a party of men went ashore to visit the Aborigines' settlement in Oyster Cove. About a dozen got into the boat, which had some difficulty in landing. In the words of one of them, this is what took place:

Some ten minutes' walking brought us to the settlement, a quadrangle with a range of wooden buildings on three sides. The first person we saw was 'Mary Ann' the Queen, a fine, portly, smiling lady about thirty years of age. The King stood close by. He is stoutly built, and about five feet and a half high. Only four men were visible. We saw some half dozen ladies, but with the exception of Her Majesty, they had all passed their prime. Some youngsters were caught taking a survey of us through a partly opened door, but when our eyes were turned they all beat a retreat. The men were all neatly dressed. The women wore a sort of sack made from thick blue wool. Only one wore a printed dress. One of them wore a very neat sort of woollen dress, fastened round her waist by a bright leathern strap. Most of them had for their head-dress a tall conical woollen red cap. One lady had a silk handkerchief bound round her head, inside of which above her left ear, was stuck the well-worn pipe ready in case of need. They asked for tobacco — cigars they would not smoke — and complained of their own tobacco being bad. Mary Ann, it appears, can read with fluency, and asked for books. She wanted 'something lively'. She had read 'Uncle Tom's

Cabin' and pronounced it 'very much true!' Books were promised her. Our stay was cut short by hearing the 'bell pealing', and after many bows and shaking of hands with the ladies, we finally took ourselves off, accompanied by His Majesty. These singular beings are fast dying out; only nineteen are now left of a race who once competed with the white man.

By 1854 realisation of what inhumane treatment the Aborigines had received at the hands of the white race was beginning to sink slowly into the consciousness of the inhabitants of the island, and the *Hobarton Mercury* seems to display genuine regret in this short paragraph about them:

To what a melancholy state have the Aboriginal tribes of this island been reduced, may be imagined from the fact that out of the hundreds who, twenty years since, trod proudly their native soil, only five men, eleven women and two boys remain to lament their premature termination of their race. Notwithstanding the care and attention paid by the Government to this miserable remnant of a once dreaded race, their confinement to one locality, so adverse to their peculiarly erratic habits, has tended in a great measure to annihilate them. In a few short years the Aborigines of Van Diemen's Land will exist only in history.

Prophetic words, indeed. On 8 May 1876 Truganini, the last surviving full-blooded Tasmanian Aboriginal, died in Hobart.

Our race is fast decaying; — far and wide
Extend thy riches, and increase thine heirs,
Oh, let us die where our forefathers died,
That we may mix our wretched dust with theirs.

6

The Bushrangers

We are the boys that fear no dangers
And what you term us is bush-rangers;
If it is our lives you do demand,
True to our guns, then we must stand.

We are all young and in our prime,
To meet our hardships we incline
And if our blood you mean to shed
Life for life before we yield.

'Tis in the bush we are forced to go —
You settlers prove our overthrow
To rob and plunder is against our will,
But we must have a living still.

Now to this country we are come,
Banished from our native land,
And if we can't go back no more,
We will rob the rich to feed the poor.

This piece was found in the pocket of one of seven individuals who were found guilty of bushranging, and sentenced to death. Written in blood, it almost sums up the sentiments of the hordes of 'armed banditti' who hindered the development of the colony from its earliest days.

The bushrangers were an even greater menace to the settlers than the Aborigines, both black and white suffering equally at their hands. A trail of havoc and destruction was left behind them wherever they chose to descend. The bands were invariably made up of escaped convicts, runaways, bolters and absconders who had managed to elude capture, and in order to exist took up arms and lived a lawless life until they were usually caught and executed.

An editorial in the *Hobart Town Gazette* in 1825 made these comments:

> We have long observed with regret and a feeling not altogether different from indignation, that the most decided criminals, who from time to time are banished by the Courts of Australia as unfit to any longer blend with that of Society which they have insulted and disgraced, are sent to the Penal Settlement in this Colony — where they inoculate with their venom all who happen to partake with them of captivity, and whence they not unfrequently escape to stain their hands with human blood, and by becoming bushrangers, to place the safety of all our provincial residents at stake.

Michael Howe, a bushranger who styled himself the 'Governor of the ranges' had a cruel and treacherous nature. With his band of eight runaways he terrorised the countryside until the latter part of 1818, when he met his death in a running battle for his life in October of that year.

There was news of a band of bushrangers being pursued in 1824, very likely a gang led by Matthew Brady and James McCabe, a pair whose exploits were causing general alarm. They were very active during 1825, and numerous sightings were made of them as they robbed and pillaged their way through the island. Big rewards were offered for their capture. In October they appeared at the house of a Mr Meredith at Oyster Bay, which they robbed of bacon and hams, and later they were seen at Green Ponds near Austins Ferry, where they wounded the occupants of a house they intended to plunder.

McCabe was caught the same month, and was described as being in a destitute state, wearing only a pair of 'trowsers' and a red shirt, neither shoes nor stockings. The rest of the gang, under the leadership of Brady, continued their lawless career, and in December made a desperate attack on the Sorell gaol. In January 1826 they robbed the home of Mr Lord at 'Laurenny' on the Derwent, and in March also committed outrages and murder at the house of Mr Dry, Brady and a party of fourteen making the attack. Brady's luck, however, was running out, for shortly after this daring man was caught by Mr Bateman.

Another bushranger still at large was the murderer Jeffries, described as 'that monster in human shape'; a man feared more than all the others put together. An account taken from a letter from a Launceston correspondent, dated 1 January 1826, tells this story:

We have three or four fellows out on this side, and yesterday morning they went to the house of a native youth named Tibbs, about a mile from this Town, and in sight of it. They robbed him, and it is supposed murdered and disposed of the body of his stock-keeper. They shot Mr Tibbs in the neck, and what is more than all, they took his wife away with them, with an infant at her breast, and she has not been heard of since. Since writing the above, I have heard that Mrs Tibbs has arrived in Town, but without her child, the villains having murdered it.

Jeffries was later heard of at George Town, where the mangled remains of Mrs Tibbs' baby were found. Mercifully, further news from Launceston in February was to the effect that all of Jeffries' gang was in custody. From the gaol, Jeffries was reported to be writing the history of his life, 'in which he describes crimes of as deep a dye, perpetrated by him in England and Scotland, as even those committed by him in this Island'.

Even the prisoners would not associate with Jeffries, so much was he loathed by all. After his capture he was placed in the same cell as Brady, who had always shown compassion for the defenceless. Brady told the turnkey that if Jeffries was not taken out, 'he would be found in the morning without his head'. Before his removal to another cell Jeffries voluntarily gave up two knives which he had concealed about his person.

Brady and Jeffries were to meet again on the gallows where they were executed early in May with three other bushrangers, Bryant, Perry and Thomson. Immediately after Brady and Jeffries were taken from the gallows, two 'plaister of Paris casts of their countenances were taken by Dr Scott, R.N. the Colonial Surgeon'. It was lamented at the time that the Act of Parliament allowing for dissection did not extend to the colony, 'not more for the advantage of science, than with reference to other considerations'.

James McCabe, who had been taken first, was not executed until towards the end of May, along with seven other contemporaries. 'All the eight unhappy men died truly penitent, praying most fervently; McCabe in particular offered up an earnest ejaculation,' which it was hoped would be heard by his associates still at large, so that they might see the error of their ways. Six more men underwent the awful sentence of the law the next morning.

Only three bushrangers were now believed to be at large — Tilly, Bird and Dunne. Dunne, who was apprehended in October 1826, had a showy personality, and at his later execution 'appeared on the scaffold dressed in a singular costume — a long white muslin robe, with a huge black cross marked thereon, before and behind; his cap was of a similar character. He walked with the rosary in his hands'.

The *Colonial Times*, on 19 January 1827, strongly censured the way Dunne and his companions were followed to the grave: 'It has always been our opinion, that a man who expiates his crimes upon the scaffold, should be interred with as little formality as possible — be they rich, or be they poor — be they great or be they humble — be they free, or be they bond — the same order should be observed.'

Early in 1827 it was announced that the passengers who had arrived by the vessels in harbour were not a little surprised to learn, after the accounts which had reached them in England, that there was not a single bushranger now at large in Van Diemens Land! The colony rejoiced briefly in the 'abolition of bushranging', until the following year when an £80 reward was offered for the capture of a party of armed bushrangers who had plundered a house near the Esk River. Mention is made in 1830 of two bushrangers who escaped after being escorted from Oatlands, due to the negligence of a constable of the Richmond district.

Another bushranger named Britton, who had been one of the terrors of the countryside for many years, came into prominence in 1833, when three men, presumed to be in his party, were seen in January of that year. It was later reported that Britton had visited the home of a resident near Launceston and taken every moveable valuable. In September five bushrangers who had infested the Eastern Tiers for nearly four months were captured near New Norfolk. Early the next year four more were caught, found guilty of burglary, and sentenced to execution at Launceston. With the exception of Britton who was still at large it was a bad year for the marauders, with four more being captured by some prisoner constables.

Apparently owing to all this zeal on the part of the authorities, there was a scarcity of bushrangers until 1838, when the *Colonial Times* felt compelled to issue the following warning:

Absconding from chain-gangs is becoming of daily occurrence, indeed from one gang in the interior, fourteen men absconded last week. Accounts from Port Arthur state that six prisoners rushed the watchmen, knocked them down, and have taken to the bush. From the want of energy and decision on the part of the Government...we fully expect to see bushranging again disorganizing the whole state of society.

True to those words a fresh outbreak did occur within a very short while, and a new batch of marauders began their plundering of the colonists in the interior. In April a gang of bushrangers were seen prowling about the Coal River, and a man was shot in an attempt to break into a hut. The same month news was received of a fatal collision near Campbell Town between a party of bushrangers and a number of constables and soldiers, which resulted in the death of three men on the side of the law. Rewards were again offered in an effort to stamp out the menace.

Four bushrangers were captured and condemned to death in May for robbery. Three were executed but the fourth man was reprieved, owing to a 'strange formality'. He had been a free man before being sentenced to the chain gang, which evidently placed him above the twice-convicted felons. The executions were public, which brought forth the comment from the *Colonial Times* that 'as examples public executions are useless'.

During 1839 and 1840 the position was just the same, with many accounts of men escaping and later being caught, although there was always a number of absconders out in the bush at any given period.

In 1841 two runaways from Westbury, Hogan and Armitage, alarmed that district. They were reported as being 'well-known to all the people in the vicinity...are on terms of intimacy with most of the assigned servants, are well-acquainted with the localities, and are resolute men into the bargain'. These men later visited the Traveller's Rest, plundered a man there, and 'made quite a laugh of the police'. In August a bushranger who had escaped from the Jericho road-party was executed in front of the gaol.

By October the bushrangers Beard and Fisher had 'commenced their summer sports' by the plunder of a settler at Lake Sorell, helping themselves to flour, tea, sugar and a few other useful articles. They behaved with politeness, despite being armed with a double-barrelled percussion gun and two brace of pistols each.

The owner of a schooner, the *Water Witch*, arrived at George Town in January 1842 with the news that his vessel had been seized by three bushrangers at Port Sorell. He did not gain much sympathy, as the capture of this vessel was regarded as a disgrace to the master and crew. Fresh alarm arose in April at the report that Westwood had absconded from Port Arthur with six of his Sydney comrades.

Now appears upon the scene that 'superstar' of bushrangers, Martin Cash. At this time he was captured, after having been at large for some time. With his usual recklessness he ventured into town early in May, and was caught by a couple of constables who took him into custody. That is only part of the story, however, for on 26 December 1842 Martin Cash made his famous escape from Port Arthur, and for the next nine months led the authorities a merry chase. Martin Cash was a tall, powerful man, and an excellent bushman, which enabled him to find his way through dense bushland never before trodden by the white man. He was a born leader, and soon formed the band of Cash and Co., consisting of Cash, Kavanagh and Jones.

In January 1843 the bushrangers paid a visit to the house of a settler at Bagdad, but as the alarm was quickly given, they left without stealing. The Governor came forward promptly and offered a reward of £50 and a pardon for the capture of each of the men. A farm at Broadmarsh next had the misfortune to be robbed by Cash and his men. As a result the owner had all his assigned servants taken from him by the authorities in the middle of harvest, probably because the bushrangers were allowed to escape.

Cash and Co. next visited Mr Stoddart's house, the 'Woolpack', at Macquarie Plains, where they tied up the inmates and took away a quantity of spirits, after exchanging shots with the constables, leaving one for dead. Afterwards they robbed the premises of a Mr Cawthorn. A chase on foot took place by strong parties of the military and constables, and it was believed their mad career would soon end. A report said they had two women with them.

It was reported in February that the bushrangers were still at large. 'On Saturday last, Cash and Co. fell in with Mr Cook... above Green Point, near Mt Dromedary, and robbed him of his watch and a beautiful double-barrelled gun, coolly remarking that they were only taking the latter on loan...Cash wore an old great coat, buttoned up to the chin — a fancy of his own, as he had plenty of clothes.'

Meanwhile other bushrangers at large were reported captured, but Cash and Co. continued to dominate the scene. 'We hope, that on this day week, we may have to record their capture; especially as Martin Cash's wife, a drunken creature, has, it is averred, proceeded to join her husband. If she does join him, his career will soon be stopped.' This was the fervent prediction of the *Colonial Times*.

In March there were three robberies in one week. A police report stated that three men, 'supposed to be Cash, Kavanagh and Jones, act in a manner so cool and cautious, yet so determined — and altogether with a system so judicious and orderly, that they seem to have gained boldness and confidence in proportion to their iniquitous successes'. In April Cash and Co. made their appearance at Jerusalem.

The bushrangers were seen on the Clyde in May and were described as having a miserable, haggard appearance, being badly clothed and with scarcely a shoe between them. It was hoped that the career of these lawless men was drawing to a speedy close. For the remainder of the month they were more than usually tranquil, although they found time to pay a visit to Captain M'Kay on the Dee and 'dine with him'.

Cash and Co. were still at large in July, although two other bushrangers, Jeffs and Conway, had been captured and were tried at Launceston and found guilty of murder. On a Tuesday in August the Mail was stopped and robbed by Cash and Jones at a lonely spot near the top of Spring Hill.

Their good fortune now deserted them, for the end of August was to see the downfall of the gang. On 29 August the notorious bushranger, Martin Cash, was taken in Hobart Town and lodged in gaol. Dressed in sailor's garb, he and his companion had been noticed by a watch-party. During the struggle which followed a constable named Winstanley was shot by Cash and died two days later.

In September was 'the trial of Martin Cash — a prisoner of the Crown, for having shot one Peter Winstanley, of which he languished and on the 31st August, died'. Cash and Kavanagh were both sentenced to death and were to have been executed in the same month, but they were given respite for another week. Then came the news that Kavanagh 'has been spared at the moment when death was apparently his only hope'. He was reputed to have been a notorious criminal from the age of seven years. Cash's fate was still in the balance.

Meanwhile the city prison was crowded with offenders, chiefly runaways from road gangs, and Cash and Kavanagh were among them. To relieve the monotony this pair got up a little 'melodramatic episode' which could have had tragic consequences. Cash rather liked abusing the soldiers, and while passing the time this way in the day-yard he was joined by several other prisoners. It was found necessary to send for the head gaoler. While this officer was speaking to Cash, Kavanagh approached from behind, looking as though he was going to strike Mr Capon. He was seen by the sentry, who pushed him back with his bayonet, but it made Cash so violent that they had to confine him, heavily ironed, in a cell, fastened to an iron ring.

Obviously the strain was beginning to tell, but there was a long wait ahead for Cash, as it was not until December that he knew what the future had in store for him. The *Colonial Times* broke the news: 'We are informed that Cash's doom is now sealed' (which did not sound very hopeful), but the paper went on to say that it was the decision of the English judges that the sentence of death passed upon the prisoner be revoked on condition that he be sent to Norfolk Island where Kavanagh was already serving his sentence.

It is strange that Cash's life should have been spared when so many other lawbreakers had been executed for lesser crimes, but his superb bushmanship and daring had excited much admiration among the people and given him the image of a popular hero. Perhaps under happier circumstances, and given the opportunity, he might have proved himself among the community. His well-preserved grave can be readily found at Cornelian Bay Cemetery, Hobart, where the headstone gives the date of his death as 26 August 1878, and his age as sixty-seven.

Jones, the remaining member of Cash and Co., was still at large in February 1844, and was travelling with another band of outlaws. One of the last acts he and his companions committed was to attack a house at the Black Brush and tie up a man, putting his wife on the fire to make her confess where the money was which they suspected the old people possessed.

Fortunately for all concerned his capture and that of two of his companions was announced in March, 'the capture being effected in a very masterly style by District Constable Morton of the Brighton Police'. Jones was reported to have been shot in the head and arm. In April he and a companion, James Platt, 'underwent the last sentence of the law on the accustomed scaffold! The crowd was immense; and it was expected that Jones would address the populace, but he appeared too deeply absorbed in prayer to heed aught but his awful condition — he died and made no sign'.

This did not put a stop to bushranging. Many men were still at large and continued to terrorise the countryside. The same year a gang of armed men supposed to have escaped from Port Arthur visited the farm of Roderic O'Connor of the Lake River, where they bailed up fourteen men and after taking some goods departed. Four men were captured later on. Another three bushrangers paid a visit to a resident at the River Isis, but their behaviour was not violent, in contrast to two armed men who plundered another residence near Green Ponds. Britton, another notorious runaway, was re-captured and taken into custody once more, while another absconder was captured right in Hobart Town.

Conditions were hardly any better in 1845 when the settlers in the interior were reported to be anxious due to the exploits of two men, Priest and Smith. Another offender, Jacky Jacky, 'a bold man possessed of more than ordinary intelligence', had parted with his comrades and was roaming at large by himself, committing robberies at will. However, both he and Priest were captured in September.

It was the same story in 1846, with a fresh batch of absconders seemingly replacing those which had been taken by the police. On the morning of Good Friday eight men made their escape from Port Arthur in a whale-boat and were at large for a few months before capture. Bushranging became so commonplace that it hardly warranted a headline, although a reward of £100 was offered by the Government in March 1848 for the capture of four bushrangers. This brought quick results, for four armed men were captured shortly afterwards at Swan Port. They were executed at Oatlands in May.

By this time, however, the 'Desperate Fingal Bushrangers' were creating a great disturbance. Somehow they managed to escape from the colony, and two constables were sent to Adelaide in the *Henry* in an attempt to catch them. They were captured at Yorke Peninsula and were brought back and lodged in safe custody in the Hobart Town gaol. It was later revealed that they had escaped from Van Diemens Land in the American ship *Barclay*.

There was no change in the situation over the next five years; in fact, by 1853 the position seems to have become even worse. At the beginning of the year two bushrangers, mounted and heavily armed, were sacking and pillaging in the northern part of the island. Seven men had just absconded from Port Arthur, and the constables were in hot pursuit. Two men, named Dalton and Kelly, had been captured and charged with murder. 'About 2000 persons assembled in front of the gaol at Launceston, a greater crowd than was ever witnessed on such an occasion before,' to see their execution.

Another notorious character was caught in September, a success which was marred by the report of four armed bushrangers breaking into the hut of a poor man at Woodcutters Hill, stealing all the clothing they could find, as well as his wife's ring. Two more men were sentenced to death in 1853.

After fifty years of settlement bushrangers were still committing crimes at the close of 1854, despite the boast of the *Hobarton Mercury* that 'all the rogues are gone to the gold colonies'. At that stage people must have taken the prediction that 'one day Van Diemen's Land will become the most respectable of all the Australian colonies' with a very large grain of salt!

7

'Tassels on a Blind Cord'

Hangings were taken as a matter of course by the inhabitants of Van Diemens Land with many people making a pastime of watching the event. All too frequently comments like: 'At an early hour on Monday morning we renewed our dreary walk to the scene of death' appeared in the early press of the colony. After witnessing the death of ten men, one man remarked that the suspended bodies looked like 'tassels on a blind cord'.

Multiple executions were the order of the day, with the victims being not only bushrangers, escaped convicts and the like, but people from all walks of life, although mainly the 'lower orders', as they were called, suffered. With so many crimes other than murder listed as capital offences, the hangman had a very busy time. In fact one executioner who had officiated at the hanging of no less than 170 persons during a period of seven years let it be known that he was anxious to obtain an increase in salary, along with the other Government officers, and even hinted at giving up the post altogether!

Shocking murders were committed almost daily; dreadful affairs which make it seem unbelievable that ordinary people could live among so much carnage. A bloodthirsty attempt at murder took place even in the Police Office, in the presence of the police and magistrates. A man who was undergoing examination on a charge of beating a boy in a dangerous and inhuman manner, put his hand into his pocket just as the lad had given his evidence, took out a razor, and slashed it across the boy's throat. The man was handcuffed by the constables and taken to gaol. The child was later reported to be in a fair way to recovery in the General Hospital.

Prior to 1824 convicted men had to be sent to New South Wales for trial, a formality which was often dispensed with, the offender being given rough justice at the hands of a local military jury. Those that did return from Sydney after sentence in the court there were sent back to Hobart Town for execution. One unfortunate man, under sentence for sheep-stealing, threw himself overboard soon after the vessel came to anchor and drowned rather than face death by hanging. This was not an uncommon event.

A description of a hanging carried out on seven men tells of a cart arriving with seven coffins. As the criminals were led one by one from the cell, their arms were tied behind their backs, and the cap of death was placed upon their heads. Meanwhile the church bell continued to toll at distant and solemn intervals. All were penitent. Some prayed aloud on the scaffold, while others sang hymns, one verse beginning 'Oh Lord, turn not thy face from us'. It was a scene which caused many tears to be shed among the spectators.

For those who missed this performance another nine men were 'turned off' on the following Monday. This account of the proceedings in the Supreme Court in December 1825 gives an idea of what went on there:

One of the most lamentable sights which can be exhibited in any country took place this morning, in the placing at the Bar of the Criminal Court seventy-one human beings, to receive their sentences for crimes of every degree of turpitude, committed in a country where the population is so comparatively small, and where the inducements to crime are so few. Of these unhappy men twenty-five received sentence of death, many of whom will most probably suffer this awful doom... (It is only due to His Honour Chief Justice Pedder to express our humble admiration of the patience and humanity which His Honour shews upon all occasions where the life or liberty of a fellow-creature, without distinction as to situation, is placed in his hands.)

His Honour did not receive too many testimonials as a rule, but of course it always paid to be on the right side of the judge! On another occasion Chief Justice Pedder passed sentence of death on 'nearly twenty unfortunate culprits begging for their lives — while the stern voice of justice forbid the judge to listen to the tender one of mercy'. Of these men, none was guilty of murder; they were principally there for stealing sheep and cattle. Two men were sentenced to death for robbing another man of one shilling, and one for stealing 17s 6d.

In 1829 thirteen out of eighteen criminals sentenced to death at the Criminal Sessions held at Launceston 'expiated their crimes' by losing their life. The Reverend Dr Brown had paid them every attention since their condemnation, and their behaviour was said to be 'very suitable to the occasion'.

Between the years 1823 and 1826 upwards of 100 executions took place in Van Diemens Land. Of thirty-seven men sentenced to death by Chief Justice Pedder in September 1826, only two were convicted of murder, the others being hanged for sheep-stealing, robbery, absconding, forgery, bushranging and burglary. One man who had actually killed another was sentenced to be burnt in the hand and discharged! The two men condemned for murder were Aborigines, Jack and Dick. The account of the execution is particularly distressing:

> Dick, one of the Aborigines, suffering under a loathsome cutaneous disease, was carried up the ladder by the executioner... Screaming most bitterly, he was sat on a stool to drop him into eternity. Jack, the younger, prayed most fervently to the Almighty. The old black died very hard: and the cord having slipped from the younger up to his elbow, he reached up his hand and bled profusely from the nose.

Another victim who paid the penalty for sheep-stealing was an emigrant a few years out from Scotland and of very 'respectable connexions' both there and in the colony, where he left a widow and two young children. James Rowles, a little humpbacked man, an indoor assigned servant to a shopkeeper in Elizabeth Street, forfeited his life for robbing his master in the daytime, during divine service.

> Thus an example was made of this man — the first instance under such circumstances in this Colony, as a caution to assigned prisoners, as well as all servants, in whom, more or less, confidence is placed by their masters or employers. Let them remember it was the confidence reposed in him, and broken so shamefully which precluded him from mercy, rendering his crime so obnoxious in the eye of the law.

Mary MacLachlan was charged in 1830 with the wilful murder of her newborn son. The prisoner had given birth while imprisoned in the female house of correction and had strangled the child, afterwards concealing it in the water closet. A vast number of witnesses were examined and after an investigation which lasted from the morning until late in the evening the prisoner was found

This advertisement for a 'Series of Select Balls' appeared in the *Colonial Times* on 30 June 1853 *(Archives Office of Tasmania)*

BALS D'HIVER.

MESSRS. HAND & FORRESTER beg respectfully to announce to their Patrons, Friends, and the Public in general, that it is their intention to give a

SERIES OF SELECT BALLS

During the present season. The first will take place **THIS EVENING**, the 30th instant, in Harrington-street, at the

ACADEMIE D'APPOLLON.

The Doors will be open at Half-past Eight P.M, Dancing to commence at Half-past Nine P.M. Admission, by Ticket only, for a Gentleman 5s.; for a Gentleman and Two Ladies, 7s. 6d.

Tickets can be obtained at the Academy; at Mr. Panton's, "The Golden Gate," corner of Collins and Harrington-streets; at Mr. Grenville's, Perfumer, &c.; and at the "Waterman's Arms," Liverpool-street.

PROGRAMME OF FIRST BALL!

Part I.

1. Country Dance (Triumph.)
2. Quadrilles (First Set.)
3. Polka (Jullien.)
4. Waltz, *a deux tempts.*
5. Quadrilles (Caledonians.)
6. Schottische.
7. Quadrilles.
8. Scotch Reel.
9. Waltz.
10. Quadrilles (Lancers.)
11. Country Dance.
12. Polka.
13. Mélange.
14. Quadrilles.

Part II.

1. Quadrilles.
2. Waltz, *a deux temps.*
3. Quadrilles (Lancers.)
4. Spanish Dance.
5. Polka.
6. Schottische.
7. Country Dance.
8. Quadrilles (Caledonians.)
9. Scotch Reel.
10. Quadrilles (First Set.)
11. Waltz.
12. Polka
13. Schottische
14. Country Dance (Sir Roger de Coverley)

Hobart Town, June 27.

1647

guilty and sentenced to be executed on the following Saturday morning, her body to be then dissected. This was only the second instance of a female being tried for murder in the colony, and she was the first convicted of the offence.

It was a brutal age and there was much evidence of sadism among the men who held authority. Three men awaiting trial for the attempted murder of a flagellator were taken into custody so that the earlier prescribed punishment of flagellation which had been ordered for them could still be inflicted. As the regular flagellator was of course unable to perform his duty the boatswain of the *Sir Charles Forbes* most kindly offered his services, 'and this "amateur flogger" was accepted, and really did perform the office, *con amore*'.

Two absconders from the penal settlement at Macquarie Harbour were executed in August 1831. There was a very strong suspicion that these two men had murdered the companions with whom they escaped. These men, Macavoy and Broughton, admitted that they had cut up the body of a man named Fagan, and roasted it, except for the hands, feet and head. This made it lighter to carry as well as making it keep longer.

At the execution of two men convicted for having shot at and wounded a soldier of the 63rd Regiment the behaviour of the men was considered most strange as 'both protested their innocence and on mounting the scaffold continued their cries of being murdered'. This was in 1832. Of another execution it was said: 'The fatal bolt was drawn at twenty minutes past eight o'clock and the five unhappy men were launched into eternity.' This execution took place in front of the gaol in 1833; those hanged were two men for carnally knowing a child under ten years, two for bushranging, and one for an unnatural act.

A trial which excited very considerable interest in 1833 was that of Ann Edwards, tried for an attempt to murder her husband. The fact that she was to be executed the day after her trial created much public sympathy. The husband, a dissolute man, had given much provocation and was still very much alive. She had acted in a fit of passion, not with premeditation. After the attack on her husband the woman had immediately given herself up. The sentence was later remitted, thus sparing the public the revolting spectacle of the execution of a female which they would have undoubtedly attended all the same.

Many innocent people were hanged on the slightest pretext of a crime. A man who went missing for a few days for reasons of his own, although his disappearance was attributed to domestic causes, was presumed murdered. Two men taken up on suspicion of his

Top: The Bank of Van Diemens Land, Macquarie Street, in the 1830s *(Allport Library)*. Bottom: Old Government House, Macquarie Street, as seen from the river. This woodcut was printed in the *Courier* on 12 September 1829 *(Archives Office of Tasmania)*

murder were about to be tried when the 'victim' turned up, which was regarded as being a 'favourable circumstance', as execution was usually carried out a week after the trial.

Three men on their way to take their trial for murder of a woman were brought to town in a cart, in company with the fourth of the party who had turned King's evidence. 'What must have been the feelings of these unhappy wretches, the three knowing the one intended to swear away their lives... the one knowing, on his oath, his companions depended for existence. These men ate together, all huddled together in the same cart, and very likely, were allowed to converse together.' The *Times* asked these questions, but there would not have been the opportunity for the men concerned to have answered them before meeting their inevitable end.

The execution of Greenwood for absconding created universal disgust in Hobart Town. Every voice was raised in disapprobation against it. Only in such a place as Van Diemens Land could it happen. He had been caught and sent to prison. The magistrate (Mason) awarded him one hundred lashes for absenting himself, and 'mercifully' sent him to trial for using means to prevent his capture, knowing that he must be found guilty and hanged. The inhumanity exercised against him was deplored by all who had any feelings of compassion. The magistrate, who sent him to degrading torture at the triangles, then sent him at once to trial for the greater offence. Spectators shuddered at the spectacle of the man's mangled and lacerated body when led to execution. The *Colonial Times* gave this account of the butchery:

We have been credibly informed, that the back of the poor unhappy wretch Greenwood was in such a lacerated state, that the wound burst and the matter exuded through his shirt. What a dreadful state to send 'a man and a brother' to meet death. The Sudds and Thompson affair was cruel, but Greenwood's case appears to us to be very much more so — 'You shall be first flogged, and then hung' — what; corporeally punish a man — inflict such wound as shall prevent his mind from being calm, and then in the turbulence of mental agony, when he can scarcely think of worldly affairs, much less of spiritual, whirl him into eternity to meet the Lord and Saviour without being prepared by the solace of calm and penitent prayer. Horrible, most horrible!!

On sentence being passed on five men for robbery in 1835 none of the prisoners, except one, seemed in the least touched with remorse. He, indeed, declared his innocence, but the rest of them uttered vehement execrations against an informer. One said he had had that day plenty of law but no justice; another said that the sooner he was hanged the better, for after the false swearing he had heard he was sick of life. Many uttered those last words; some received their fate with scarcely any emotion, while others died admitting the justice of their end.

A horrible murder of a young woman named Mary Ann Mills, who was the wife of a coachman at New Norfolk, occurred near the town. The deed was 'perpetrated by the monster taking off her garter, making a slip noose with it, and strangling her'. The trial of Samuel Guillem on the charge of her murder took place on 10 March 1837 before His Honour Chief Justice Pedder and a military jury. Forty-six witnesses were subpoenaed. Mrs Mills, who was delicate in health, went for a short ride in her husband's coach, but feeling ill, got out to walk back home. She never returned, her body being found near Terry's Paddock. Her gloves were still on her hands — an important point, as Guillem, in service of William Jarvis, later was said to have told another prisoner in the gaol at New Norfolk that Mrs Mills could not scratch much as she was wearing gloves. Two other females had been murdered in the same district shortly before this case without anyone being brought to justice. Guillem suffered the extreme penalty of the law. He made no confession but did not deny the crime, and he begged that he might not be asked on the scaffold whether he was guilty or otherwise.

At another morbid trial the following month two men, McKay and Lambe, were charged with murder. The Chief Justice passed sentence for them both to be hanged the next Monday morning, and when dead, their bodies to be hanged in chains. The *Cornwall Chronicle* gave an account of the gibbetting:

> The body of McKay, hung at Hobart Town, arrived at Perth at two o'clock yesterday afternoon, under charge of Lyons, the Sheriff's Bailiff, and a constable, arranged in the usual iron casing, and ready for exhibition on the gibbett, twenty feet high, at about forty yards from the main road, to which the body was securely attached about four o'clock, in the presence of that Officer, the Commandant, and a number of spectators. Lyons, it is said, stated at Perth that he expected to meet the body of Lambe on its way over, for a similar exhibition, on his return to Hobart Town, and that McKay made some confession under the gallows, that caused the delay of his execution. McKay acknowledged the justness of his sentence, and said that it was Lambe, and not himself, who shot Mr Wilson.

The year before the *Times* had expressed the opinion that

the 'greatest of all evils consequent on the independence of Van Diemen's Land was the formation of the Supreme Court of Civil Judicature in this Colony. There will not be found one individual in the whole Island but will coincide with us in this opinion'. That opinion, under those same circumstances, would still stand today.

Hangings were not always carried out humanely. From clumsiness on the part of the executioner, one man's sufferings were dreadfully protracted, the rope agitating violently for more than ten minutes. The Chief Justice was said to have wept when condemning a mere lad scarcely eighteen years old to death for shooting an overseer. 'When the boy was brought into the presence of his dying victim, he shed tears and said he was sorry for what he had done. "Ah George," said the dying man, "it is too late now." It was considered very strange that such conflicting feelings should be shrouded in the bosom of the same individual. To deliberately kill and then weep over the victim!' The boy was condemned to death without hope of mercy.

Another man, sentenced to death, his body to be then dissected, exclaimed in hard defiance at the verdict: 'Thanks be to God! You cannot dissect my soul, though you may dissect my body!' He had been convicted for murder. Of two men sentenced to hang one said nothing, but the other declared his innocence, saying that three witnesses against him had perjured themselves. The aptly named *Tasmanian Weekly Despatch* reported the execution of another two men for the murder of a shepherd, 'who were hanged in the usual manner and with the usual effect, yesterday morning, at half-past eight'. There were many murders among the prisoners at Port Arthur, with the guilty parties always paying the penalty.

The novelty of an execution at Oatlands in the midlands was experienced in April 1844. A runaway, described as a fine young man, appeared to die instantly, while the other, a murderer, a man of slight build, struggled for a few minutes. The young man's body was buried in the ground of the township, but the other was delivered to the surgeon for dissection.

There was another murder at New Norfolk of a young woman. The girl had been preparing her mistress's linen and had gone into the lower kitchen to change an iron, after which she was not seen alive again. The remains were later found under circumstances that strongly suggested murder. Three men were executed about seven or eight months later, after a number of postponements. A woman, Eliza Benwell, was charged with 'feloniously, wilfully, and with malice aforethought' being present and 'aiding, abetting, and assisting' three prisoners in the murder of Eliza Saunders. The prisoner pleaded 'Not guilty, my Lord.' She was hanged in

September 1844 before a large crowd including many women. There were children there also, playing marbles and leap-frog to amuse themselves. The 'miserable creature appeared almost insensible'.

Arson was also a capital offence, and an elderly man was hanged for this crime in 1846. The morning of the execution was wet and miserable and scarcely a dozen people attended. No confession was made by the prisoner. Twelve men were sentenced to death in the first three months of that year. The execution of Charles Benwell was held before 2500 individuals, including a considerable number of women and children, in 1847. He denied his guilt up to the last moment. The body, after hanging for the usual period, was cut down and taken in a shell to the Colonial Hospital for dissection.

One prisoner was tried for murder, along with others, of a man at Port Arthur. This particular prisoner was acquitted and on his way to Port Arthur, having freed his hands from his handcuffs, struck a witness to the trial on the head with a billet of wood. On seeing the blood of his injured victim he put some in his mouth and swallowed it, saying that it was the sweetest thing he had tasted for many a day. Another prisoner from Port Arthur was executed in front of the gaol for making an assault upon a religious catechist. No fewer than 700 persons attended the execution of three men in January 1848. Two were hanged for murder and one for a murderous attempt.

Reports of executions seem at times to have been written up for the press like sports reviews, with special emphasis on the number of spectators. The more sensational the case, the more the people flocked to see the hanging.

For having wilfully set fire to a barn belonging to the Government at Impression Bay a man suffered the extreme penalty of the law. He was described as 'a very ignorant man, of a very low range of intellect, but in no respect a maniac. He walked with a firm step, but a violent tremor came over him as the rope was being adjusted, and a remarkable change in his features gave indication of the mental agony struggling in his breast. The spectators were less numerous than on any previous similar occasion for a long time past'.

The perpetrator of the 'Kelly Street Murder' underwent the dread sentence of the law with plenty of other wrong-doers lined up for the same fate, waiting their turn. Many women and children were present among a large crowd of spectators in front of the Court House when a man was executed for an assault upon a constable. A couple of 'black-faced robbers' died at Launceston in 1850, while four days later another pair made their exit before a large audience.

Murders appeared to be on the increase, instead of the reverse, even though the year was 1851. The lifeless body of a man was found about 200 metres from the bridge at New Norfolk. James Smith, employed by Mr Shoobridge, was stabbed after drinking with a woman at the Golden Lion. Three men were taken into custody after the body was removed to the Star and Garter Hotel. The sudden assassination of the landlord of the Turf Tavern in Murray Street resulted in a verdict of wilful murder against a man named Williams.

A savage murder of a child in Hobart Town occurred in 1852. The victim, a girl little more than two years old, was the daughter of the landlord of the Old Commodore in Brisbane Street, the father being absent at the Victorian goldfields. Mary Sullivan, aged about sixteen, born in the county of Kerry, Ireland, and who had been sentenced to fourteen years' transportation, had been taking care of the landlord's children. She strangled little Caroline and threw her into a water butt. Hundreds of people wended their way to the gaol and waited to witness the hanging, only to find that it had been postponed until the following day. A vast crowd collected again the next morning.

Mary was described as walking with a firm and resolute step to her hanging, her face and general demeanour indicating a total absence of fear. Her hands were pinioned and as the executioner made her turn round with her face to the gaol she moved her head back to look at the crowd. A large woollen cap was then drawn over her head. The executioner appeared to carry out his office in a way which nearly drew forth loud execrations from the crowd, particularly when, on his re-appearance, he 'chucked' the rope which was round the prisoner's neck.

The executioner was quite a showman usually and liked to give the crowd as many thrills as possible. If the victim could be induced to say a few words, all the better. After all it was a free performance. And the star performers did not have to act their parts!

The hangings continued on with the years, and people still gathered eagerly to watch, with the victims often protesting their innocence up to the moment before they dropped out of sight. In 1853 it was considered a pleasing fact that, although the number of executions in the colony had not been few, none of the native born had been capitally convicted.

A small number of people collected at an execution at Launceston, when it was believed that it was to be the last hanging to take place on the present permanent gallows. Later it was announced that these gallows, 'which had so long disfigured the northern wall of the gaol, have been removed at last'. In 1854 an important news item in the *Guardian* was that Mr Justice Horne had opened the criminal sitting at the Supreme Court the week before, and as there was not a single prisoner on the calendar for trial, a pair of white gloves fell to the portion of the judge. It could hardly be believed that in the very metropolis of a penal colony such a pleasing event could occur.

It was only a temporary respite, unfortunately, as at an execution at Launceston the same year, 'the attendance of women and children to behold this horrible spectacle was more numerous than on former occasions'. Another 1000 turned up in front of the Hobart Town gaol a few months later to witness 'the disgusting exhibition' of the hanging of two men. The onlookers were chiefly female.

'Verily we have a strange Government, everyway worthy however of a Penal Settlement,' exclaimed the *Colonial Times*, when drawing attention to a tender in the official *Government Gazette* calling for the fixing and unfixing of the scaffold, and for a supply of coffins and carts for removing the bodies at all executions in Hobart Town 'for one year, from the 1st of June next'. It was considered a wonder that the rope and grease were not tendered for also!

Back in 1829 the *Colonial Times* suggested cynically that criminals should 'carefully avoid bringing on your trial late in the evening, so great is the danger of being in the hands of a Jury when they are hungry; in this case business is always dispatched... "The lank-jaw'd Judge will hang the guiltless, rather than eat his mutton cold." '

8
The Factory:
Female Prisoners and Emigrants

'The best articles of traffic in this Settlement would be respectable females,' a gentleman in Van Diemens Land wrote in a letter home to England in 1824. He added, in all seriousness, that one speculator proposed to take from 100 to 200 women as a first order, and was so certain of disposing of them to advantage, that he only stipulated that they should be under fifty years old. Offers were made to remit cash, advanced as freightage, with the least possible delay. A further incentive was that the Governor had offered a bounty on the importation of from fifty to one hundred acres of land.

The Home Government was made aware of the great disparity in the numbers of the two sexes in Van Diemens Land, believed to be ten men to one woman, and so began sending out suitable females to the colony, hardly any women being confined to the penitentiary at Millbank as formerly.

'The female prisoners per the *Princess Charlotte* were landed yesterday morning, and afterwards assigned to the service of the inhabitants and settlers. They were landed generally healthy especially considering their long voyage.' This was reported in June 1820. These women would have been eagerly sought after as servants for the privileged class. A shipment of women arrived on the *Providence* in 1826, all selected from the prisons in London; a 'cargo of the fair sex' was the most desirable consignment which could be made to the women-starved inhabitants of the island. Most of these young women were of a superior class to those which had been sent previously. The *Providence* also carried between thirty and forty families who had come out as free settlers.

Convict women who were confined at the female barracks were

considered quite unsuitable as assigned servants. It was not uncommon for a 'lady from the factory' to be given a seat in the stocks for a few hours to try to teach her better manners! One woman who had been granted a ticket-of-leave and acted as midwife to the best families in Hobart Town lost this privilege due to the accusations of the Reverend Bedford. On his next visit to the barracks to teach the joys of a virtuous life to the female inmates, they turned on 'Holy Willie Bedford' in revenge for his denouncements and tried to maim him permanently. If it had not been for the prompt assistance of the constables standing near he would have been 'ruined' for life.

This factory, as it was called, was considered useless for the rehabilitation of the convict women, and an entirely new system had been adopted by the Governor-in-Chief at Sydney, which it was hoped could be followed also in Van Diemens Land. Every encouragement should be given to marriage; no female prisoner was to be prevented from marrying, and the females in the factory were to be sent out whenever their services were required. The Reverend Bedford was said to be opposed to this move, perhaps for very private reasons of his own, but his objections were later over-ruled by Governor Arthur in 1832.

Meanwhile a House of Correction was opened in 1829, being 'that most important and useful establishment of punishment for the disorderly branches of the female prisoner population'. This had the approval of the *Colonial Times*: 'Instead of idleness and sloth, the more industrious occupation of wool-combing, spinning etc., with the additional amusement of hemp-picking, have superseded the more agreeable occupation of tossing each other in blankets, and picking up love-letters, tea and sugar...'

The regulations that were to be followed in the establishment promised few diversions for the prisoners who were to be kept there. The women were divided into three classes. Those in the first class, who were permitted to wear a dress without any distinguishing mark, were to be employed as cooks, task-women and hospital attendants. Second class women, whose dress had a large yellow 'C' on the left sleeve, were used to make clothes for the establishment and to attend to 'getting up the linen'. Third class prisoners were prominently distinguished; a large 'C' figured in the centre of the back of the jacket, on the right sleeve and on the back part of the petticoat. These women were to wash for the factory, the orphan schools and the penitentiary, and to work at carding and spinning wool.

The diet was equally dulling. Breakfast consisted of a quarter of a pound of bread and a pint of gruel; dinner provided a half pound of bread with a pint of soup; and supper was made of a quarter of a pound of bread and a pint of soup. The soup was made in the proportion of twenty-five pounds of meat to every one hundred quarts of liquid, in addition to vegetables. Ox or sheep's heads were suggested as sources of meat.

The object of encouraging matrimony among the prisoner population had been attended to by the authorities, even if it did not receive the wholehearted approval of the Church, and marriages were taking place. On one occasion there were 'no less than fourteen couples dressed in gay attire, approaching the Temple of Hymen... all eager to be made happy, and to increase the physical force of Tasmania'.

There was one exception, however. One lass, who had appeared as willing as her companions to 'embrace the happy deity', exclaimed 'No!' just as the ring was being placed on her finger. When asked the reason for this strange turn of mind, she replied that her man was not able to keep her. The disappointed bridegroom-to-be immediately answered, 'Oh! you ungrateful wretch! Are not all the clothes on your back mine?' The woman was removed to the vestry where she took off her borrowed plumes. Away went the fine bonnet, feathers and the rest of the finery, to be replaced by the factory dress, and in lieu of enjoying the pleasures of matrimony, she went back to the crime class for two years. The change of mind was apparently because the man was not the one she had been expecting to marry. In this case it was felt that 'the heroine acted with becoming spirit, the poor creature supposing she was to be wedded for life to imbecility, without hesitation chose the better part, to lead a life of chastity'.

It was not long before the factory became the subject for censure; attention was called to the manner in which the children in the establishment were taken care of. Not only were a large number of women cooped up in an 'infinitely worse than useless state' but their poor children were forced to suffer also; the blame lay with the Governor and with the Superintendent of Convicts.

Female emigrants arrived in September 1832, and although welcome in the colony, they were said to be 'most injudiciously selected from the improper mixture of respectable characters and others'. It was hoped that now the Female House of Correction had become a place of bitter and severe punishment, the inmates would reform and try to become useful members of society, rather than stay there.

Even when they did reform, the odds were heavily weighted against them. It was a notorious fact that some families exchanged their servants once a month throughout the year, and could return them to the factory on any caprice or for trivial cause. The poor servant had no chance whatever, when the complaint was heard before a magistrate, to offer any defence on her own behalf.

In 1833 a report reached the colony from England of the first 'lady speculation' to have left the northern hemisphere for Van Diemens Land, ships being sent out freighted with young females on a 'matrimonial adventure'. On their arrival Governor Arthur had personally examined the condition and treatment of 'these children of the State', and twenty-five who had received offers of marriage were ordered by His Excellency to enter into that estate.

These would have been the young women who had been imported by the *Edward Coulson*, and their behaviour on board was considered to have been exemplary. The greatest possible pains had been taken to select well-conducted virtuous females who it was hoped would be proof against the arts of seduction. They were given a temporary home by the Government at the Orphan School.

A different picture was given by the *Courier* of 'the very numerous emigrants that have arrived by the last two or three ships, especially the *Strathfieldsay*, from Dublin [who] are now crowding the streets of Hobart Town. While several have met with engagements, the great majority, we regret to say, are still without employment, and from the destitute condition of most of them, they must soon be objects of real charity...'

Another consignment of free females was landed from the *Strathfieldsay* in August 1834, and 'of all the disgusting, abominable sights ever witnessed, nothing equalled the scene which took place on this occasion'. They were subjected to every indignity and humiliation by a mob of animalistic men who pursued them from the ship to wherever they were able to seek refuge. They could not have been accorded worse treatment, even if they had been convicts. As well, by now insufficient applications were being received for assigned servants, so that many female prisoners were forced to remain shut up in the factory for long periods, having nowhere else to go.

The arrival of the *Sarah* in February 1835 presented a novel feature in immigration, the whole of the passengers having arrived without any problems, their characters unstained! The committee under whose arrangement they had been forwarded was highly praised. With the population at that time consisting of about 24 000 males, and only 10 000 females, the cargo the *Sarah* had brought was felt to be beneficial not only to the comfort but also to the morals of the colonists. About 140 single women and twenty families had arrived, and on the first day upwards of forty young women had been employed.

The system under which the emigrants had travelled was remarkable. It consisted of not allowing the married men to sleep with their wives! 'The whole of the families and children had their sleeping berths altogether distinct and apart from the men, but what is more novel — the husbands were the guardians and the protectors of their wives and children, and at the same time the single women; for this purpose, the men kept regular watch during the whole journey, so that there were always three husbands on deck guarding the women, and to each hatchway was stationed one of the married men...'

The next shipment of female emigrants early in 1836 shocked the colony with the terrible conditions which they had endured. The *Boadicea* brought out 260 free females, of which 160 were said to be under the age of sixteen. Emigrants with large families had also arrived, and these were without friends and food. Part of the live cargo of the *Boadicea* included abandoned orphans from the Irish orphan schools, as well as other children.

Prison discipline was also under fire. A number of children with convict mothers invariably were to be found locked up in the women's cell in the gaol, which was three metres square; free as well as convict women were confined there before and after their trials. An instance of what it was like to be taken as a woman prisoner in those days can be gained from the following account. A convict janissary knocked at the door of a house one night about twelve o'clock, the door being opened by a woman with a sick child in her arms. Without ceremony the janissary took the child and, walking into the bedroom of its parents, gave it to the father, saying, 'There young man, take that, for I want the woman to go to the watch-house, on a charge of conniving in the robbing of some peaches.'

In 1838, the mismanagement of the Female House of Correction at last came under investigation. It was evident that any servant who came from the factory proved the uselessness of this establishment in the matter of reform. The deaths of several infants brought the matter before the public. A child had been taken from its mother on her admittance to the factory; at that time the child was quite healthy and strong. Through criminal neglect it had later died as a result of diarrhoea and fever, produced by being kept in such a crowded unhealthy place, without air and exercise. There was no doctor available in the factory to attend to these poor children.

But the female prisoners still poured into the colony. Another 126 women arrived in January 1839 by the *Majestic*. This was the worst cargo ever shipped into the colony, with the women generally believed to be very abandoned characters. One woman was reported to have been kept in irons nearly all the voyage in a sort of cage which was occasionally used on board women's ships.

By 1841 discipline in the factory had deteriorated to such an extent that it was being laughed at by nearly all, while many actually preferred the life of lazy incarceration within its walls. Lady Franklin changed all that in 1842 when with ten other ladies she took over the management of the female convict establishment. A new prison in the Brickfields was planned for all the assignable women, and those who landed from the ships, until they were disposed of. The remainder were to be kept at close and constant labour in their respective yards, according to their sentences. 'Those in the lowest crime yard were to be employed in breaking stones for the finishing course on the roads, not larger than the yolk of an egg, to be passed through an iron riddle according to Macadam's plan; a certain task to be fixed and finished daily, under the penalty of an extension of sentence. The other crime yards were to be employed at washing, sewing, spinning and making various sorts of clothing for the Orphan School children, which her Ladyship said may be all made by the Factory women.'

The Brickfield factory got into the news again in 1846, because of a ladies' petition. Ladies who attended the Brickfields in search of servants were imploring that something be done to the road leading to the depot. It was almost impossible for their carriages to get there from the main road, as the road was crossed and intersected by dangerous ruts and holes. Without Lady Franklin's inspiring leadership, the ladies' committee was obviously not nearly so invincible.

A celebrated woman, known as 'Jemmy the Rover', made her escape from the Female House of Correction in 1848. Her only instrument was an iron spoon which had been left in the cell, which she sharpened by rubbing it against the wall; she then cut out one of the iron bars over the door. She squeezed her way through and in the yard she piled up a number of tubs against the wall until she was able to reach the top. With a blanket which she had torn into strips she lowered herself twelve metres down the other side. She got clear away and has not been heard of since.

Married female prisoners were frequently deserted by husbands who, being originally free or conditionally pardoned, left the island. With no provision being made for their wives' maintenance, this left the Government responsible. It was another problem created by the number of women still arriving in the colony. More female convicts reached Hobart Town in 1850 by the *Earl Grey*. The Comptroller-General notified the public of their expected arrival so that people would be at hand when the women were distributed as assigned servants. No allowances were ever made for the cause of these women becoming what they were — the appalling conditions prevailing in England. Transporting them halfway across the world, then confining them in noisome prisons, was not likely to make them worthwhile citizens overnight, nor for that matter was consigning them to act as unpaid slaves to the settlers. It was extremely hard for them to change their habits so they were usually in or out of the factory, and the newspapers always had some little story to tell of their misdeeds:

> Whilst a decently attired female was giving herself some airs in a draper's shop in town one day, a lady entered, accompanied by a constable. The first-mentioned fair one turned pale, and resigned herself to the arms of the officer, by whom she was taken to the watch-house! She was a pass-holder servant, and had just absconded having taken the loan of her mistress's purse.

It was not much help to be a free emigrant lass, either, especially if she was not addicted to work. A young girl was charged by her master, under the Hiring Act, with misconduct by disobedience of orders. Apparently, when the dinner hour had arrived, her mistress discovered that nothing was ready and no preparations had been made. When asked about this, 'saucy Mary became insolent' and refused to work at all, so that her mistress was forced to do her refractory cook's dirty work. Her master branded her 'a most perfect nuisance' before she was sentenced to one month's imprisonment in the House of Correction, also forfeiting all wages due to her.

After a spell in the factory, Mary was not likely to have shown any improvement. Another 300 women were sent out from the Shetland Islands in 1854, apparently as free emigrants, although by that time they may have had a slightly better chance to make a decent life for themselves than those who had suffered before them.

9

Paupers, Pensioners and Political Prisoners

Ah, who is he with downcast head,
With hollow eyes and tottering tread,
And visage pale as fear?
'Tis Poverty! I know him well,
For with him I've been forced to dwell
Full many a dreary year.

Poverty became more apparent in the colony with the increase in population. By the year 1829 the population of Van Diemens Land alone was as great as both Van Diemens Land and New South Wales together had been in 1817. At that time there were 17 165 souls in New South Wales, and 3214 in Van Diemens Land, amounting to 20 379.

It was the influx of the wrong types of emigrants which affected the economy of the colony so adversely, and the rumour in 1833 that nearly 10 000 pauper emigrants were on their way from England was enough to cause much consternation. The rumour was correct, although the number might not have been so large. Arrive they did, and from then on the streets of Hobart Town were full of gangs of housebreakers and petty street robbers. Scarcely a night passed without some thefts taking place.

In 1827 the *Hobart Town Gazette* advocated that the emigration of the poor agricultural class of England should be encouraged. It considered that the two essential requisites for the prosperity of a young and rising colony were labour and population. The lack of labour in Van Diemens Land was as severely felt as lack of wealth. The settler who had capital could not use it in improvements because there were not sufficient labourers to carry them into effect. Agricultural and farming men were badly needed to bring the price of farming labour down by causing competition. The prisoner, while he remained without some indulgence, was unable to compete, being bound down at the pleasure of the local government. The prisoners becoming free by servitude at that period were not sufficient to supply the demand.

However, the *Gazette* hastened to add, the free emigration of the poor was not in preference to the importation of prisoners. The benefits from the prisoner population to the colonists were too immense for the ports to be shut against them. They were the principal support of the colony, the Commissariat supplies for the feeding of the prisoners forming the grand depot of colonial meat, which financially helped the colonists. But as the supply of prisoners from England was not equal to the wants of the colony, the deficiency should have been made up by free labourers coming out. The tune was to be changed later on.

Emigration was increasing rapidly, however, with nearly 100 passengers arriving from England in November 1830, and another 100 expected daily from the Swan River settlement. The ships were also bringing out cargoes of less welcome arrivals in the form of idlers of all kinds, described as 'Do-littles to absolute Do-nothings at all', and all bearing that sort of recommendation which was seldom disregarded by local governments. The *Times* was referring to the practice of sending young men from well-to-do families out to the colonies, where the 'good-natured John Bull' created places for them, according to their influential connections back in England. 'Even if ten times as many drones are sent to join our hives as have already found their way here, they will be freely invited to partake of the honey, until, by and by, we shall discover to our cost and sorrow, that not one particle remains for ourselves.'

Another imposition on the colony was the arrival of the Chelsea pensioners in February 1832. Although increase in the population was still considered to be advantageous, in this case it was felt to be an exception to the general principle. It was extremely difficult to imagine what benefit, either to themselves or others, was likely to be derived by their having been sent out. No one could give a satisfactory answer to the question, 'What are they good for?' They had not the means to become masters, and there were very few who were fit as servants. Their pittance of four years' pension, the sum for which they had compounded for all future demands upon their country, would be spent in nine out of ten instances among the publicans, before they even thought to make a single enquiry about their forty-one hectare grants. Even if it were otherwise, their capital

TOP LEFT: A Tasmanian Aboriginal girl, 'Jenny', a typical representative of her race (*Tasmanian Museum and Art Gallery*). TOP RIGHT: Bushranger John Gregory, believed to have been a member of Brady's gang (*Allport Library*). BOTTOM: An etching by Benjamin Duterrau, showing George Augustus Robinson with Tasmanian Aborigines (*Tasmanian Museum and Art Gallery*)

ALBERT HOUSE

would be quite inadequate to cover the expenses of a settler's first establishment.

Added to this, the colony had been blessed with the first fruits of the far-famed Immigration Committee, with the arrival of the *Lindsays* with her live cargo. Only time would tell what difficulties had to be contended with 'in consequence of the wild speculations and theories of men who could not reduce any one of their ideas to practice'. It had been decided that the money from the sale of lands in the colony was to be spent to pay for the passage of free emigrants, and £20 sterling per head was paid to Captain Fenton for the *Lindsays* stock in trade. How these men were to be disposed of had not yet been discovered. The formation of a society for the advice and assistance of emigrants upon arrival was imperatively required.

The town was teeming with free mechanics by 1833, which the people thought could be used to the best interests of the colony by removing the whole of the loan gang in the area and giving this work to the free men instead. Another shipment of free emigrants was expected by the *Thames*, and their arrival was anticipated with dread. Already the streets were thronging with paupers of all descriptions in 1834, and it was felt that some public measure should be adopted to check the danger which threatened the stability of the colony.

In November 1835 a vessel arrived from Buenos Aires with emigrants. In 1836 several Malays were wandering the streets as well, apparently without homes, dragging on a lingering existence. It was thought that if these poor wretches had been brought by Indian vessels, it was the duty of the Government to see that the captains did not break the laws of England by abandoning sailors in foreign ports! With the Emigration Committee in such low repute, it was wondered whether they had recommended the emigration of these foreigners! Six Malays were later sent to the common gaol for having refused to work on board the ship to which they belonged.

The distress among the poorer classes in Hobart Town was alarming, and winter was expected to be the means of thinning the population. Work could not be obtained, and numbers of honest, deluded emigrants, with their families, were starving upon bread far less in quantity than that given as rations to the chain gang men. The free emigrants had worse treatment than the convicts. One woman, unable to pay a fine, was incarcerated in the gaol with criminals of the worst kind, in one and the same den.

All of the single immigrants who had arrived by the *Orleana* in 1842 quickly obtained good situations, and it was hoped that those who were married and had families would soon be similarly suited.

TOP: The Hobart Town gaol at the corner of Murray and Macquarie streets, as it was in 1835. BOTTOM: Flogging a condemned prisoner. This cartoon appeared in the *Cornwall Chronicle* on 9 September 1837. *(Both from the Archives Office of Tasmania)*

A house of refuge was needed where the people could be placed after landing in the colony, and it was suggested that the Government should provide one by the time the next immigrant ship arrived. This would allow 'female heads of families', who could not go on board ship to hire servants, a more convenient means of doing so.

Another importation that year by the *Ocean Queen* added to the population three parsons and two lawyers. 'The Colony would have been more benefited by five stout ploughmen,' was the unequivocal opinion of the *Colonial Times*. As well, German emigrants from New Zealand arrived in 1844, in a state of great poverty, and refuge had to be found for them. A subscription was started for their relief with the hope of raising £100.

However, by 1846 people began leaving Van Diemens Land in ever increasing numbers, among them many useful artisans and labourers. Prisoners that had become free by servitude were leaving also, probably only too anxious to leave such painful memories behind them. It was estimated that 2790 people had left the colony for Port Phillip during the year 1848, with 280 leaving for Sydney, 415 for Adelaide and 307 for other places.

Pauperism had increased under the probation system, an evil which it was felt the colony would feel for years after the system had ceased, unless attention was drawn to the fact. The Legislative Council made an effort to throw the burden of pauper convicts upon the Home Government. The total number of paupers maintained in the hospital at the expense of the colony during the year 1846 was 696. 'Three of these unfortunates, at one o'clock in the morning, [were seen] following their occupation; and in the vicinity of St David's Cathedral, no less than three or four afflicted with blindness were plodding their cheerless, sightless way in the pursuit of alms. . .' This dreary, hopeless scene indicates the plight of these poor people in 1848.

A Government pension scheme was instigated in 1850 to provide for the widows and children of those who had died in the civil service of the Crown. It was well known by anyone who had lived long in the colonies, that there were many examples of women's sad transition from comfort and abundance to difficulties and even destitution. It was very difficult for women of refined birth to fend for themselves in those days, and some sought advice from the newspapers. 'A distressed needlewoman asks whether she may venture to emigrate to Port Phillip. We think she may, if she will place herself under the direction of Mrs Chisholm. This lady resided for some years in the Colony, and is competent to give an opinion upon the qualities, mental and physical, necessary to ensure success. . .'

The reason for most people leaving the colony in the early 1850s was of course the gold rush, but there was a small increase of immigrants in 1853. Upward of 560 persons, of which 345 were Government immigrants, arrived that year, with another twenty-four assisted immigrants, mostly farm labourers, gardeners and bricklayers, arriving a few months later. On the other hand, 250 of the Chelsea pensioners had volunteered to go to Victoria and left by two steamers. Large crowds of people thronged the wharf to see them go. Many of the wives of the men showed their attachment to their husbands and their unwillingness to part with them.

Judging by this account in the *Hobart Town Guardian* of the arrival of some emigrants from Scotland in 1854, there does not appear to have been much improvement in the handling of these people:

Duncan Munro, Margaret Munro, his wife, and Isabella Campbell, as their names wery plainly import, emigrants from Scotland, and recently arrived in the *Sir Allan M'Nab*, now in the service of Mr Palmer of New Town, were charged by Constable Stafford, with disturbing the peace at New Town by shouting and making strange noises. But Mr D.C. Esdaile deposed that the defendants, who were honest newly imported Highlanders, had no intention at all of disturbing the peace; and that they were talking rather loud in their native (that is Gaelic) language, which so marvellously bewildered this intelligent (?) guardian of the peace, worthy Stafford, that he took them all at once into custody. Of course, they were forthwith discharged. Of these simple-hearted creatures, one of the females could speak no English and the other only very little — indeed Mr Palmer, their employer, was in anxious attendance at the office, and gladly took them home with him...We are really ashamed of the proceeding...

Other unwilling emigrants to Van Diemens Land were the political prisoners, notably the Irish State prisoners, who arrived in 1848. However, they were not the first to suffer for their beliefs. News had been received in the colony in 1837 that Lord John Russell had declared before the House of Commons that all the machine breakers found guilty of the offence in the southern counties of England, and transported in the year 1831, had been pardoned by His Majesty. Dreadful suspense was suffered by the men before being officially informed of their release.

Ninety-two Canadian political offenders had been transported to Van Diemens Land in 1840. These English-speaking exiles were sent out following the uprising of 1837-38 in Upper Canada; the cause for which these rebels had fought, under William Lyon Mackenzie, being 'nothing less than political liberty'. Of the 143 prisoners who embarked at Quebec, aboard a three-decker transport vessel, the *Buffalo*, one died on the voyage. Ninety-two Canadians and Americans were put ashore at Lower Sandy Bay in the vicinity of the present Wrest Point, the rest being sent to New South Wales. Thirteen prisoners died in exile, forty are known to have received pardons and returned to North America in the late 1840s, while a number remained behind in the colony. At least three were reported to have married and settled down in the land of their captivity.

These men were first employed in repairing the streets of Hobart Town, and were later taken inland to gangs building the Hobart to Launceston road. The *Launceston Courier* in January 1842 gave the news that two of these men had absconded and were illegally at large. It was thought that they were among the party which seized the *Water Witch* at the River Forth, but this rumour was not confirmed. A report via the *Sydney Herald* in 1844 brought the information that a free pardon had arrived by the *Mary Sharp* for all the Canadian political offenders transported to the colonies.

Five Maori prisoners arrived in Van Diemens Land on 16 November 1846 by H.M.S. *Castor*. Imprisoned for rebellion in New Zealand, they were believed to be chieftains, although there was no positive proof of this. At first held at the prisoners' barracks in Hobart Town, they were described as 'simple-minded men, but not deficient in intelligence', who asserted that they were only 'fighting those who came against their country'.

Their only complaint at this time concerned the very bad water which they were forced to drink (along with the rest of the inhabitants of Hobart Town), as they were accustomed to drinking from the crystal springs of their homeland. Later on they were sent to Maria Island, where one died, apparently of consumption. He was buried there at Darlington, and a headstone erected over his grave bears the date 9 July 1847. The four remaining prisoners were returned to Auckland by the *Lady Denison* on 12 March 1848, at the special request of Lieutenant-Governor Denison.

The Irish State prisoners, patriots who had tried to free their countrymen from exploitation by the English, arrived in Van Diemens Land in October 1849 by the *Swift*. On this occasion Messrs W. Smith O'Brien, Pellew McManus, Patrick O'Donohue and T. M. Meagher* disembarked. Mr Naire, the Assistant Comptroller-General, went on board to ask them to sign a document not

* The spelling of the names varied from time to time.

to attempt to escape from the colony, or to go to public meetings, or private parties. If they agreed they should have the advantage of ticket-of-leave men. Meagher and O'Donohue signed, but the other two refused, and it was considered probable at that time that one would be sent to Port Arthur and the other to Maria Island.

They had been treated as gentlemen for the whole of the journey out, being given private cabins, a saloon, and with little restriction on their actions. The vessel had touched at the Cape for water, but those living there so disliked the arrival of a ship with prisoners that the Commandant had advised the captain to leave within twenty-four hours.

Mr O'Meagher went to Campbell Town, where he was to live, Mr McManus to New Norfolk, Mr O'Doherty to Oatlands and Mr Martin to Bothwell. Mr O'Donohue was allowed to live in Hobart Town, but had to report himself monthly to the police magistrate. Every civility was said to have been shown to them throughout the matter. Mr Smith O'Brien, having refused to accept his ticket-of-leave, was sent to Maria Island.

Mr Patrick O'Donohue sent a letter to the *Hobart Town Courier* to counteract the rumours circulating about him:

Short as my time here has been, falsehood is busy about me; it has been rumoured that I had formed a connexion with a newspaper here, the very name of which may be obnoxious to some people. With your kind leave, Sir, I beg positively to deny this slander; I have not, nor will I ever connect myself with any newspaper, or political party or clique in this penal colony. All I seek is employment in my own profession, and patiently to endure my lingering exile with becoming fortitude.

In April 1850 the *Neptune* arrived with convicts from the Cape. John Mitchell, one of the Irish State prisoners was among them, the rest being mainly men transported for minor political offences and sheep-stealing. Earlier in March Mr Smith O'Brien was going to be removed to Port Arthur from Maria Island, where the stable attached to the former residence of General Lemprière was to be his home. This news very likely prompted his attempted escape in the cutter *Victoria* in August, which resulted for him in a penalty of £60 and costs against the master and mate of the ship. The superintendent of Maria Island was later dismissed from the Convict Department for having treated Mr O'Brien with too much consideration. A letter alleged to have been written by Smith O'Brien to a member of the House, complaining of having been placed in solitary confinement by the Governor of Van Diemens Land, was supposed to have been intercepted and opened in the presence of the local authorities.

Smith O'Brien, later at Port Arthur, was reported in October to be leaving there for Hobart Town, but before doing so he requested the superintendent there to communicate to the proper authorities that he was now willing, in compliance with the wishes of his friends in the colony, to accept the indulgence of a ticket-of-leave. He arrived in Hobart Town by steamer in November and was received by a deputation as well as by upwards of 200 people waiting upon the Commissariat Wharf to see him land.

Mr McManus had obtained His Excellency's permission to live in Launceston, while Mr O'Meagher was living in Hobart Town. Patrick O'Donohue, now the owner of the newspaper, the *Irish Exile and Freedom's Advocate*, had been involved in a brawl with John Moore, a printer of Macquarie Street. They were both taken to the watch-house but later allowed out on bail by the district constable. O'Doherty and McManus also were in strife and had both been admonished by the police magistrate at New Norfolk and discharged for being absent from their respective districts without leave.

In January 1851 the *Government Gazette* contained a formal notice of the revocation of the tickets-of-leave held by McManus, O'Doherty and Donohue. The same month, it was stated that His Excellency had been pleased to remit two months of the imprisonment he ordered O'Doherty to undergo. Patrick O'Donohue had left town in the steamer for Port Arthur to fulfil the three months' imprisonment awarded to him.

The *Irish Exile and Freedom's Advocate* was to make an impassioned appeal on behalf of O'Donohue:

The gentleman who established this Journal has ceased to be connected with it. Mr O'Donohoe is no longer its Proprietor or Editor — he no longer enjoys even 'comparative liberty' — he is no longer free, even in a limited sense, to exercise his faculties in order to procure an honourable and independent living — he is now a probation prisoner of the Crown. What crime has he committed? none — his imputed offence was virtue itself. Actuated by generous impulses, he paid a visit to his political companion and chief, Smith O'Brien, and for this, and this alone, Mr O'Donohoe has been divested of his only earthly means of living, and he himself cast among a vile class of prisoners in a penal settlement and, in his case, this has been done without even a trial! His treatment at the hands of the Local Government for his alleged infringement of convict bye-laws is cruel in the extreme...

The *Hobarton Guardian* strongly censured the Lieutenant-Governor on his treatment of the Irish State prisoners, one remark stressing that it could hardly be credited 'that any sane man, even if he were a second Nero, would punish men as Sir William Denison has the State prisoners'. It was felt that a most humiliating insult had been offered to the magistrates who had tried McManus and O'Doherty, and that the sentence passed by His Excellency was most severe, and many doubted the legality of his depriving those men of the ticket-of-leave granted by the Secretary of State. Sympathy for the prisoners was overwhelmingly in their favour, not only in Van Diemens Land, but in Sydney and the United States of America as well.

In February 1851 the *Irish Exile and Freedom's Advocate* excitedly told its readers:

> We stop the Press to inform our readers that the Judges have given their decision in the case of this gentleman — Sir William Denison's act was illegal!!! Mr M'Manus was discharged from the Court. We have only room to compliment the Colony upon having a Court whose independence can no longer be questioned.

Upon his discharge McManus proceeded to Launceston, and then in their issue of 8 March, the paper had another exciting disclosure to make:

> The drama progresses and the plot thickens:— Mr M'Manus has escaped! Escaped, we rejoice to say, from the fangs of unrelenting cruelty, and the bonds of vindictive tyranny! And not only do we rejoice; but every man, woman, and child, who has a hatred of oppression, and a love of justice, will exult also in the escape of this much injured gentleman from a condition worse than death...

At the Supreme Court, also, on behalf of the expatriate Patrick O'Donohue, a writ of habeas corpus was moved for, which resulted in his removal from Port Arthur in April. A reward of £50 was offered by the Van Diemens Land authorities in the Sydney *Government Gazette* for the apprehension of McManus, but it was too late. The report of his arrival in San Francisco came in September, the same year.

In January 1852, after sending a letter to Mr Mason resigning his ticket-of-leave, Mr O'Meagher was reported absent, and was presumed to have escaped from the colony. He was next heard of in America, where he had declared his intention of becoming a citizen of the United States of America. John Mitchell was gazetted as an absconder in June 1853, with a reward of £2 'or such lesser sum as may be determined upon the convicting magistrate' offered for his capture. 'Don't they wish they may catch him!' gloated the *Colonial Times*. It was later learned that Mitchell was on his way to join his compatriots in America. Mrs Mitchell, with her family and a servant, left the colony, where she had been living, and had taken passage on the *Emma* which sailed for Sydney in July, where she was expected later to take ship for America to join her husband.

Patrick O'Donohue, who had lost his ticket-of-leave the year before on a charge of drunkenness and been sent to the treadmill, had now regained his indulgence. He, too, made his escape in 1853, and was reported in June to have been seen at Tahiti, en route for California.

In 1854 the *Hobarton Guardian* scotched the rumour that Smith O'Brien had escaped, 'which is not of course the case, nor likely to be, so long as that gentleman gives his word to remain. We had the pleasure of having seen and spoken to this truly patriotic gentleman yesterday, who appears in good health, and is likely to reside for a time in Hobart Town; but we hope soon to have the pleasure of announcing his and Messrs O'Dogherty and Martin's free pardon'.

Smith O'Brien changed his residence in May from New Norfolk to Richmond, for reasons unknown to the public. That month came the good news 'that the royal clemency had been excited in favour of the State prisoners indiscriminately in the Colony'. However, in June the *Government Gazette* published the notice for conditional pardons of O'Brien, O'Doherty, and Martin, to the effect that they could leave the colony and go where they pleased, except to England, Ireland and Scotland.

The *Hobarton Mercury* in 1854 gave a full account of the farewell address to William Smith O'Brien. A deputation had been appointed to present the address to him at the Freemason's Hotel. 'The feeling which seemed to pervade all present was that of sympathy and esteem towards the gentleman, whom they had met together to honour and to congratulate on his partial restoration to that liberty, that freedom which advocating for others deprived himself...' He was later entertained by about thirty of his friends at the Bush Hotel at New Norfolk, before leaving for Launceston, where the same demonstrations of esteem awaited him, before he left for Melbourne by the *Lady Bird*.

O'Doherty and Martin had faded out of the picture, but there was a final word about Smith O'Brien in a news item in the *Hobarton Mercury* in January 1855:

Among the passengers between Malta and Gibralter by the *Candia* which has arrived home with the Indian Mail, was Mr Smith O'Brien, returned from transportation. He arrived from Australia via Madras. He was a firstclass passenger on board the *Candia* and entered into familiar conversation with those on board on every topic except politics. He looked care-worn. He was obliged to leave the *Candia* at Gibralter, as he is prohibited by the terms of his pardon from visiting the United Kingdom. It was believed that he purposed visiting some part of Italy. He appeared sad on leaving the steamer; and, while wishing 'Good-bye' to those who were bound for England, he remarked, that he scarcely knew what countryman to call himself...

10

Butchers, Bakers and Candlestick Makers

Muffins and crumpets, hot in the morning from seven to nine o'clock, and in the evening from four to six o'clock, were available during the season for the good people of Hobart Town in 1834. Families taking twenty-four loaves of loaf bread and upwards weekly were entitled to have their bakings done free of expense. There was a choice of French, English and Scottish breakfast rolls, hot every morning, for those who had their particular tastes, from Mr Wilson, baker and confectioner, in Collins Street. Around the corner in Elizabeth Street, Mr Hedger the pastrycook had a mouth-watering assortment of pastries constantly on sale, with mock turtle, gravy and vermicelli soups and savoury pies, hot every day till ten o'clock at night. Bride and funeral cakes of the best description could be supplied on the shortest notice also by Mr Hedger, who did most of the catering around town.

According to the advertisements this was the type of service given to the public, but the *Colonial Times* had a habit of contradicting the claims of the advertisers in their own columns, with such remarks as: 'The bakers of Hobart Town keep up the price of bread higher than even in London, the dearest spot in the civilized world, for that necessity of life — here the four pound loaf is charged one shilling, although the expense of labour and fuel is not by any means so great as in London. Our folks are not satisfied with less than one hundred per cent.'

Depression of trade was severely felt in the colony from 1826 onwards, and attention was called many times to the high prices and unfair practices of the merchants who tried to increase their profits. The butchers, bakers, grocers and others were accused of dishonest conduct by selling with light weights. Some of the bakers had heavy bread in their windows, while they kept light bread out of view, either under the counter or in the next room.

In 1830 butcher's meat was not only scarce and dear, but bad as well. Lean beef was fetching fourpence, and stall-fed beef sevenpence and eightpence per pound, with mutton four, five and sixpence per pound. Butchers bought a sheep for a few shillings a head, yet retailed the joints at sixpence per pound, which was regarded as scandalous. 'It must be a fine time for such butchers as have a good family connection to supply with meat, and the price fixed by themselves,' was the general feeling among their customers.

Colonial laws made matters even harder for those in need who tried to raise a little money on the side. A poor woman who sold three pounds of mutton without having a licence was fined £10 and costs, although the meat was purchased from a licensed butcher.

A tallow chandler, who professed himself to be the principal and superior maker of candles, came under strong censure for not being able to fulfil his extensive orders. His reason was that with his solitary six moulds he could not supply the public with his superior wax wicks until the winter had gone, which was bad planning seeing that they were in greater demand during the winter months. It was said that the customers of an opposition chandler never had cause to complain, it being an invariable rule with him to keep such a stock on hand as would meet in a few hours' notice any demand required in the colony.

The rival chandler naturally took advantage of the publicity, and was quick to offer to the people candles of colonial make, manufactured with colonial fat, which was reputed to be preferable to all others, well seasoned and in any quantity. Beef and mutton fat was bought in any quantity from those in this business. Candles made of mutton fat must have somewhat diminished the romantic appeal of dining by candlelight, although pure sperm oil was obtainable at eight shillings and sixpence a gallon for those who preferred oil lamps.

The inhabitants had been agitating for a regular market in the town for many years, which would help to eliminate the price difference between so many essential commodities. Finding a suitable site was one of the obstacles. It was not until 1833 that tenders were called for the erection of stalls at the market place, which at last was almost completed, and it was hoped that an Act of Council would now be passed to prevent hawking in the streets.

In February 1834 the new market was opened for the first time, with a splendid show of all kinds of provisions. It was well attended and was expected to be well supported, being open on Wednesday and Saturday. Hawking was still allowed to the detriment of the market, and it was feared that the £600 expended in the building could be considered as so much money thrown away.

Colonel Arthur's market place opened for a second time in 1835, according to proclamation and Act of Council, and yet the inhabitants would not attend there.

The commercial state of the colony was anything but flourishing, and failures were being announced almost hourly, with the constant fear that the depression of trade and the scarcity of money would become even more severely felt. The system had brought the colony to a standstill, it was claimed, and it was hoped that before it was totally ruined the leading merchants would adopt measures to allow the internal trade to be carried on. Usury was the order of the day, and from fifteen to fifty per cent was being obtained 'according to the consciences of the traders in money'.

Although the season in 1836 was excellent, both for grass and stall feeding, the people were crying out for meat for the approaching winter; but Colonel Arthur's impounding law had destroyed all the carcases, and there were no beasts to fatten. However, by 1838 the settlement at Port Phillip was beginning to have a decided influence on the colony's supply of meat, and sent 408 fat wethers that year to Van Diemens Land, to be disposed of by private contract to Mr Kirkby, the butcher. The price of wheat, flour and bread kept rising considerably, and the two pound loaf was now one shilling, while people were beginning to find rice a good substitute for bread, especially as milk was then abundant.

The depression of the times was being felt severely as well in Launceston, and in 1842 it was reported from the statement of several shopkeepers in town that the gross amount of sales for the previous twelve months did not equal the amount of profit earned in a corresponding period of three weeks. It was hoped that 'things would take a turn'. Things seemed a little better in Hobart Town, with every week the butchers advertising superior colonial beef, mutton, pork, lamb and veal.

The shopkeepers in Liverpool Street, who paid heavy rent, keeping first-rate articles and giving full weight and measure, could not compete with the erratic competition of the itinerant vendors who lined the streets on Saturday night. Night hawking was still tolerated by the law, and those in legitimate trade suffered. However, improvements were taking place in the shops, and for the Christmas trade in 1845 goods of a reasonable price and excellent quality were in abundance. Despite this trend, the price of bread continued to rise.

The occupiers of the market decided to give a social entertainment to the citizens, to which the Lieutenant-Governor and Legislative Council were also invited. It was to be free of all 'political appearance and bias'. The public banquet at the new market to celebrate yet another opening took place in January 1854. By August sour flour was causing a glut, which probably rebounded on the market, and measures had to be taken to prevent another epidemic like the last which had made many people very ill.

Millers were essential for the well-being of the colony from the earliest days and were particularly welcomed as settlers. In 1819 Mr Terry brought a pair of mill-stones in the *Prince Leopold*, as well as a variety of utensils for 'the purpose of erecting a water mill at a place fixed upon for that undertaking', which happened to be New Norfolk. Mr Terry served the community extremely well for many years, where he was 'much and generally esteemed'. His mill has been long a ruin, but the mill-stones are still in existence and have found a final resting place outside St Matthew's Close at New Norfolk.

The Commercial Flour Mill was in full operation at the Old Wharf in Hobart Town in 1841, a mill capable of grinding nine bushels per hour, and it had a good dressing machine attached. Another new steam flour mill had been erected in Macquarie Street by Mr Turnbull, the distiller. It was hoped that the day would soon come when no more wheat, but only flour, would be exported from the colony, and the offal used in the feeding of cattle. Mr Walker, the miller, who had been accused of monopolising the wheat market, had also erected a very powerful flour mill upon his estate a few kilometres from New Norfolk.

In 1821, in the factory at George Town, cloth from the coarse wools of the colony was being made, as well as leather for shoes. Parchment, equal to any imported from Great Britain, was being manufactured as well, selling at the *Gazette* office at ten shillings for a large sheet. There was an upholsterer and mattress maker, who, inspired 'with a just sense of the very generous and distinguished support' which he had met with since beginning business, moved to the corner of Elizabeth and Brisbane streets in 1823. Funerals furnished on the shortest notice and on the lowest possible scale of profit was part of the service offered by this enterprising businessman.

Most of the goods on sale in the shops, however, were imported from England. A gentleman who returned to the colony in 1818 with considerable merchandise, consisting of Bengal and Madras piece goods, informed the public that the shop was open for inspection and sale in Macquarie Street, at prices much lower than any sold during the last three years, while J. & J. Solomon advertised superior cassimeres, wool and worsted hose, along with Taddy's Superior Snuffs, strong English vinegar and other goods in 1826.

The Veranda Stores also kept a variety of mourning and common caps, snake frills, collars and tippets handsomely worked, with ladies' London-made dresses and spencers, consisting of plaids of the different Scottish clans, all 'most fashionably made'.

Mr Wise, the druggist, respectfully informed the public of the receipt of new stock whenever a cargo ship arrived, and kept on hand purified Epsom Salts, balsam capiva, alum, julap, sugar of lead, powder of hellebore, aether, scammony and Peruvian barks, among the other essentials on his well-filled shelves. Select China goods, for those who had the taste for gunpowder tea in lacquered catties, preserves and orange flower honey, dry ginger, as well as bamboo blinds, fire works, silk jackets and nankeen pantaloons, were to be found in Hobart Town. For the gentlemen, duck frocks, red flannel shirts, and chinsurah segars were no doubt much in demand, together with colonial clump sole boots, 'collashes' and all kinds of colonial work. Colonial hats, made by the 'spirited and enterprising townsman', Mr Champion of Melville Street, for service and durability of texture could not be beaten by any imported at the same price, namely ten shillings.

Important reductions were made at Howe's summer sale in 1836, when several pieces of good dark green merinos, serviceable for poor people, were priced at one shilling per yard. Boas, warranted free from moth, were from £2 to £3 each, while a few richly figured silk mantau dresses were sacrificed at thirty shillings each!

With the advance of the years a staggering amount of merchandise was imported into the colony, with a certain number of luxury items for the wealthier clientele. For the fashion-conscious ladies, Watchorn's Emporium was the right place to visit. Several cases of rice straw bonnets were on view in 1838 at the Emporium, together with very elegant Tuscan and Dunstable cottage bonnets with the following recommendation: 'The shapes are *une mode à part*; they are infinitely more becoming, as well as more *distingué* than the original Cottage Bonnet.' Ladies lasting kid and leather shoes and Adelaide boots, parasols and check French ginghams would have been fingered and eyed by the women, whether rich or poor. Watchorn's Emporium catered for the more practical needs of the public as well, with the best assortment of whaling slops in the men's department.

On their arrival in town, settlers were advised to call on William Pudney, tailor and draper, of Liverpool Street, as they would always find on hand an assortment of clothing made precisely to order.

Mourning was executed at the shortest notice, with a considerable reduction made when ordered for a whole family. There was no need for anybody to be ill-dressed, especially when a blue serge shirt, a regatta shirt, a pair of lined moleskin trousers, a Manilla hat and four pairs of sox could be had for a one pound note, from a new shop which had opened in Murray Street in 1845. Cabbage-tree hats of course were a stock item, just as oil casks, staves, anchors, chains and trypots were always to be had at the ship-chandlers. If the cabbage-tree hat did not suit, there was always a good range of straw and palm leaf hats to be bought in time for the regatta from Theophilus Lightfoot, the tailor and habit maker. And just the thing for the winter to cope with the muddy roads, were gent's stout bluchers, stout clumped Wellingtons, and patent Napoleons.

New inventions which came onto the market in England event-ually found their way out to the colonies. A confectioner in Murray Street, Mr Webb, imported a Master's patent freezing machine in 1849, which arrived in time for the summer months. This would have been a great boon during the hot weather, and Mr Webb's cream and wafer ices must have been in popular demand. The machine also supplied cylinders of pure ice from spring water for the cooling of wine, lemonade and butter, and kept a constant supply of iced water in the hottest season. Twelve months' supply of the patentees' freezing mixture enabled Mr Webb to keep the public well served.

No settler in the interior would have been without a container of Holloway's Ointment, which had made extraordinary cures of snake bite in South Australia, and was now to be found in all the colonies, although manufactured in England. Holloway's Pills were even more sensational and were supposed to cure almost everything from typhus fever, dropsy in the chest, to 'a case of weakness and debility of four years' standing'. The ointment used conjointly with the pills were reputed to cure coco-bug, sore throats, sore heads, wounds, chiego-foot, chilblains, cancers, fistulas, piles, yaws, tumours, bad legs, bunions, the bite of 'muschetoes', and so on and so on! About the only cure it did not claim was that for inflammation of the eyes, suffered by gold diggers and others, but fortunately Dean's Invaluable Eye Lotion, at five shillings per bottle, was available at the druggists.

Of all the business establishments in the colony, the brewers and publicans would have been given the largest following by the inhabitants, whose drinking habits were notorious by any standards. In January 1820 the foundation stone of an extensive brewery was laid by R. W. Loane at the bottom of his premises in Macquarie

Street, adjoining the town rivulet. Another large brewery was also in progress on the farm of Mr G. Gatehouse at New Town, the malthouse of which was nearly completed. Seven years later this brewery was to receive a valuable investment of hops from England, and also a 'known and approved receipt for fining, strengthening, and keeping beer', with a good brew anticipated by the public. However, the Hobart Town brewery on the corner of Davey Street had kept them well supplied with draught beer, brewed from malt and hops in Van Diemens Land, the price of which had been reduced to ninepence per quart in 1822.

The distillery, which had been recently built at the Cascades, had for some time been distilling spirits. A little private enterprise as well was going on at Vinegar Cottage in Liverpool Street where a few puncheons of fine-flavoured Jamaica rum were offered along with a general assortment of British manufactures.

In 1823 Mr T. Gorringe of Green Ponds was licensed to brew beer and ale. The increasing number of breweries in the island had the people in a happy frame of mind. Another practical brewer, Mr Fergusson, arrived in the *Comet* in 1829. Mr J. L. Roberts commenced a brewing establishment in the same year in Argyle Street, and it had succeeded in producing a beverage which was highly spoken of. It was remarked at the time that the colonial brewers could encourage the local hop-growers by not giving preference to the use of English hops. In 1845 Mr Walker started and nearly completed a new brewery adjoining his mill in Collins Street, so there was no shortage of worthy brewers to serve a very thirsty public.

A very potent brew advertised in 1823 was Tasman's Stingo. The fame which this beer had justly acquired 'in consequence of its genuine and peculiar manufacture from the best barley malt and hops' had induced the landlord of the Britannia Hotel always to have a plentiful supply from the Tasman brewery, at a period when rums were so expensive and pounds so scarce, and the value of health so generally understood!

Drunkenness had been rife in the colony for many years, and in 1825 the *Hobart Town Gazette* drew the attention of the people to the fact 'that more liquor and beer are vended in what are elegantly called "Sly Grog-Shops" than in all the Licensed Houses'. Every publican's premises were open to the police, and publicans were fined heavily, to the tune of £40, for allowing gambling in their rooms. The Act for suppressing the sale of spiritous and fermented liquors had earned the approval of many, especially as four men and one woman had died due to excessive drink in a couple of weeks, an occurrence which was probably quite common.

An attempt to make wine from the grapes in the colony was made by Mr Broughton, of Prospect, New Town. Those who tasted it pronounced it very little inferior to 'Champaigne', and suggested that it should be distributed throughout the two colonies and England. At the annual licensing in September 1832, upwards of fifty new public houses received official sanction for the coming year, creating, together with the licences already held, a total revenue from this branch alone of about £7000.

When the revellers at the sly grog-shops became drunk and noisy they were given a finishing glass which soon knocked them out. In this state they were robbed, cast out into the street, and then picked up by the constables. When they came to, they found themselves in the watch-house. This finishing glass consisted of a strong poison. When rum was being drunk, a large quantity of laudanum was administered and swallowed without being discovered. With other spirits, different kinds of poison were administered. The whalers were usually the victims, as they often had the most money.

The publicans of the licensed houses were apparently victimised by the police, however, for the Sunday clause of the Licensing Act meant that no publican was safe. If his door was open on a Sunday, and a friend or visitor was simply sitting in his parlour drinking a glass of grog, a district constable would be sure to catch him, and the publican fined £5. The magistrates were accused of having no discretion, as the constables' object was to secure half the fine if the publican was found guilty, which was a very profitable move on their part. For many years a 'crusade' was remorselessly carried out upon the licensed victuallers, several of whom were regularly victimised.

However, the police had their work cut out trying to keep control of the sly grog-shops, always the subject for censure by the *Colonial Times:*

Of all the pests which exist in this town and throughout the Colony generally, amongst the very worst may be classed the sly grog-shops, in other words — the brothels. The mischief of these nuisances is incalculable...Allurements furnished for young men of a superior grade in society...also afford a harbour to assigned servants both male and female, encouraging them to pilfer and peculate, in order that they may indulge in their vicious propensities.

Several of the householders in Bathurst Street had asked the police to attend to two houses of notorious ill-fame, from which came at all hours of night 'shrieks and cries of murder and other discordant noises, rousing the peaceable inhabitants from their quiet repose'.

Colonial brewing went on regardless, with porter now being brewed in the city. Not so praiseworthy were the number of private stills which were being discovered. A district constable found one in full operation, situated in a gully about three kilometres from the Springs, and another the same day in the possession of a carpenter who lived in Goulburn Street. Information had been laid against both parties. The lowest penalty was £100 and costs. Another offender who had an illicit still in Butler's Paddocks at the rear of the barracks was fined £100 and sent to gaol in default. A second offence by a ticket-of-leave man for illicit distillation earned him nine months hard labour in chains.

The brothels never stopped being a nuisance. There were houses alluded to and well-known as 'flesh-houses', 'where in low singing and dancing rooms the lowest and vilest of both sexes nightly enact scenes of the darkest profligacy'. This was no assertion unsupported by evidence. People were always being brought to hospital insensible from the effects of excessive drinking or from hoccussed liquor.

As well as the merchants in the town there were the people who plied their special crafts, among them the farriers and black-smiths, rope-makers, boiler-makers, carpenters and others. Useful toys were made for children by Mr Burton of Elizabeth Street, such as 'nice little horses for the young gentlemen'. The furniture in Government House, said to be of 'exceeding curious manufacture and very valuable', was made at the penal settlements. A new pottery had been established in 1850 at Longford, while also in the north a gentleman who had given much attention to the electrotype process of copying copperplate engraving had an excellent business.

Of the professional gentlemen in the town, the services of the surgeon dentist would have been an essential need for those who required 'Artificial Teeth and Palates'. Ferro-metallic teeth of 'surpassing beauty and durability' were obtainable in 1837, when Mr Martin respectfully told the gentry of Hobart Town that he would continue 'to supply the loss of teeth, from one to a complete set, to answer all the purposes of the original'.

11

Operations of the Plough and Sickle

His echoing axe the settler wrung...
Rude was his garb, and strong the frame
Of him, who plied his ceaseless toil.

The greatest gratification obtained by any of the settlers in Van Diemens Land would have come from taking up holdings of land and experimenting with crops, plants, and any agricultural and horticultural pursuits which took their fancies. It would have been like making their own 'voyages of discovery', sowing and reaping a virgin earth which had never been tilled before.

Crops grown not long after the settlement had been formed were not very successful because of the lack of skill of the convict labourers and other members of the colony. It was the settlers that had been bred to the land, and who brought their age-old knowledge with them who later found out how fertile the island really was. The influential colonists had been granted the best tracts of land, and those that followed after were all too frequently given heavily wooded lots, which took the small farmer years to clear before the land became arable. The ones that persevered later reaped their benefits, however.

The culture of the hop was recommended as one of the first ventures which could be undertaken. The very favourable climate for brewing through the greater part of the year was likely to benefit any settler with a family of children and servants, as well as his neighbours.

A gentleman wrote to the *Hobart Town Gazette* in June 1816, offering the method by which the hop was cultivated in England,

and as a further inducement to cultivation held out this exciting prospect:

How much more delicious to the parched and thirsty Labourer in the field of Harvest season, would be the cheering and sprinkling cup of Ale to the draught of Grog? What sums of money would be left in the Colony, or applied to other uses, was Ale and Beer the general beverage? What excesses would be avoided, and Crimes less likely to be committed? It would be to the interest of every Settler to Endeavour to have a Barrel of good Ale in his house instead of Gallons of Rum.

This suggestion apparently was taken up with enthusiasm and much experimentation went on. In 1825 a most luxuriant crop of hops, the finest ever grown on the island, was gathered on the estate of a gentleman living at New Town. The following year, in February, a plat of hops, which were planted only the September before, were luxuriant and healthy and averaged half a pound of excellent hops from each pole. These were grown in a garden at Pittwater. By 1829 it was proved without a doubt that 'the climate and soil of this Island are peculiarly well adapted for the growth of hops'. English hops were then plentiful, although colonial hops were being sold at three shillings per pound.

That year the usual procession of the hop pole was borne through the streets of Hobart Town by some labourers from Mr Shoobridge's garden. The crop in general that season was very luxurious. Those employed in the picturesque occupation of hop-picking at New Norfolk in March 1854 were getting threepence per bushel, just double the amount paid the year before. There was still abundant employment for pickers in that locality, marking the beginning of an industry which was to make the Derwent Valley famous as a hop-growing district.

Apples were to make the island equally well known later on, and in February 1820 this was in evidence as a greater show of apples than had ever before been experienced were grown in the colony. It was remarked that 'as there is every appearance of this useful fruit becoming very plentiful...we have reason to expect to hear of good cider being made at no distant period for the Public's use'. This was regarded as rather a novelty, and there is a touch of awe in the announcement in 1823 that 'there was now in the garden of an inhabitant of this town, an apple tree in full blossom'.

Agricultural matters were occupying the attention of the settlers with increasing interest, and the astonishing luxuriance of some fruit trees about town was causing much comment. Apple stalls were to be seen at the corners of streets in Hobart Town by 1833; previously there were none, although there were usually two or three orange stalls about town bearing imported fruit.

An agricultural society was formed in 1822, giving medals to persons who grew four hectares of wheat, barley, artificial grass and vegetables, as well as other produce. The culture of the potato was being particularly attended to also, while by 1825 a plentiful supply of grapes, walnuts, greengages and cherries was being produced, as well as an unprecedented crop of apples.

Tobacco was also being grown in Van Diemens Land in 1825. A Mr Joshua Fergusson had no fewer than two hectares of fine Virginia plants at Tinderbox Bay 'under the care of an American black', who made the prediction that with a little care the colony could produce Negro-head in less than five years, as fine as ever was imported from India. Linum, the flax-seed, was growing spontaneously on all the hills and in most of the valleys of Van Diemens Land, in many places with more luxuriance than under the best cultivation in England, while hemps grew as well as in any part of the globe.

All these interesting discoveries had not prevented the men on the land from being jubilant the year before when they learned that the maize crop in New South Wales had been cut off due to caterpillar infestation, making the cows, oxen, horses, sheep and asses die. This calamity meant that the senior colony was forced to 'enlist the succours of recently neglected Tasmania'.

This attitude seems hardly creditable to the 'junior Colony' by today's standards, but in those early days Van Diemens Land, which was often alluded to as Tasmania even then, was very aware of the fact that it was the second place to be colonised. When the other settlements in Australia were formed and began to prosper, Tasmania, cut off from the mainland by Bass Strait, was forced to lag behind.

The competitive spirit was very much in the foreground at that period, with no thought of what was to come in the matter of prestige relating to 'territorial eminence'. Enterprise within the island was at a high level also, with the merchants of Hobart Town already buying the produce of the settlers on the Port Dalrymple side. An agricultural company was projected in 1827 for exporting the produce of the colony, and to bring back goods for consumption. Establishments were to be formed at Hobart Town and Launceston, with the necessary warehouses.

There were naturally setbacks to the harvest and marketing. Settlers on 'the other side of the Island' had to sow wheat twice over in 1826 due to damage on low grounds from late heavy rains.

The weevil, introduced into the colony by wheat which had not been shipped clean, was being most destructive. Artificial English grasses did not withstand the dry warm weather, and in some thin soils, burned up. It had been proved that early-sown seed upon high land produced the best and fullest crop, having the advantage of being well up before the dry season set in. The harvest in 1829 was prolific, though an unusual quantity of smut was reported, which was accounted for by the unceasing wetness late in the season. The reaping charges had been reduced from fifteen shillings per acre to nine shillings, 'including victuals'.

A settler at the Ouse River suffered considerable loss in 1831 owing to the effects of the blights, which destroyed 300 bushels of his wheat. In the interior practical farmers were turning their attention to feeding sheep upon turnips and hay. This was a much approved old English system, and by feeding off a certain number of full-mouthed sheep on a turnip field the settler was able to improve the condition of his land.

A fine sample of rye was grown by a farmer at the Coal River, which was encouraging, especially as those on the land were having difficulty in competing against imported produce. An indignant settler wrote to the *Colonial Times* in 1833: 'I see. . .that the people of Sydney are sending us back our own wheat turned into flour, and then absolutely underselling our millers. . .' Exploitation of the farmer had already begun, and the enterprising merchants were more interested in quick profits and their own concerns than those of the primary producers.

The *Colonial Times* had the interests of the farmers at heart and must have been at boiling point when it wrote this article on their behalf:

> The cannibal New Zealanders have become cultivators of the soil and actually undersell us in our own market!!! Notwithstanding the boasted superiority of Britons, their free institutions and manufactures, we find a set of copper-coloured savages, without capital, or any of our glorious privileges, such as taxes, quit-rent, revenue of any sort, attornies or usurers:— nay, what is more, without a Government, Executive or Legislative Council, or even an 'Act' of Parliament, Colonial or other, sawing timber, growing flax, planting potatoes, sowing Indian corn, and all at a cheaper rate than it can be grown in a Colony with such in-numerable blessings as we find attendant upon our civilized mode of Government.

No wonder the settlers were becoming disheartened. In the town monopoly in the wheat market had been taken over by Walker and Company, who had obtained the flour contract for the following twelve months; with the price of wheat so high, and likely to remain so, the company had chartered the *Boadicea* to go to India and bring back a cargo of what was considered Indian trash. Although the harvest was abundant that year there had been numerous complaints from several districts about smut-affected wheat. 1836 was not a good year for the farmers.

An immense crop of thistles had taken root in every creek and cranny, not only on the outskirts, but in Hobart Town itself, by 1838. It was hoped that the town surveyor, 'a bonnie Scotsman', would not let his love of his national emblem prevent him from taking the necessary steps for its eradication. He took the hint, but the thistles had discovered the antipodes to be very much to their liking and have been thriving ever since!

'A bountiful Providence has blessed the Colony with a most abundant Harvest...During the last ten days there has been a reasonable supply of rain, by which the operations of the plough may proceed as quick, and as far as there are hands to be found.' This was the position in 1840, with the promise of a 'plentiful harvest for man and beast' predicted again for the following season. For fruit and vegetables, 'the season had been somewhat backward as to the progress of vegetation, but had been highly propitious as to its fertility and abundance'.

The next year was a time of crisis, however, with the announcement of another failure among the first class agriculturists. The *Launceston Examiner* reported that a gentleman who had 1500 acres under wheat crop that season had asserted that the cost of production would not exceed two shillings per bushel.

Matters proved worse in 1845, although the year started well enough. By September a long drought had affected vegetation, with a plague of caterpillars taking over in December and committing havoc in the fields and gardens near the town. New Town Road was actually blackened with them, with lime being the only suggested means of destroying them. They were also just as much a menace in the north of the island. A settler whose crop of wheat was intermixed with oats and barley was surprised to find later that the caterpillars cleared out all the oats and barley and left the wheat untouched.

A horticultural show was held in 1846 at the Music Hall, Collins Street, where flowers, fruit and vegetables were exhibited under the direction of Mr Lipscombe. 'The Band of the 51st played several favourite pieces to a pretty good assemblage of visitors.' This must have been a very proud moment for the producers. Other opportunities for the farmers were becoming apparent all the time, and it was pointed out that it would be a profitable move if someone were to open a pickling establishment in the colony. 'Kidney beans, green walnuts, cauliflowers and small onions can be produced in this soil and climate — to use the expression of a competent judge "against the world",' was the opinion of one. The market was scantily supplied that year owing to another drought, so the project had to wait awhile.

However, progress was slowly taking place, easing the load of the farmer; in 1853 a reaping machine was in use on a farm at Curramore. This was apparently one of its first trials, and it was said to have 'cut ten and twelve acres of barley and oats per day'. The farming communities were consolidating their own interests and sticking together, with the Glenorchy Ploughing Association holding its annual ploughing match along with its fellows. The Gardeners' and Amateurs' Horticultural Associates held their first summer exhibition in the new market on the anniversary of the discovery of Tasmania.

Agricultural and horticultural science was being keenly studied, which was to benefit the colony. Not only were important discoveries being made by the men on the land, but the botanists, naturalists, geologists, explorers, and those just interested in 'fossicking about' were contributing to the general wealth in their own particular way. The report in 1822 of pipe clay being discovered, superior in quantity and to any before found in the colony, was encouraging. A fine spring of fresh water was discovered by the road men digging gravel between the Halfway House, Black Snake, and the Sorell River. Pure water was of inestimable worth in 1823. A year later three seams of coal were found in the banks of the Coal River, which flows under the picturesque stone bridge at the little township of Richmond. This was another good find.

Despite this last discovery coal was not plentiful in Van Diemens Land. What coal there was to be had was very expensive. In July 1847 a letter in the newspaper called attention to a deposit of coal at Mr Cawthorne's farm on the Derwent, a few kilometres above New Norfolk. The river cut through several strata of clay, gravel, indurated and slate clay, marl containing lime and magnesia and shale; below these lay a bed of the finest wood coal. At that time it was under two metres of water, the river being high. All the same, Mr Cawthorne had about a cart-load dug up, which was enough to show its high quality.

Another discovery of coal was made in 1849 at Proctor's quarry, near the Cascades, Hobart Town, but borings later proved unsuccessful. Meanwhile a good specimen of coal had been discovered at New Town near the government farm. The owner of the estate began to sink for coal, but no further news was given of the venture, so it apparently proved unsuccessful also.

Quicksilver as well had been found at Bagdad on a farm tenanted by a Mr Tooth, and silver ore was said to be found at Safety Cove, near Port Arthur, but whether or not it was ever investigated seems to be a secret. Of interest to spelaeologists was the discovery in 1844 of a large cavern on the banks of the Tamar, near Spring Bay. It was described as being so large that no one had yet penetrated it fully, and it was worthy of scientific exploration. Another cave was found in the south in 1854 near Glenorchy.

Forestry experts had not taken long to discover the worth of the timber growing in Van Diemens Land. 'Valuable scientific analysis of the Blue Gum of this Colony compared with other timber ranks with the strongest and fully bears out the high opinion which it has hitherto borne amongst our shipwrights,' it was stated in 1852. A consignment of Macquarie Harbour pine, which doubtlessly had been hewn by half-starved convicts labouring in appalling conditions was sold by auction the same year at the Constitution Dock in Hobart Town. The lot contained 21 340 metres in logs and planks, some of them beautifully knotted and veined and said to be admirably suited for picture-frame making and other ornamental purposes.

A fascinating discovery made in 1851 by a correspondent to the *Launceston Examiner* was of a piece of earth, dug from his land, which he called native soap. It somewhat resembled fuller's earth, but was darker in colour and softer, with a strong smell resembling soap. It could be used for washing clothes, only requiring to be dissolved in hot water overnight.

Gold! That was the most exciting discovery of all! The *Launceston Examiner* was the first to give the news of gold being discovered in Van Diemens Land. It was found at Westbury, tested and pronounced pure. The year was 1851. Actually, Van Diemens Land had been gold-conscious for quite some time. A specimen of gold ore had been brought to the colony by Captain Clinch of the *Flying Fish*, who had obtained it on a trip to Melbourne in 1847. It had been found by a shepherd who had refused to name the locality it came from.

News of the gold strike in California was brought by the Sydney mail to Van Diemens Land. 'A strange revolution is at present taking place in California — a gold region has been discovered on the American fork of the Sacramento, and all California is rushing thither to dig. Half the population of San Francisco has already gone... The yellow fever increases here daily...'

111

Who's for California? The Vandemonians soon took up the cry. Vessels were soon fitted up to go immediately. However, the first thought seems to have been concerned with the scarcity of provisions which there must have been in California, with no cultivation going on as all were digging for gold. Another field had opened up for the disposal of Van Diemens Land wheat or flour, as it was only about seven weeks' sail from the colony.

Captain Haig, who for many years traded along the coast of California and was well acquainted with the country, advertised his intention of chartering a ship, should enough emigrants offer themselves. The United States of America was expected to form a government there so it was thought to offer great advantages.

News from California was coming in all the time, sometimes less flattering than it had been; the unfavourable weather had hampered the efforts of the adventurers, and gold was not so plentiful. Provisions had become cheaper, and supplies were closer to hand. The number of gold seekers was daily increasing, however. On the wharves at Hobart Town the carpenters were very busy, as the trade in wooden houses had become very brisk, with the men giving up their employment to leave for the 'Land of Independence', presumably taking their homes with them. Neither was there want of enterprise on the part of the skippers in taking them to find their pot of gold on the other side of the Pacific.

By May 1850 sixty-two vessels had left the island for the gold coast of South America since the discovery of the precious metal. The *Hobart Town Courier* issued a special supplement devoted to news from California. Samples of gold were being brought back for inspection, one weighing seventeen troy ounces, which had been found at the rich 'gulch' at the 'Dry Diggins'. One man who had returned from California was persuaded to show some gold-dust while he was drunk and was promptly robbed of it. Gold-dust robberies were to become very common. Seventy-one troy ounces of Californian gold were offered at a novel sale, while another piece of gold, heavy enough to make a skittle ball, was on sale at Mr Elliston's mart in Hobart Town.

In the midst of all this furore, there came the news that the whole line of the Onkaparinga River in South Australia was said to show auriferous deposits, and that a company had been formed at Adelaide, headed by seventeen of the leading colonists. Later news reported the fact that 'not a tenth part of the number of persons employed at the diggings were earning anything at all... Between Parramatta and Penrith, 600 or 700 were going up and very large numbers returning in a very wretched state of destitution'.

Reports of good strikes were coming in from everywhere, even from New Zealand. A specimen of quartz was forwarded from New Norfolk, where it had been found just beyond the township; it was now certain that the presence of gold in the colony was a fact. At a public meeting in Launceston it was agreed that a reward of £500 should be paid upon the discovery of a goldfield capable of being profitably worked. The people were beside themselves with excitement, with the merchants in the town doing a roaring trade selling 'gold-diggers' trowsers', as nearly everybody was off to the diggings. By now the localities were changed, with prospectors coming from America to Australia, although not a large number of Americans were expected to visit the colonies.

Beautiful specimens of Victorian gold were being shown off in Van Diemens Land, dazzling the inhabitants; accounts of yet more finds in the island were being brought to notice all the while. Even a small quantity had been found on the New Town side of Mt Wellington!

In February 1852 a letter was received in Hobart Town announcing the discovery of gold by James Grant near Fingal. The *Cornwall Chronicle* stated that two men had left with them a sample of gold, said to be obtained in the Fingal district, and claimed the reward of £500 for the discovery. The discovery was recorded, athough the money was not paid. Many others were also to claim for the reward, including James Grant. There were said to be a thousand and one false reports, with accounts from the Tower Hill diggings at Fingal getting the most publicity. Between forty and fifty people were said to be there, although apparently they were not persevering or industrious enough to develop the richness of the soil, which was believed to be similar to that in California but of a different kind of strata.

A gold proclamation was issued by the Governor in 1852 warning all people against digging for gold in the neighbourhood of Fingal without being duly authorised by Her Majesty's Colonial Government. It notified that such regulations as may be found expedient would be published from time to time as circumstances dictated. However, the *Advertiser* viewed the matter as being merely precautionary and only intended to assert the Royal authority, 'being no degree required by any success on the part of the prospectors'.

The *Colonial Times* conceded in January 1853 that although gold had been found without any doubt in the colony it was in such small quantities that the sense of working the area was questionable. 'Should it turn out that gold-digging could be profitably carried on, its political aspect would be materially altered.'

The large reward offered still kept the search going feverishly, and by the end of the year a public meeting to promote the discovery of gold in Van Diemens Land was convened by the promoters of the gold discovery reward. 'A subscription list was opened on the spot, and a goodly sum was raised before the meeting separated.' The committee approved of two exploring parties, one to take the route by Marlborough and the other by Port Davey, with three other parties expected to be following suit later.

Very likely most benefits were being gained by those who stayed behind and provided the amenities. Two gold escort carriages had been completed by a coachbuilder in the town and sent off to Victoria to be used for sending gold and specie to and from the diggings.

The price of gold at Hobart Town was around sixty-five shillings a troy ounce. The Fingal diggings were now almost abandoned, although for two years a few had found profit in surface washings. A new discovery was reported in 1854 near the settlement at Port Cygnet, but by that time the people of Van Diemens Land were leaving the island in droves to try their luck on the Victorian fields.

At the height of the gold-digging fever an effort had been made to discover the origin of the word 'nugget'. It was supposed to have originated at the Ophir diggings in New South Wales and was probably a corruption of 'ingot', which was itself a corruption of 'lingot' — 'a little tongue'. 'A little tongue,' maybe, but with a great deal to say. It told the fortunes of some . . . and the ruination of many!

12

Animals and Native Fauna

Domestic animals were greatly valued by their owners in the early days of the colony, particularly because their progenitors were brought out from England at great risk and expense. Actually, an animal was worth at least a human life, as those who indulged in sheep-stealing knew only too well. Sheep, especially, played a large part in the export trade, with wool being a constant and never failing resource to offset the effects of the drain of taxation.

It is on record that a quantity of merino lambs were landed in Hobart Town in April 1820, although a considerable number had died on the journey. These merino ram lambs, which had been imported by the Government, were later distributed by lottery to the sheep-owners who were to receive them. The wool of the colony was much sought after, particularly by the manufacturers in the west of England where it sold well, despite the depressed state of the country. By 1823 care and preservation had made a marked improvement in the quality of the wool.

'Sheep appear to be the mania,' was the thought expressed in 1825 at the news that a man at the Macquarie River had shipped sixty fine Saxon sheep, while a further shipment of eighty full-grown pure merino sheep had also arrived. The benefits to be derived from exporting wool were now sufficient to encourage extending the colonial breed of fine fleeced wool, and by 1829 the French were taking all the English coarse wool they could get, which was not suitable for the fine British fabric, thus leaving this market open for wool from the colonies. In a published address, advice was given to the settlers on growing and properly cleansing and selecting their wool before sending it overseas.

Imported cattle from the mainland were beginning to be hazardous to the people, due to the reckless manner in which the wild cattle from Port Phillip were driven through the Government Domain to the slaughterhouse at all hours of the day. It was dangerous for the citizens to promenade on the Domain, besides being unhealthy owing to the filthy conditions of the stockyards.

One pleasant story reported at the time concerns the 96th Regiment. About fifty men were exercising in the Domain, marching in double column, when to their surprise and consternation, there came rushing upon them an enormous wild bullock.

Intent, as good soldiers always are, upon the manoeuvres they were performing, the furious animal was not descried until he was close upon the column, when with the quickness of thought, the officer in command gave the word 'Fix bayonets, right about face!' and in an instant the bullock was enclosed in a 'hollow square'. The scene was now extremely interesting; the bullock was evidently taken by surprise at the novelty of the situation, and apparently wishing to gain some further information on the subject, he thrust his nose against one of the bayonets and not admiring its cold sharpness, he also 'right about faced' and with an indignant and scornful flourish of his tail, he marched out of the square, and fled bellowing into the bush.

The practice of landing cattle from Port Phillip and Adelaide was to lead to the inevitable tragedy. A bullock broke away from the drovers at Wapping and raced down Collins Street, where a young boy was passing. The bullock rushed upon the child and gored him in the face, the tips of the horn going into his eye, and he was thrown about a metre into the air. The child later died. The tragedy apparently was not taken as a warning by the drovers as further incidents occurred frequently with near-fatal consequences.

The city was thrown into great excitement by a number of wild cattle being hunted through the streets in 1853. A sentinel on duty at Government House was gored, and the bullock afterwards got into the Government garden, where it was said to have been shot by a detachment of four soldiers sent from the guard room. Another man was knocked down and had his ear bruised off by the horn of a bullock. The following month, three infuriated bullocks bolted from the Government paddock down Argyle Street, and when near Liverpool Street, one of them rushed at a man and knocked him down. Retaining his self-possession, the man caught hold of the animal's horns. When the bullock retreated a few steps the man sprang to his feet and ran for safety behind a cart. The people passing at the time suddenly disappeared! A short time afterwards two horsemen drove the animal back to the paddock.

Horses, naturally, were the greatest asset of all and were brought out from the earliest days of the colony, some of them having been shipped from the senior settlement as well. Notices of lost stock in the *Hobart Town Gazette* listed the recovery of the 'Entire Horse', which had broken from his tether at Blue Hills, near York Plains, in 1819. A fine 'Black Entire Horse', of the well-known Clydesdale breed, was auctioned in the mart in 1824, and two years later there was some excitement when Captain Lamb imported one of the most magnificent blood horses in Europe, the animal being bought by Mr Willis of Wanstead Park.

The native breed of horses was being lauded in 1829 for being able to support the fatigue of a long journey. Travellers frequently rode a distance of fifty or even sixty kilometres without stopping for refreshment, and it was no uncommon thing for a horse to perform the journey between Hobart Town and Launceston in two days, a distance of 200 kilometres. The horse was said to be wonderful for rounding up wild cattle, allowing the rider to gallop up and down the steepest and most rugged passes with little rest from morning till night. This hardiness was partly attributed to their living so much in the open air night and day, rather than being enervated by the warmth of the stable. Another shipment of English blood mares was landed the same year, this being for the wealthy members of the community who could afford such luxuries. However, the value of good draught horses in the colony was as high as £75.

In 1846 a captain in the Indian Army visited Van Diemens Land especially to buy horses, which showed that the claims of the colonial horse-breeders had spread far and wide. It would have been a big loss to a settler to lose a horse as one did. It was stung to death by nettles. The owner had been hunting cattle on horseback, and when he jumped a log his horse landed in a bed of nettles. It fell backwards, rose, but fell again, rolling over and over, screaming with pain. Another valuable horse, which had cost its owner £150, was fatally bitten in the lip by a black snake near Prossers Plains.

With horses, of course, went carriages. In 1828 a light phaeton was advertised for sale, having lamps and brass mountings, suitable for one or two horses. This was typical of the vehicle available as suitable for the roads of the colony, being both substantial and light.

New livery stables, a novelty in Hobart Town, were opened near the market place in 1831. Valuable stock was often sold by auction, including such items as a pair of ponies 'accustomed to run in a phaeton or carry a lady', an elegant pony phaeton, strong, with shafts and pole, as well as that 'well-known ladies' pony "Taffy", the most useful and docile animal in the Island'. A splendid new britska with complete harness was on the market, as well as elegant carriages and gigs. Horses, gigs and carriages could be hired to go to any part of the town or country.

Horses brought employment to a great many people. Unhappily, the working horses were not given the care and attention received by the coach and carriage horses, or the more pampered blood horses. The *Colonial Times* in 1826 drew the attention of its readers to 'the inhumanity with which horses, oxen and other animals are treated here...There is not a day but the most brutal instances of ferocity are witnessed in the public street. It would be well if some spirited individual would make an example of the first ruffian who is witnessed treating the wretched animal, subject to its brutality, with the cruelty which every day occurs. By a recent Act of Parliament, this offence is subjected to six months' hard labour at the Tread Mill'.

Again, in 1829, cruelty to horses, daily witnessed at the wooden jetty, was denounced by the *Times*. It probably had little effect, as even as late as 1834 the police were being urged to act upon the clause in the new Act which authorised summary punishment to those who treated the miserable, half-starved animals working all day long in the streets with cruelty.

By 1826 it was apparent that dogs were becoming a menace, and the attention of the settlers and stock-keepers was called to the danger of multiplying the race. Several years before, the breed used for hunting the kangaroo was so scarce that it brought a high price, which made their increase very desirable. By 1826, however, they had become too common. Along with those which the natives had owned they had become wild in the woods, ravaging the flocks and the herds. It was feared that the natives' dogs would be the origin of a wild destructive race of ravenous animals of the island.

Regulations to restrain the increase of dogs were enforced from 1830. Dogs roaming the streets often bit passers-by, innumerable hordes of them infesting the town both night and day, making it imperative that some expedient should be adopted to reduce their numbers. A good watch-dog was necessary, but the strays were useless and dangerous. The dogs still increased in number regardless of the attempts to control them, and by 1834 it was quite obvious that wild dogs were the greatest drawback to the prosperity of the settler. They were prowling 'the little Antipodean metropolis' in even larger numbers by 1838. So numerous had they become a year later that it was recommended that they should be taken out, a dozen at a time, and sunk in the river, at some distance from the

Notices printed in the *Courier* on 6 February 1855 *(Archives Office of Tasmania)*

HOBART TOWN IMMIGRATION SOCIETY.

Office—Opposite the lower gate of Governmen House.

ALL PERSONS availing themselves of the agency of this Society, under the Bounty Regulations, can get out their relatives and friends, or obtain mechanics, servants, and labourers of any description from the United Kingdom, with despatch, and at a very moderate advance of money ; which by the Society's arrangements is provided to be repaid to them.

By Order,

4110   HORACE ROWCROFT, Secretary

 ## BLACK BALL LINE
OF
AUSTRALIAN PACKETS.

PASSAGE ARRANGEMENTS
FROM ENGLAND TO VAN DIEMEN'S LAND.

THE CELEBRATED BLACK BALL LINE of AUSTRALIAN PACKETS.

SHIPS.	REGISTER.	CAPTAIN.
LIGHTNING, new.........	2093	Forbes.
OLIVER LANG, new	1275	Manning.
CHAMPION OF THE SEAS, new	2280	Newlands.
BONNIE JEAN, new Aberdeen clipper	2000	M'Carthy.
SCHOMBERG, new	2300	Duguid.
MARCO POLO...............	1625	M'Donnell

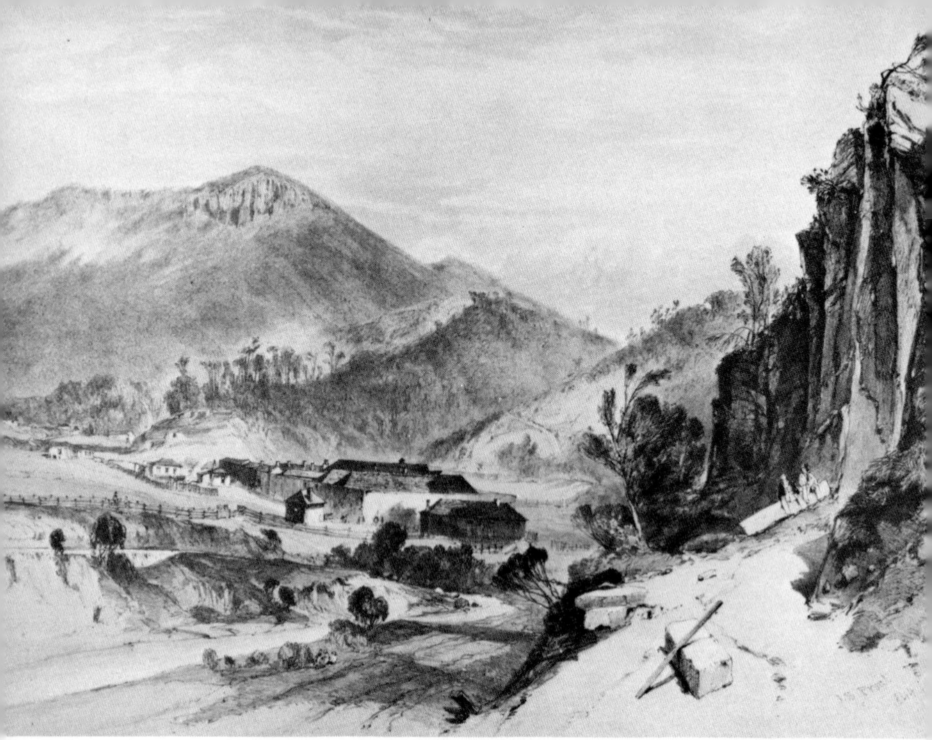

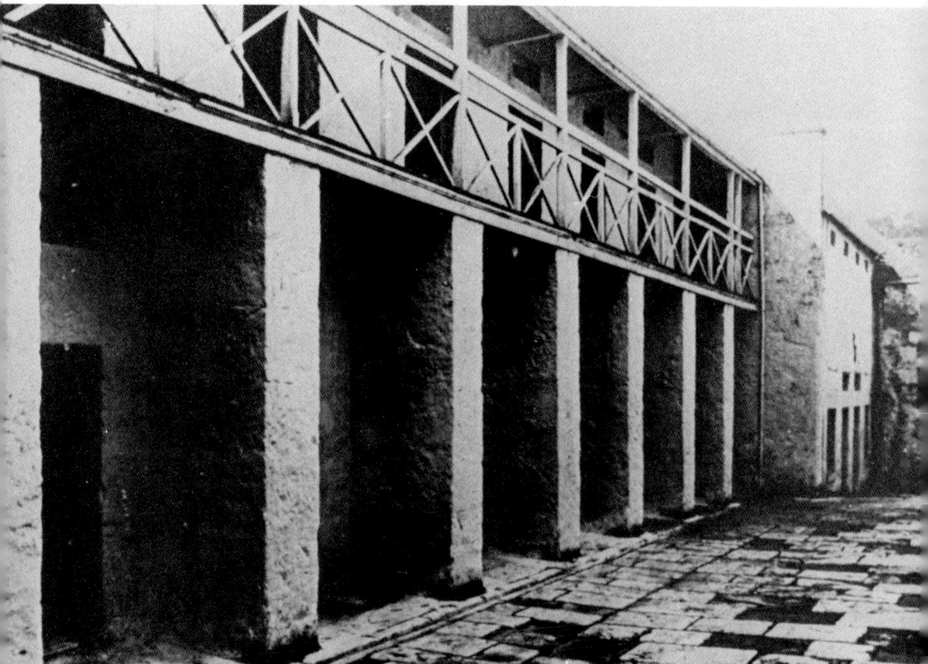

town. Soon afterwards a number of dead dogs were to be seen floating up to the jetty at the rear of Government House.

At one stage Mr Mather of Liverpool Street went to the Police Office and complained of the cruelty which was exercised towards the dogs condemned to slaughter. They were being buried alive in many instances. A small hole used to be dug, and the animals were thrown in by the constables. A little dirt was scattered over, then the constables jumped upon them, with the half-slaughtered dogs setting up a howling, shaking the ground with their struggles.

People were fined for permitting dogs to be at large without being under the control of some competent person, but it had little or no effect on the problem. In 1843 serious accidents were still being caused by the animals, and the *Times* was imploring the Government 'to take the proper measure for putting an end to the frightful accidents which are almost daily occurring by the unrestrained ravages of savage dogs'.

An Act to repeal the Dog Act was introduced in the Legislative Council in 1848, but it did nothing to alleviate the situation, as four years later it was reported that 'curs of all and every variety of shape and breed are running about in all directions, and less than one-twentieth portion of the total number are unlicensed beasts'. There is still plenty of evidence that this problem has never been completely overcome.

Native fauna was a constant source of curiosity to the inhabitants. The kangaroo was a staple part of their diet, relished and enjoyed despite its curious form. An uncommonly large kangaroo was reported to have been caught in the neighbourhood of New Norfolk, in August 1823. The hindquarters alone weighed seventy-six kilograms, which was the only part used for food. There was much carnage of these animals, and their skins were prized.

Kangaroo skins were described in the English journals as having great value and rarity, with advertisements calling the attention of noblemen and gentlemen to boots made from these. An advertisement appeared in the *Colonial Times* in 1826 asking for twenty to thirty thousand kangaroo skins, which must have resulted in wholesale slaughter of the animals by the hunters to fulfil the demand.

By 1847 there was a scarcity of kangaroo skins in the colony, which added one hundred per cent to their value, the tanners giving twenty-two shillings per dozen for them. A remarkable feature of this 'peculiar quadruped' must be its regenerative powers, for it has managed to survive up to the present time. Another native animal which created great interest was the Tasmanian tiger, which was then known as the cat tyger, hyena, or hyena tiger. It is mentioned

TOP: The female factory at the Cascades, from an 1844 lithograph by John Skinner Prout *(Allport Library)*. BOTTOM: The separate treatment division at the female factory *c*. 1868 *(Tasmanian Museum and Art Gallery)*

in the *Hobart Town Gazette* in 1819, where it is described as a ferocious animal which had killed a sheep in the night. In 1821 a large hyena was killed on a farm at the River Plenty.

More information was given in a further account in August 1823:

A few nights ago, a hyena tiger, an animal so rarely seen in this Colony, but of the largest size, was found in the sheep-fold of G.W. Gunning, Esq., of Coal River. Four kangaroo dogs which were thrown in upon him refused to fight...and he had seized a lamb when a small terrier of the Scottish breed was put in and instantly seized the animal, and after a severe fight, to the astonishment of every one present, the terrier succeeded in killing its adversary.

The tiger, now believed extinct, apparently became more elusive after this incident, and reports of sightings were far from plentiful.

An extraordinary occurrence took place in 1845 at Mt Direction, when two eagle hawks tried to lift from the ground a little boy of about three years of age. A Mr Raycroft heard the child's screams and frightened away the birds. The child, although lacerated on the head, recovered. An odd battle between an eagle and a child's kite occurred at Bournbank, near New Norfolk, in 1852, when the children of Mr Jeffrey were flying their kite. The eagle, a female, was later caught and killed.

The duck-hunters that year had a bumper season, when the wild duck were said to be more numerous than had ever been known since the colony had been formed. Twenty-seven were killed at Muddy Plains, and twenty-two were bagged at Single Hill. A man at Lauderdale had earned £1 a day for some time in supplying Hobart Town with ducks and teal. They were considered excellent eating, but where they came from no person knew. They sold readily wholesale at two shillings per couple.

The early inhabitants appear to have been in the habit of killing any native animal, whether it offered a threat to human life or not. A platypus, an extra fine specimen weighing about three kilograms, was shot at Degraves' millpond in 1850. Mr Degraves intended to preserve it and send it to England.

Venomous reptiles have always incited the greatest fear for those walking in the bush, and there are many stories about snakes in Van Diemens Land. Three snakes which were destroyed in 1822 were found to contain an astonishing number of different species on being opened. One 'frightful reptile' measured about three metres long and was about twenty centimetres in circumference, having two birds of the 'whattle' kind inside. Few instances were heard of up to that period of any fatalities from snake-bite, with only one death of a child being recorded.

In 1823 a labourer was bitten on the leg by a snake. At the house he cut out the poisoned flesh, but as all of the venom was not removed, a second attempt was made by his master. After a little gunpowder had been thrown into the wound, it was burnt with a hot iron, and a bandage was placed tightly round the leg above the bite. The poor man underwent this torturing and painful operation; it probably saved his life, which he expected to lose. He recovered in the Colonial Hospital, very likely as much from the treatment as from the bite!

Another snake story which was told in 1831 has a rather macabre flavour:

It may not be improper to state that about ten months since, a man when reaping in a field was stung in the middle finger by a snake. He had sufficient presence of mind to chop off the finger, and in four days he was able to proceed with his work as usual. Unfortunately for himself, he had the curiosity to look at the finger that had been cut off, and which was in a state of putrefaction; putting it to his nose to smell it, he was instantly seized with a violent headache, and died in less than an hour, supplying a convincing proof that poison, when finding its way in any manner to the brain, is of a most dangerous and injurious tendency.

Two snakes were shot at George Town near the lighthouse in 1844. One was a female and was found to contain no fewer than sixty live young ones. Snakes do appear to have been more prevalent in the north of the island. A thirteen year old boy, driving a team of bullocks at Delamere, West Tamar, was bitten by a black snake and died on the same day. However, a shepherd living at Westbury was bitten for the eighth time by a snake and recovered. It was reported in 1848 that these reptiles were on the increase in the northern part of the island.

In 1851 a man at Roseneath was bitten by a snake between the forefingers of his hand. A doctor pronounced the case to be hopeless. However, the patient had a bottle of Underwood's Lotion by him and applied it to the wound. In two hours he recovered! Another man who was bitten by a snake near Ross drank a large dose of olive oil on the recommendation of a neighbour and in a few hours 'found himself tolerably well'.

Animals and insects were also being gradually introduced into the environment. The introduction of bees had been very successful.

A suggestion by a settler that the silkworm would easily adapt to the favourable conditions in the colony was noted, particularly as the mulberry trees on the island were more thickly leaved than they were in Europe. Finally, a wryly amusing note is sounded in this innocent comment on the importation of one small animal into the colonies. 'Having heard that rabbits are being bred in various parts of the country, and knowing from experience that their favourite food is parsley, we hope that a few remarks on the mode of culturing this vegetable may not be considered uninteresting...' It soon became very obvious that the rabbits' favourite food included a great many other edibles beside parsley!

13

Health Hazards
and the Town Creek

The health of the people living in the interior and rural districts
was much better than that of those living in the towns, particularly
Hobart Town. The overcrowding of the gaol, the lack of sanitation
and low standard of cleanliness among the prisoner population
added to the already polluted environment. Medical knowledge
was not at an advanced stage in those early days, and home cures
would probably have been just as effective as any recommended by
a physician. It was a case of kill or cure in most instances.

A correspondent of the *Launceston Examiner* sent in the following
story in 1852, and although it sounds very much like a 'leg-pull'
there would have been more than a grain of truth in it. Amputation
was the favourite method of treating broken limbs, and many
settlers with a simple fracture often found themselves crippled for
life, provided they survived the operation of course.

A Colonial surgeon of a certain district in Van Diemen's Land
was visited by his brother, who was a Government official, and
while looking out of the window one fine morning, the following
'colloquy' passed between the pair. 'John,' said the Government
official, 'this is a sweet place, but how is it that I see so many
of the fellows with wooden legs? I never saw so many, I think,
in all my life before!' 'Oh,' said the surgeon, 'I take 'em off.'
'Good God!' rejoined the former, 'then I suppose that if a poor
fellow comes to you with a scratch on his leg, you take it off?'
'Oh yes,' said the other, 'whip 'em off — least trouble!'

Medical benefits in the 1820s seem to have consisted merely of an offer by a Dr Murdoch to attend 'poor lying-in women' free of charge, on application being made a few weeks before confinement; a newspaper article on the efficacy of vaccination; and instructions in lifesaving methods for the resuscitation of persons who had suffered drowning.

A major step forward, however, was the importation of an instrument purchased by the Government, a stomach pump. It 'removes and destroys poison taken into the stomach, relieves apoplexy, occasioned by ardent spirits (a power which renders it peculiarly desirable in this Colony) — conveys nourishment into the stomach, in cases of obstruction in the passes, it scarifies and cups, relieves the nipples of women who have lost their children, and is used for many other purposes'. It successfully saved the life of a young man at the General Hospital less than two months later by extracting a quantity of sugar of lead from his stomach.

Hobart Town was by then 'honoured and adorned by a Hospital for the public benefit'. It was not known for some time how the hospital discharged its filth. It happened to be into the rivulet used by the populace for its water supplies!

A warning was issued that a mixture called Paregoric Elixir taken for colds and coughs 'had killed more people than it had cured, in cases of cough, merely from the opium it contained; and that neither that nor the opium ought to be administered except by the advice of a medical man, who had the case before him, and could judge of the degree of inflammation present'.

By June 1827 it was recorded that the number of deaths which had occurred within a few weeks was unprecedented in the colony, and that during one week there had been upwards of ten deaths and funerals in Hobart Town from the prevailing disease of catarrh. Now the bell was continually tolling. Some people had experienced two or three severe attacks, some never before having been affected with any illness in the colony since its formation.

Another dreaded complaint was dysentery. A 'highly accomplished and amiable young lady', who had only arrived in the colony three weeks before, died of this after a short illness of only seven days. She was accorded an extravagant and poignant obituary in the *Colonial Times*. An 'effectual cure for dysentery', guaranteed never to fail, was published the same month. Had anybody bothered to give the poor young lady a small tea-cup of that mixture three times a day?

All kinds of theories pertaining to health were discussed with varying degrees of earnestness. The following one is quite delightful:

Medical experience every day suggests the folly of wearing tight stays. Pulmonary complaints are engendered, and consumption and certain death follow. Surely, after this, our Dandies and fair Belles in Tasmania will see the folly of spider-waists; notwithstanding the argument that they are justified by law, under the Acts for enclosing wastes and other common lands.

Those who were apt to become low-spirited and listless in damp weather were recommended to wear silk waistcoats, drawers and stockings, these being 'the most powerful of all cordials'. Flannel was also good, but nothing was so powerful as silk. This was because silk is a good conductor of electricity, and forked lightning or thunderbolts could not pass through dry silk, however thin. It was explained that the reason why people felt oppressed and drowsy in moist or rainy weather was 'because all moisture greedily absorbs people's electricity'.

Infant care was another important subject in the young colony, where new babies were frequent. A sensible suggestion was put forth which it is hoped was heeded by all mothers:

In a climate such as we enjoy in Van Diemen's Land, we would not willingly smother these little creatures in heaps of flannel and cotton garments, neither would we trammel their little feet and legs with what the nurses call long clothes. The ungainly walk and awkward gait... in a great measure can be attributed to this swaddling system. In the words of old Chaucer, we should say, 'Why do you mothers vex your children so?' Short coat them.

By 1831 the suspicion that the recurring complaint which had been so prevalent in Hobart Town for sometime past was not due to the climate but to some other cause, was beginning to sink into the consciousness of the more intelligent. 'Why is its influence confined to the narrow bounds of our streets?' was the question asked. 'We hear nothing of the sort in any part of the Interior, but on the contrary, the most excellent health seems to exist in all parts of the Colony... We have all along entertained...the firm opinion that unless some means are adopted by the Authorities to supply the lower part of the town with wholesome water, we shall at all times be subject to visitations of a similar nature.' Doctors were of little help in the debate, as they disagreed among themselves, even though it was pointed out to them that 'only water-drinkers suffer from the malady'. Others that drank wine or beer seemed to be immune.

The position became worse with each succeeding year, with five of the inmates of the hospital dying in two days, which was a higher average than London. 'Either the medical treatment adopted here differs from that practised in England, or our boasted healthy climate is anything but what it is usually considered,' was all that could be offered in explanation. The health of the Bridgewater chain gang was also very unsatisfactory. Fifty men were sent to the hospital at New Norfolk, and several deaths occurred. It was felt that 'an investigation ought to be set on foot to examine the various cases and to try to discover the cause of this scourging calamity'.

Illness was very prevalent in Hobart Town in 1835, and it was said that the medical gentry had never had more patients. 'There was a kind of fever going about, which was most sudden in its appearance, the body becoming almost suddenly freckled with scarlet spots,' with sickness and vomiting following. If taken in time the fever could be checked. Some people said it was caused by eating fish, but there were cases where people became ill without having eaten fish for months. Some of the medical men stated (at long last) that it was the impure water which brought on the illness, and that should dry weather set in dreadful consequences could be expected from lack of water.

November was the usual month for the prevailing sickness which, for want of a better name, was termed 'influenza'. Scarcely a person escaped, and it was reported that 'the country folk need only come to town, and in all probability, within a few hours, they will be coughing, sneezing, weezing, and teazing themselves to their heart's content'.

The sickness was compared with a similar epidemic which had preceded and succeeded the last cholera scourge in England. Healthy people suddenly succumbed; the hidden mysteries of this illness frightened everyone. Bleeding was considered the best means of treatment. 'Old, young and middle aged were indiscriminately exposed to its infliction... it being absolutely painful to hear the coughing at church and chapel; in the evening it was especially distressing.'

In 1838 positive orders were received from the Home Government to remove immediately from the colonial hospitals all free and ticket-of-leave men. The cause of this peremptory order was that the colonial Government was indebted for a few thousand pounds to the Commissariat for medicine and attendance for the free in the hospitals. The non-payment of the sum resulted in this action. The *Colonial Times* spoke out against the enforcement of this order:

What is to become of the invalids, the maniacs and the pensioners at New Norfolk — nay, what is to become of the lame and blind now in the Hobart Town Hospital? Are the whole of these poor wretches to be turned out of house and home, and left destitute to perish in the streets, because they are not convicts?... Assuredly, one half of the civil funds raised from the people is for the purpose of paying for the superintendence of the convict population, and if the Colonists pay some fifty thousand a year for that purpose, it is somewhat hard if their free poor cannot obtain temporary relief among the convicts in the hospitals.

The medical profession was not held in very high esteem by some of the people. This suspicious enquiry came from a correspondent to the *Colonial Times:*

A certain medical officer not twenty miles from New Norfolk has purchased the reversion of several farms in the neighbourhood, on the deaths of the present owners, and part of the consideration is that he shall 'physic them gratis'. In case of the deaths of any of these parties, surely there must be a Coroner's Inquest?

A more optimistic view was provided by the announcement of the introduction of a novel invention into the colony — a respirator, which had been recently invented in England, and was on show for one week at the office of the *Colonial Times*. It was said to be 'beneficial to disorders of labored respiration'. However, it does not seem to have had much effect in checking that annual epidemic, the influenza, which was very widespread during 1840, although not as sweepingly fatal as the year before. Several deaths had occurred, and among the children the suffering was great and there were many deaths.

Fever in the gaol, believed to be typhus, had broken out, although the doctor said it was dysentery and diarrhoea. The only positive action seemed to be the adjournment of the Court for a fortnight. The careless manner in which those that had died in the Colonial Hospital had been buried was brought to light, but the curious facts apparently brought little reaction from the authorities. The fever continued to rage among the 'lower orders', especially among the prisoner population. The General Hospital was crowded, the penitentiary overflowing, and the gaol quite full.

The fever waned briefly in March 1840, then flared up again in June and July, raging at the hospital, which had twenty-nine cases. The public was made aware of the situation, although that very likely only served to give more alarm. There was death in the prisoners' barracks, where a room approximately seven by four metres was said to contain fourteen sick men: 'similar to the live stowage deck of a slaver'. No surgeon stayed inside the hospital walls.

With the coming of summer a smell began to emanate from the penitentiary. A new wall in Bathurst Street was in the course of being undermined, and when the wind blew across the penitentiary the stench was so powerful that the residents on the opposite side of the street could not leave their windows open. 'No wonder that Fever is so prevalent, when such abominations are permitted by the Government.' This cry from the newspapers went on and on but was unheard.

Complaints were coming from everywhere. The gaol at New Norfolk, 'a miserable, damp and disgraceful den', also deserved some attention from the Government. Free men, incarcerated there for months, 'suffering in every way and laying in a stock of rheumatism from which they never recover, are tried and acquitted, and what recompense can they get? — None!' Even the gaoler was suffering from the damp.

Other than receiving free vaccinations at the self-supporting dispensary, the public seemed to receive nothing from a totally unsympathetic Government. However, slight improvement in skill was showing among the medical profession, with a successful operation being performed upon a whaler, whose arm was removed after being accidentally pierced by a lance. This was believed then to be the second instance only in which this important operation had been successfully performed in the colony, the first being by Dr Scott some years before.

But the recurring theme was fever. The cold damp weather of October 1842 was very favourable to the spreading of the epidemic, which soon became very strong, and several deaths occurred. Scarlet fever was feared also. It was said to attack not only children but adults as well. If steps were not taken to stop an epidemic of that occurring also, it was thought it would be impossible to place limits on its ravages.

The new Colonial Hospital was finished in 1844, 'and beautifully finished too..fitted up for the reception of male patients who had beds and bedding and sundry other external requisites for their miserable situation'. The internal and most important arrangements were sadly lacking. To make matters worse that year, a prison ship in the river was reported to have the 'scourge of the human race' on board — smallpox. Fortunately, every necessary precaution must have been taken to prevent its reaching the people, presuming the rumour to have been true, as no epidemic occurred.

A report was given on the New Norfolk Hospital and the need for a few more improvements:

Huddling madmen into a yard, exposing them to the glare of the sun all day, and then at night locking them up in solitary cells, is in our opinion a strange method of curing madmen. We doubt whether the most sane among us would not become insane — stark staring mad — under such treatment, especially when we take into consideration the manner in which the victualling department is carried on.

A few months later it was reported that nearly the whole of the insane of the New Norfolk establishment had revolted and had completely overcome their keepers. The men armed themselves with whatever came to hand, including bricks and stones. The keepers were put on the defence, and the mad men 'showed their determination of destroying Dr Brock if he came within their reach'.

However, positive experimentation was going on. A letter from New Norfolk in 1847 told the result of an experiment made with sulphuric ether by Dr Weston upon a dog. 'The dog did not appear to evince the slightest pain from any of the methods adopted to test the efficacy of the inhalation of the vapour, although they were of a severe kind. Half-an-hour after, when the effects of the ether had ceased, a repetition of the experiments produced the usual manifestations of pain . . .'

In October of the same year a surgical operation by inhalation of ether was successfully employed by Dr Bedford to amputate the right leg of a boy of six years of age. The stump remained healthy and healed rapidly. Another successful operation followed soon after, then three more. Other operations were also being carried out under the influence of chloroform at Launceston as well as at Hobart Town.

Now amputations were carried out more easily. One man's leg, which had been broken in three places by a waggon, was taken off under the influence of chloroform at the Ship Hotel. This limb was severed at the hip joint. An antidote for snake bite had also been discovered, the 'recipe' still being a secret. In 1849 about fifty gentlemen attended St Mary's Hospital to witness the extraordinary powers of the antidote.

In the midst of these discoveries, influenza was still 'disturbing the peace and quiet of the good people of Hobart Town and its neighbourhood'. Sickness was also very prevalent in May 1853, with several cases of scarlet fever occurring also, although these were confined to children.

Nearly thirty years had to elapse before the vital subject of drainage and sewerage was raised. In November 1853 that fact suddenly became apparent to the inhabitants:

Fever breaks out first and becomes more prevalent and fatal in the neighbourhood of uncovered sewers, stagnant ditches and ponds, gutters full of putrifying matter, nightmen's yards, etcetera. The effect of want of cleanliness and bad drainage, where their action is not sufficient to produce scarlet fever, is shown in the disease of the digestive organs, and predisposes the human frame to receive some of the most common and fatal maladies to which it is subject...

This knowledge did not bring immediate relief to the people, and apparently little action was taken to alleviate their misery. In January 1854 there was the alarming news that some people near Cascade Road had become ill with what was said to be 'very similar to Asiatic Cholera'. As well there was the possibility that vessels arriving in the harbour from places where smallpox was raging could introduce this scourge to Hobart Town. Smallpox had been widely reported in New South Wales, and in an attempt to avoid it spreading to Van Diemens Land, medical practitioners had been supplied with fresh vaccine lymph for free vaccination of the people. Strict quarantine was recommended for visiting seamen, but whether it was enforced is another story.

The town creek, the villain of the piece, had been under the noses, in every sense of the phrase, of the inhabitants since the settlement had commenced. It had been a pure mountain stream in those early days, but the influx of settlers and the constantly increasing population in time reduced the rivulet to a sewer. Attention was called to this by the *Hobart Town Gazette* in 1825:

Is it, or is it not, the duty of some appointed individual to prevent the banks of the creek within high-water mark from being hour after hour mis-employed as a substitute for Cloacina's edifice?... Are dead animals allowed to be thrown into, and hogs to wallow in, that water, which is so principally connected with the health, cleanliness and consequent comfort of this increasingly populous Town?... Female delicacy is sacred; and every man, whatever may be his rank or station, is bound to protect it from offence. But can any Lady walk from the jetty past the stone pile commonly called Bostock's store, without blushing for those who commit, and equally for those who suffer to be committed, one of the most disgusting nuisances? There should be a structure which shall be nameless, created near the wharf or market-place, for the convenience of all that have 'no local habitation'. Perhaps the best site for it would be the beach adjoining Bostock's wall, because the tides would act as purifiers.

Complaints concerning the want of pure water because of the pollution of the town rivulet went on from year to year. In 1829 the residents were crying out that there was scarcely enough water in the creek to fill their tea-kettles, much less their washing-tubs, because of the quantity of filth continually dumped into the only current which supplied their domestic needs. There was also the offensive smell all summer from the filth conveyed from the gaol and left on an embankment, preventing it from escaping to the sea.

The Government made a third attempt in 1830 to convey the sources of Browns River into the Hobart Town creek. This was done under the superintendence of an experienced navigator, a ticket-of-leave man, with thirty men in his charge. He had no doubts that he would succeed, having already accomplished over two kilometres of the distance. If he succeeded he would have the remainder of his term of transportation rescinded and would possibly receive a handsome present.

He had not succeeded by 1831 as the washerwomen who lived by the side of the creek were then complaining they could no longer use it for the purpose of washing. However, by 1832 there was a plentiful supply of pure water. The ordinary people were still not much better off, as some persons, described as 'little men in office', had chained the pump handles so that no one could get a single drop of water for love or money.

People were still crying out about the impurity of the water in the town ditch, which they were obliged to drink. Four-fifths of the population was compelled to drink this water. Most Government officers lived near Macquarie Street, which was well watered, but the populous area was supplied with filth of the worst description. 'Not only were pig-styes washed before the greater part of the inhabitants obtained their supply of water, but it was common to allow tan-yard filth, and the shores of every description, to embouge into the creek.'

By now the town rivulet water supply was being compared with the celebrated Fleet Ditch in England. The *haut ton* were freely supplied at the public expense with the very purest water, for instead of water being carried through the main streets, the small water channel was turned and twisted to take a circuitous route for the use of Captain Montagu and a few others of the privileged at the Battery. Water did not pass into a well which had been sunk at Wellington Bridge; Captain Montagu's Basin, as it was called in derision, situated almost two kilometres from the town, was always profusely supplied. The Government mill was also damming up the whole of the ditch for hours, so that this 'muddy necessity' of life was unobtainable altogether.

The people at New Norfolk expected to be supplied with pure water, an aqueduct being cut which would bring a portion of the water of the Lachlan River to the highest spot of the town, much to the envy of the Hobart Town residents.

No change took place for Hobart Town until the arrival of Sir John Franklin. The inhabitants were delighted when Sir John personally inspected the creek in March 1837, as it indicated that he was anxious to benefit the community. His visit did cause the town to be much better supplied with water than formerly. The next year he approved of a design for the establishment of a water company in the town.

This company was still not established in 1839, and the old problem was just as acute, with the town ditch in such a putrid state that the stench was disgusting. The pump at the bottom of Macquarie Street was being used for filling water carts, thus quickly emptying the well and depriving the residents of its proper use. The people of New Norfolk were still expecting pure water six years after it was first promised. Finally, it was announced that the Government had made a move to obtain pure water and was to build a capacious reservoir with proper filters, costing above £8000.

Another dangerous situation which had often faced the residents was the lack of water to fight the fires which occurred frequently. An account of a disastrous fire which entirely destroyed a town building in December 1841 shows clearly this extra anxiety:

Two circumstances were obvious — a melancholy deficiency in the supply of water, and the want of a superintending master-mind to guide the well meant efforts of the crowd; there were by far too many masters. Sir John must appear very foolish with his Water Act, when such a serious loss occurs within a few hundred yards of his own door, almost entirely from the want of water.

It was known that the quantity of water from Mt Wellington to the Hobart Town rivulet was sufficient to supply a population of more than 50 000. Accurate data had proved that the rivulet produced 800 tonnes of water every twenty-four hours. That quantity entered the pipes at their source, but three-fourths of it was lost by bad management on the way to the reservoirs.

An offer was made in March 1844 by Mr Degraves to the Government to construct a reservoir eighty-five metres above high water mark. It was accepted. The water was to pass through a filter to deliver it clean into main pipes leading down Macquarie Street to the shipping, from where it would be delivered in the quantity of a tonne in fifteen seconds! The Governor placed fifty men with overseers at the disposal of Mr Degraves, who was praised for freeing the city from having to use water from the filthy common sewer. The pipes were completed by November, and the residents had the prospect of having pure water to drink for the summer.

Other factors still prevented the people from enjoying this long-awaited benefit. The water carriers were accused of haste and dangerous speed in racing towards the different pumps. The horse, cart and pump scene daily enacted in Macquarie Street, opposite Government House, was enough reason 'to induce despatch in the conveyance of water through the City in pipes'. The forthright opinion of the *Colonial Times* was that 'there is not a village in England where such a nuisance would be tolerated six months'. Even the water carriers were complaining in the middle of winter at the repeated failure of the water supply at the pumps, which did not augur well for the droughts of summer.

A water memorial was presented to the Lieutenant-Governor, praying that he should give directions for re-opening the town aqueduct, 'as the representative and symbol of the inalienable rights of the community to a supply of fresh water, independently of all private establishments whatever'. It was signed by 2000 inhabitants. His Excellency apparently gave it consideration, for six months later he sacked the Director-General of Waterworks!

There was squabbling going on in May 1854 regarding the widening of the creek, which was still most offensive. The problem this time was that some of the landowners in the neighbourhood of the bridge in Murray Street had objected to this project and refused to come to terms with the Corporation over a few metres or centimetres of land required for the proper straightening of the creek.

The rivulet still runs through the modern city of Hobart, although it is mainly underground. Usually the flow of water is very meagre, but it has never been entirely tamed. During periods of prolonged rains it can go on a rampage and do considerable damage to the business premises which have basements built near or over it. Some of the original stone parapets of the bridges are still standing in the city area, and the Harrington Street structure has been re-erected after suffering damage in one of the rivulet's sprees.

14

Bridges, Ferries and Highways

The state of the roads! Why the roads are so bad
'Tis enough to make the pedestrians mad!
Wherever you step, you stick fast to the mire,
Quite up to the ancles, or perhaps ever higher!
The state of the roads! The state of the roads!
'Tis a state that would suit frogs, tadpoles and toads!
But beings whose tastes differ somewhat from these,
Such plunging in mud-pools, I'm sure cannot please.
The state of the roads! See the creatures in breeches,
Can scarcely escape from these deep, dirty ditches!
Then woe to the lady who wears a long dress,
Silks, satins, and mud appear all in one mess!
The state of the roads! Why when your way picking
With care — in the mud you leave your shoes sticking!
While shoeless, and bootless, and dirty to boot
Through quagmires of mud you must now make
*   your own route.*
Ye powers who preside o'er this beautiful place
Make haste to remove from our town this disgrace.
No more let our men, or our women, like toads,
Crawl, scramble and hop — through the state of the roads!

This very indignant poem was written by a lady whose initials were 'M.B.', and who lived at Sandy Bay in the 1840s. M.B. usually wrote verse of a very elevated nature, but the state of the roads in Hobart Town and elsewhere was enough to stop anyone communing with the muses, bringing them very much down to earth!

TOP: The now demolished old Custom House at Princes Wharf, Castray Esplanade, Hobart Town. The building dated from the 1820s (*Tasmanian Museum and Art Gallery*). BOTTOM: The Old Treasury, Hobart Town, in front of which stand the much-used stocks. This picture was published in 1834 (*Allport Library*)

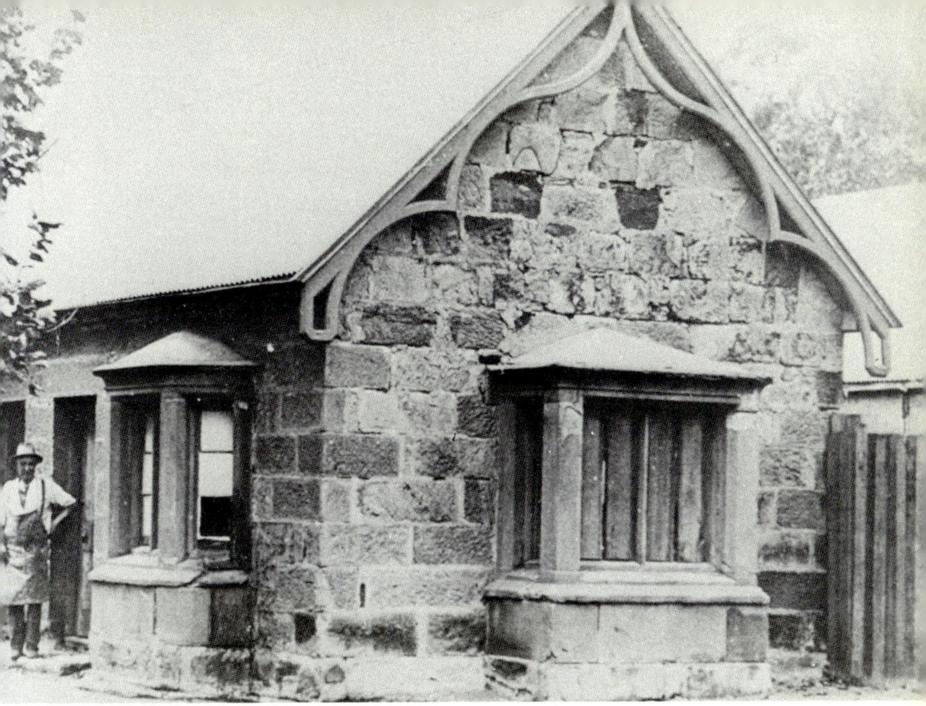

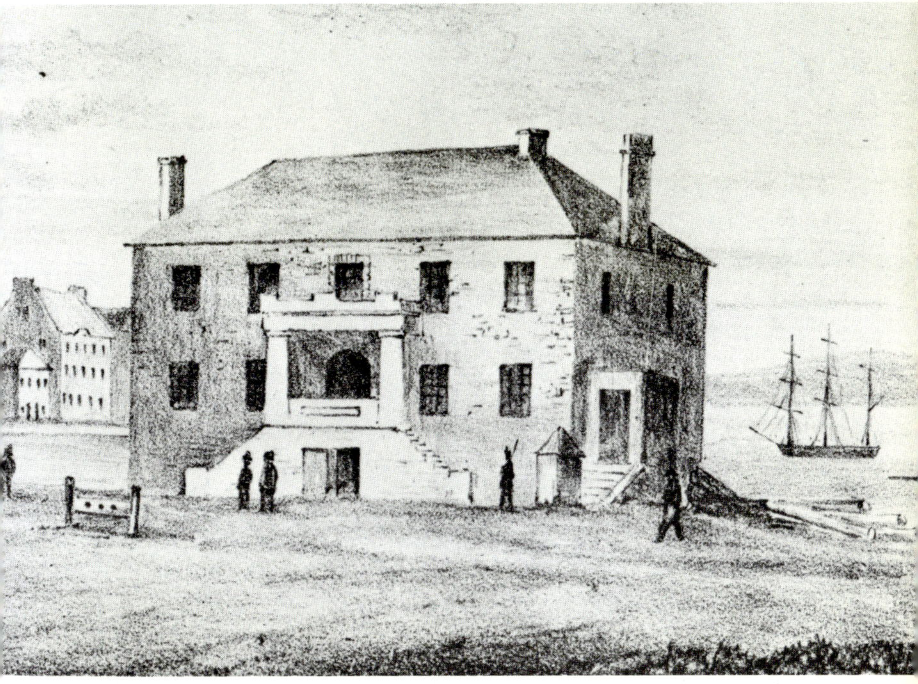

Mr JOHN JACKSON.

Before adequate highways could be constructed to take settlers to their new homes, transport in the early days of the colony was mainly by the river ferries. Unfortunately, this method of travel proved highly dangerous, because boats were often overloaded and there was little knowledge of the unpredictable behaviour of the deep, broad Derwent.

One of the most dramatic accidents occurred in February 1818, when a boat, the property of the ferryman at the Black Snake, left town with twelve passengers, a heavy cart and other luggage. It appears that the boat ran up the river, taken by a strong sea-breeze, and overturned, 'when melancholy to relate, the whole of the unhappy souls, except one, were consigned to a watery grave'. A child in arms and a young girl about six years of age were among the victims.

Another 'awful and melancholy catastrophe' happened in 1821, when the ferry-boat of Mr E. Crowder was seen by his wife to go down while he was plying it across the ferry-place at the Bluff. He was not seen again. Five other men were drowned in a ferry-boat travelling between Hobart Town and Kangaroo Point in 1824. Tragedies of this kind were all too frequent, not only with the ferries, but with any small craft unlucky enough to be upset in a sudden squall.

The *Hobart Town Gazette* in 1825 gave this advice to the settlers:

Several fatal accidents having occurred, in consequence of the unskilful manner in which the ferry-boats plying between the Jetty and Kangaroo Point continue to be built and ballasted, we are induced to offer some remarks on the subject... It is well known that stringy-bark wood, of which all the ferry-boats, or most of them, are formed, is extremely ponderous, and that the ballast usually employed is of stone, which proves both troublesome and dangerous from shifting in stormy weather; so much so, that many persons, who would otherwise visit their friends on the opposite shore once or twice a week, can never venture across the water... We suggest that all future ferry-boats shall be built of fir or Huon-pine, and furnished with masts and oars of the same buoyancy...with allowed ballast to be formed of what are technically called flat-breakers (composed of fir or some other light wood) and filled with water; because they would float and thereby increase a passenger's chances of escape, should the boat be upset.

After another tragedy at Cove Point Ferry the *Hobart Town Courier* commented: 'If anything could stimulate countrymen to erect a bridge at this place, we trust these awful warnings will suffice...' Not only were lives lost, but valuable property as well. The complete library of an ensign of the 39th Regiment went to the bottom of the river in that disaster, together with nine out of the twelve bullocks which were on board. Spirited blood horses, often transported on the ferry-boats, were also the cause of many accidents. An effort was made after this mishap to try to secure the safety of the ferries by placing a platform at each landing place, but this was not really getting to the root of the problem.

Suggestions for bridging the Derwent, a matter still troubling the minds of the City Fathers up to the present day, were put forth from the earliest years of the colony. A plan in 1827 for the erection of a suspension bridge was dismissed as ridiculous, and 'too palpable to need any further comment, than the assertion of its utter impracticability'. A wooden bridge across the upper reaches of the Derwent at New Norfolk was contemplated in 1826, although the undertaking had been talked of for many years. It was thought that no country in the world was better supplied with timber for such a project than Van Diemens Land.

Another likely spot for a bridge was at the Black Snake ferry point, where a causeway was under construction by the end of 1829. The first bridge across the Derwent was to be built from the end of the causeway. However, this did not eventuate for many years, the preliminary work being referred to as 'the Bridgewater folly, where men have been trying for years to fill up a fathomless soft mud hole, and who are as near the completion as they were three years since'. Talk was still going on about throwing a bridge over the Derwent at Bridgewater in 1841, even then with the gloomy prediction that good would probably be neutralised by a higher toll than was sufficient to pay expenses.

During this time work had been proceeding with the bridge at New Norfolk, which was finished in October 1841. This bridge thus had the honour to be the first erected across the Derwent, although the glory became a trifle diminished a few months later, when a long drought made parts of the river above New Norfolk fordable.

It was not until the year 1849 that the Bridgewater bridge was finally finished; even then the Grand Opening ended in anticlimax. 'Because the bridge was opened on Thursday, the Governor and his suite did not go to see it opened — they stopped at home.' The scale of tolls was published for the convenience of the public, the toll for the foot pass being tuppence.

Four months later the bridge was described as being barely passable and choked with ruts. Waggons were being stuck in deep holes, and other horses were put on to extricate them. The passing coaches swayed first on one side and then on the other, to the imminent danger of the passengers' lives. Despite all this criticism the Bridgewater causeway is still giving good service 128 years later, a tribute to the many prisoners who toiled in the chain gangs there, and to those who lost their lives through fever and hardship.

Other bridges were being built throughout the colony, although it pained people to witness the expenditure that was constantly being lavished upon useless undertakings at a time when both money and labour could have been better employed. Some progress had taken place, however. A bridge had been completed at Ross, in March 1822. That bridge was blown up with a keg of powder when a beautifully carved stone bridge replaced it in 1836. An elegant stone bridge, built in 1837 over O'Briens Rivulet, was hailed as a masterpiece of architecture. On the other hand, a horse-shoe bridge outside Bridgewater was reported to be in a disgraceful state in 1838, having been impassable for nearly two years.

Wellington bridge, in Hobart Town, was in disrepair, as well as the foot bridge over the creek at the bottom of Harrington Street. It was thought at first that the latter bridge had the prior claim, as it had been neglected for so long, but arrangements were made for the rebuilding of Wellington bridge. A precipice occupied the site of the intended bridge over the rivulet in Harrington Street, but as no fatal accident had recently occurred there, the wishes of the public were disregarded by the Government. That was the position in 1843. A bridge uniting Macquarie Street with the Domain was on the way to completion early in 1844 and promised to be a great improvement, especially when the slaughter-house and its filth were removed.

The highways and streets were in a dangerous state, and the poor animals labouring in the ordinary business of the inhabitants were having a very hard time. Repairs were very spasmodic, but the Government stirred itself in 1827 and made some much needed improvements. The complaints concerning the state of the roads have a very familiar ring, comparable with that being heard in this day and age. As soon as work began in one area of the town, outraged cries came from the people living in another part, objecting to having to take second place.

A causeway was needed in Elizabeth Street, which, being the principal thoroughfare, required the use of pathways much more than did Macquarie Street! Metal was being carted to Davey Street. Why was it given preference above the much more thronged thoroughfare of Liverpool Street? And so the objections continued. At the same time improvements were going forward at the other end of town in Brisbane Street, where no fewer than three men of No. 2 chain gang were working on the approaches to the bridge, built by voluntary subscription, across the Alumy creek. A new road to Sandy Bay was to be carried through a grant of land, but the fence at the end of an adjacent burial ground had been continued, blocking up the road and forming a cul-de-sac!

In June 1837 the roads were again in a 'most deplorable state'. The Launceston coach had become bogged and capsized within twenty kilometres of Hobart Town. The New Norfolk coach had become so bedded in mud that bullocks had to be used before it could be extricated. There was one loud and universal cry of: 'Who has charge of the streets, and what is to become of them?' The new ones were being destroyed, and the old ones were impassable for man and beast.

The main road between Hobart Town and Launceston was in so poor a state that a traveller who was overtaken by darkness could consider himself fortunate to escape with so small an accident as either a fall from a gig or a dislocation. Several men had suffered severely while travelling on this 'great thoroughfare'. In Hobart Town at the upper end of Argyle Street 'a poor fellow' fell into a hole and broke his collarbone.

There was a gang of men at work in 1840 excavating the sandstone rock behind Government House and filling up a space in the cove, which greatly enlarged the promenade leading from the New to the Old Wharf. As well, there were improvements in the harbour, and the *Colonial Times* recommended that 'a gentle stroll to the wharfs one of these fine and bracing mornings, before the sun has gained sufficient power to scorch the nap off one's beaver, will do anyone more good than all the physic in Mr Rowe's Emporium'.

Conditions were a little better in 1842, and a number of improvements were contemplated. The ground had been surveyed to have a railroad laid down between Jerusalem and Bridgewater. A road was also to be opened between Macquarie Harbour and New Norfolk; a probation gang had been set apart for the purpose, and the necessary stores had been forwarded. A new line of road of a comparatively level type from the Launceston road near the Crooked Billett to Hamilton had been started.

For a change, the Town Surveyor came in for some praise for appearing to be studying his business. The finishing of Murray Street to Collins Street, both as to metal and form, was the nearest to macadamising seen outside Britain. Captain Forth had very properly introduced the heavy roller and rake to keep the roads in repair.

Piling of the New Wharf was begun in 1843; it was hoped this would save the remainder of the embankment from being carried into the ocean. But the question was still being asked: 'Is it possible to find worse streets anywhere else in the world?' At Sandy Bay Road, as predicted, the man-trap across the footpath had again been opened by the rains. The new carriage road in the Domain, fortunately, was making good progress.

With the approach of the winter of 1844 the streets were still in the same state of disrepair as they were the previous year, and the *Colonial Times* spoke on behalf of the ordinary people:

> The useful and necessary are giving way to the ornamental, and the humble man in the more humble street will again have to wade his way through mud and mire to his humble home, while the comparatively rich will have his carriage drive, his approach complete, to his more stately domicile. The Town Surveyor is doing his best, but his gang should be increased in number tenfold.

In 1854 the Corporation proceeded vigorously with the completion of a much-needed bridge across the creek in Murray Street, so that the thoroughfare could be opened to the public before the start of the winter. The heavy floods of that year had done a great deal of damage, and the bridge across the Lachlan, at the entrance to the township of New Norfolk, was in a dangerous state. Much of the stonework had been completely swept away.

As well as having to contend with poor streets and roads, people had to put up with numerous other hazards, including vandalism. The ostlers were criticised in 1830 for galloping their horses dangerously through the main streets of Hobart Town. In 1833 some maliciously inclined persons amused themselves by tying ropes across the footpaths at night. 'These evil-disposed persons no doubt consider this fine fun, but an exposé will take place shortly, which will fully prove to these gentry that their fun is rather expensively purchased.'

The sons of the gentry were usually to blame for these foolish pranks, and the *Colonial Times* had little patience with them, describing their behaviour as 'silly and blackguard'. It went on to say that 'a regard for friends and relatives of these silly young men alone prevents us from publishing their names, but so sure as they appear again before the Police Bench, so sure shall all their respective names and charges against them be duly recorded in this journal'. There was one law for the rich and another for the poor; the 'lower orders' would never have got off so lightly.

The freaks of the 'Tom and Jerry' fraternity, as they were called, were revived again, in 1838, 'to the disturbance and disquietude of sundry families'. A board inscribed 'Dealer in Wines and Spiritous Liquors' was fixed over the door of the Reverend Mr Bedford's house, while another one inscribed 'Boot and Shoemaker' was placed over the entrance to Captain Forster's residence.

In 1840, Hobart Town was alive with a group which gave its war cry as 'Bricks!' Exactly how this name was derived was anybody's guess, although the gang may have come from the area known as the Brickfields. They removed lamps from building sites and performed all the mischievous tricks that vandals delight in. There was less complaining about 'these idle and ignorant young men' in 1843, and it was presumed that the lessons they had received had been of service. They had, after all, been threatened with time in the stocks!

Another danger was the furious driving through the public streets by the butchers and the gentry, seriously jeopardising life and limb. The workmen laying the water-pipes contributed to the hazards also; horses' legs, wheels of carts and other vehicles were continually sinking in the loose dirt near the corner of Murray Street. The people were asked for alms by 'blind mendicants' who became quite a menace in the 1850s, while a new generation of 'Bricks' were around in 1854, with their mischief and tricks. 'It is a pity their parents cannot find some employment for their precious young gentlemen,' the *Hobarton Mercury* complained, threatening to publish their names and addresses, but somehow never getting around to it. And of course, another custom persisted then, just as it does today. This was the habit of writing with chalk on the church walls, public buildings and any place available for desecration 'words of the most gross and filthy description'.

Public transport on the ill-made roads began with the stage coaches, two of which were brought to the colony in 1830. It was a great novelty for the people to see the handsome well-equipped coach start for New Norfolk in August 1831, it being the first thing of the sort yet produced by the colony. It ran between Hobart Town and New Norfolk, each way, daily. A New Norfolk coach also started in 1832. Safe and reliable, there were now places in it adapted to 'young influential gentlemen' and clerks in 'certain offices', so that the delicate nerves of the elegant, the exquisite, and the influential need not be endangered!

The proprietors of the New Norfolk coaches were later to take dudgeon at a remark the *Colonial Times* made respecting the dangerous manner in which the coaches were allowed by law to be overloaded. In 1836 the newspaper passed some more remarks on the subject, which would have been hard to take seriously:

We understand a Coach Act is about to be brought forward, because very lately one of our great officials was frightened out of his wits in consequence of a coach being overloaded. By the new Act it is said, we are to be taken by weight, and for this purpose, every coachman is to be supplied with a steel-yard — we wonder what, under the new law, Mr Martin's fare will be to New Norfolk! In addition to this improvement, every coach is to have a fifth wheel and a horse behind in case of accident; and before mounting the coach, each outside passenger is to make an oath before a Justice of the Peace that he is perfectly sober and a member of the Temperance Society.

Mr Baker of Murray Street started a hackney coach in 1841, which had its station near the Ship Inn. By 1844 there were others, and one of the new stands for 'cabs' was the section of Melville Street, from Elizabeth Street to Argyle Street.

In the same year strenuous efforts were being made by Mr Hyrons to benefit the public by the spirited manner in which he managed his Launceston coach, the 'Comet'. The 'Comet' left Hobart Town in the morning and reached Launceston in the evening, making about four journeys in a week.

Another company was formed in 1845 to run a second coach between Launceston and Hobart Town. This led to prolific accidents, owing to the reckless driving of the rival coaches; the habit was shared by the drivers who operated coaches to other districts as well. One driver was charged with manslaughter after a fatality had occurred.

Page's Royal Mail coach left Launceston at four o'clock one Monday morning in 1850 and arrived in Hobart Town at twenty-six minutes past three o'clock. In about a quarter of an hour, Mrs Cox's coach, which started at the same time, came in also. Thus both coaches performed the fastest trip that had ever been made upon the road.

'Why is Mrs Cox's coach like Prince Albert?'
'Because it's a Royal Mail (male).'
That was the latest joke going about town at the time.

A new coach called the 'Diligence' was also running between Hobart Town and Launceston in 1852. Traffic accidents became quite commonplace and the road toll mounted with each succeeding year. This is how they dealt with traffic offenders in 1833: 'Two bullock-drivers who were the cause of Mr J. E. Cox's carriage being upset one night, as coming down the Cock'd Hat Hill, were found guilty of being on the wrong side of the road, and sentenced to one month in the road gang.'

15

Ships and Whalers

The floating barques and merchant ships,
Much good they can perform,
Though often in the mighty deep
They tremble in the storm.

Ships were the lifeline between the home country and the colonies, and though the settlers took their lives into their own hands by taking the hazardous voyage across the oceans to the antipodes, the ships opened the way to a new world.

From the beginning of June 1816, to the end of 1823, 336 vessels had arrived at Hobart Town from different parts of the world. Just as many ships would have made the return journey home, some of the passengers making a one-way trip, while others had every intention of coming back to the colony. Cargo was arriving by the ships all the time, and they frequently commuted between Hobart Town and the other Australian ports, particularly Sydney Cove.

It was inevitable that many 'melancholy and disastrous' shipwrecks occurred. Total loss of the schooner *Sally* was reported in July 1826, with twelve people drowned. The barque *Hope* was wrecked in the Derwent River in 1827. This was regarded as an extraordinary happening, considering that the port of Hobart Town was reputed to be the safest harbour in the world.

American ships made Hobart Town a frequent place of call as they travelled between America and India, and they were usually given a good reception. Matting carried aboard these vessels was very cheap, and the settlers found it made excellent carpeting for their cottages. The captain of the American brig *Bolivar* returned to

Van Diemens Land in 1827 and became a permanent settler.

The shrewdly intelligent captain of the ship *Tybee* later introduced a new feature into the commerce of the colony. Seeing that there was a favourable opening for trade between America and Van Diemens Land, he remained in Sydney, sending this information to his employers at Salem, who were in an extensive shipping business. They sent the *Tybee* across to Hobart Town, and in exchange for American produce, wool, hides and a variety of colonial articles were taken, the Americans being able to afford to give a higher price for them than the English manufacturers. A lucrative trade was established, which was important to the economy of the colonies.

Many of the inhabitants of Hobart Town waited at the Battery in 1830 to witness the arrival of three vessels which had passed Crayfish Point. The *Nancy, Manlius* and *Elizabeth* came in sight of the Battery almost simultaneously, creating a great deal of speculation as to which would first make the town. Everyone there found it very gratifying to see three fine large vessels coming up the Derwent, within pistol shot of each other, 'pouring in upon us the riches of India — of our Sister Colony — and what is still more wanted, the most valued of all, labourers to be assigned to our enterprising Colonists'.

Van Diemens Land was also the repository of many settlers who had first tried their luck at the Swan River settlement on the west coast of Australia. In February 1831 the *Eagle*, a schooner, arrived in Hobart Town bringing seventy-two passengers from the Swan River. If there had been room on board, it was reported, double and treble that number would have embarked. Accounts from the settlement were depressing, and its prospects were becoming worse daily. There was a rumour that orders had been sent to break up the settlement and to transfer the whole population to Van Diemens Land! It says much for those early pioneers in the west that this gloomy prediction never came true.

'It's got a saw-mill on one side, and a grist-mill on t'other, and a blacksmith's shop in the middle, and down cellar there's a tarnation pot boiling all the time.' This humorous description of a steamboat was given by the *Colonial Times* in 1832. A steam engine had been shipped from England by the *Resource*, arriving at the end of 1830 for the purpose of being attached to a steam passage boat which was to be worked from Hobart Town to Kangaroo Point, and also up and down the river. This steamboat was the *Surprise*, which made its first run in 1832 to New Norfolk. Owing to the strong current and tempestuous weather, and having on board only green gum for fuel, she did not reach the Black Snake until late, when it was thought wise to return. A second steamboat was ready by the end of the year, with the new engine powerful enough to tow large ships out of the harbour even when a strong sea breeze was blowing.

Another 'beautiful craft', the *Derwent*, steamed at an average of eleven knots an hour on an experimental trip to New Norfolk in April 1840. The *Sea Horse* steamer arrived in harbour at Hobart Town in February 1841 with a 500 tonne cargo. The benefits derived by the settlers from the steamers between New Norfolk and the capital were considerable, and were said to compensate in some measure for the want of a promised bridge at Risdon and Bridgewater ferries.

A handsome steamboat called the *Native Youth* began plying to and from Kangaroo Point and the New Wharf in February 1844, and a series of summer trips by the iron steamer, the *Thames*, began in November 1846, starting with a pleasure trip to the 'pretty little township of New Norfolk'. At one stage it was specially engaged by a gentleman who, with a party of friends, journeyed to Barnes Bay on a pleasure trip. The voyage was described in this fashion:

The vessel left her berth, the Steam Boat Wharf, at half-past ten, and arrived at her destination about half-past two. The run down was delightful; a fresh breeze and an unclouded sky shows the scenery to advantage on the more elevated banks of the river in its wild and primeval grandeur; and in the valleys, cultured by the hand of man, [are] many beautiful spots giving promise of a beautiful harvest, and green pastures affording sustenance to numerous flocks and herds. A sumptuous repast and every description of refreshments were provided by Haynes and set out under an awning on deck. The cuisine was much approved. After remaining some time at the bay, where the party landed, the vessel returned, and reached her station at about eight in the evening.

Steam shipping to Australia from England was contemplated from the year 1850, and an item on steam communication in the *Courier* brought the readers up to date with the plan. 'Instead of reaching our Colonial brethren through Alexandria and Aden, we are about to put ourselves in communication with them through Chagres and Panama.' The tenders which had been made for sending the mails by steam to Australia were published by the Admiralty in 1851. By 1854 two new steamers, the *Monarch* and the *Culloden*, were regularly plying the Derwent, while two steamers, both bearing the name *Tasmania*, were operating between the colonies and crossing Bass Strait regularly.

with gear... An American man-of-war and a Consul are also expected, in order to protect the American trade and bring under control the seamen of their vessels, which, according to our beautiful police law, cannot be punished for desertion. Thus, in all probability, before long we shall have two foreign men-of-war stationed here, and thus be protected by a foreign power, when our own Government has not condescended either to give us a battery, or a single boat for our protection. Truly is England the worst of mothers to her infant Colonies. It would appear that everything the people wished was to be denied, and tyranny and oppression alone allowed to stalk over the interest of Colonies, without even a reproving word being uttered by those whose duty it is to endeavour to make the people loyal and united.

The streets of Hobart Town were enlivened by scores of Frenchmen for the ten days of their visit. The shopkeepers were rubbing their hands with glee at the large sums of money being circulated around town, as it was estimated that even the most economical French or English tar who 'kept it up' while in port would find all his arrear pay gone, as well as any he might have been compelled to draw in advance.

Whether there were any stowaways when the ships left harbour has not been recorded, but stowaways were often found on vessels. On the day an American whaler, *Newtons*, got under weigh, she was closely searched and two men were found stowed away among the casks in the hold; they admitted to having been there for ten days, and were so weak and emaciated for want of food that they could not stand and had to be sent to the hospital.

The American vessels were much admired for their trim lines. The American schooner *Petrel*, described as a 'beautiful model of a vessel', fired a gun every morning at eight o'clock, and again at sunset. In July 1843 she was gaily dressed for Independence Day with various national flags, firing salutes and causing much excitement. Many hoped that there would be a race between her and the Government schooner *Eliza* before her departure. (The *Eliza*, which played such a big part in the affairs of the colony, was wrecked in 1849 on her return from San Francisco and was cast away on Flinders Island.)

There was much competition between the captains of the numerous vessels to try to achieve the fastest time in journeys to and from the colony. The *Derwent* and *Calcutta*, two fine vessels, made very rapid voyages in 1841. The *Derwent* only took nine months and eight days to travel to London and back, while the *Calcutta*, which left Hobart Town on 24 February, arrived back in the latter part of

November, taking only nine months and one day. The *Derwent* also achieved this record on her journey the next year, while the male prison ship *Kinnear* arrived at almost the same time, making the passage in 100 days from Dublin.

Shipbuilding was a thriving industry in the colony, and many fine boats were launched. A smart schooner of about thirty tonnes burthen was launched from a yard in Murray Street, opposite St David's Church, but not into her natural element. She first had to be dragged upon four wheels by twelve bullocks through the streets to the New Wharf before breasting the dark, blue sea.

The taking of craft by runaway convicts was a frequent occurrence. A sealer living on Clarkes Island reported a schooner of about 200 tonnes lying high and dry there, having been run on shore by people supposed to have escaped from the colony. She was empty and sound; her ballast had been thrown out, apparently in an attempt to lighten her to get off.

The gold rush caused a new signal to be hoisted at the Battery — a red and white chequered flag indicating that the vessel was from San Francisco, always a very welcome sign. In 1853 there was an American Vice-Consul in the colony. By then, California was about seven weeks' sail from Van Diemens Land, and closer than England. There were plenty of crackers, loaf sugar, champagne, hams, raisins, cheese, snuff, buckets, tubs, India-rubber goods and other merchandise imported from the best warehouses in New York by the American ship *Channing*.

Equally important to the prosperity of the colony were the whalers, who were busily engaged from May to October giving chase to the numerous whales which were in Tasmanian waters at that period. In two instances in 1822 whales were caught in the Derwent within view of the town; one was caught by Mr Kelly, the harbour master, and the other by a Kent whaler. The first was expected to produce about eighty barrels of oil. Two more large ones were caught in 1823, again within view of the town. The unprecedented spectacle of a whale which had ventured up the Derwent as far as New Norfolk was seen in 1825. It was a fin-back, twenty-seven metres long. It paid with its life for its daring, and produced a considerable quantity of oil.

Usually the whaling seasons were most successful, and many were taken. A report in the *Colonial Times* in 1829 gave the news that the whale fishery was going prosperously, with one party alone capturing thirteen a month after the season had begun. May was the normal time for the whalers to set out, but quite often they started a little earlier if the time was right.

The whales were plentiful in 1832, but owing to the stormy

weather and tremendous seas the whalers could not take advantage of them. The vessels at the station were all obliged to cut and run. The season in 1834 was a good one, with nearly 500 tonnes of oil being taken as early as August. The rough men who manned the whalers were not always popular among the townspeople, however, as it was a common practice among them to defraud the merchants.

At the start of a season the whalers began busily preparing with fresh vigour their boats for the approaching fishing time. Several gangs were usually formed, some leading the way and others following shortly afterwards. In whaling parlance it was customary to express the hope that the parties would meet with 'greasy luck'. Back in port, however, a most unpleasant 'effluvia' arose from that portion of the wharf where the whalers were permitted to land and cooper their oil.

During the 1839 season a Mr Watson of the whaling establishment was brought to town seriously wounded, having been struck by a whale. The previous day a boat had been smashed to pieces and one of the crew cut in two by the fin of a whale. But despite mishaps, at the end of the season, in October, the whalers broke loose! Hobart Town was a rip-roaring place then, with the men eager to spend their money on all the pleasures offering, fighting and disturbing the peace, so that the residents were only too anxious to keep out of their way. With the close of the season that year the catch was estimated at 3000 tonnes.

In 1842 the schooner *Prince of Denmark*, on her voyage from Portland Bay, fell in with several sperm whales and succeeded in capturing one of those valuable monsters, although its head was lost during boisterous weather in Recherche Bay. Seventeen whales were secured by the barque *Cheviot* in one of the coast bays, after being out for only six weeks in 1843. The *Cheviot* again had a lucrative season the following year, when, with the *Camilla*, she arrived back in Hobart Town with forty tuns, the latter with twenty-eight tuns of sperm black oil, neither of them having been out much longer than three months. As soon as they discharged their catch they started off again on another voyage. They were wished every success, for at that time whaling was the only real source of the colony's riches.

Captain Irvine of the *Martha and Elizabeth* reported having seen about 300 whales during his passage from Sydney to Hobart Town in 1849, the largest number he ever recollected sighting during any of his passages between the ports of the colonies. Another capture of a whale in the harbour occurred in 1852, the *Courier* reporting: 'A whale which wished to view the world, made its appearance in the Derwent on Wednesday evening last, and gam-

148

bolled sportively among the shipping.' Needless to say it did not gambol for long, and after an exciting chase and fight it was caught, and was expected to yield between five and six tuns, worth about £200. The men who took part in the chase agreed to share and share alike, 'there being no Lord Warden of the Cinque Ports to claim "waifs and strays"'.

A graphic description of a whale with a tooth-ache was given by the *Colonial Times* in 1853. This particular whale, displaying all the symptoms of a jumping tooth-ache, was caught by an American whaler after an extremely dangerous chase. The boat's crew narrowly escaped a 'fowing' from the whale before it was harpooned by the mate, although even then it was reluctant to yield and its death-struggle was long and violent. However, before nightfall its blubber was in the trypot and the jaw stripped of its covering. When the teeth were extracted the cause of the whale's singular behaviour was seen. The cavities in several contained a large number of worms. The teeth were perfectly sound, but the marrow or nerve of the tooth was in many of them entirely consumed by the worms which seemed to have bred there.

Whales were not the only fish in the sea, of course, and the smaller variety were sought after to supply the market in the town. There was a plentiful catch of small salmon at the start of 1833; these were hawked about at one shilling a dozen. An increase in the population was creating a market, stirring up a little competition on the part of the fishermen. Shrimps were caught at the north side of the island and were brought over by mail coach. It was a matter of astonishment that someone did not begin shrimp fishing in the Derwent, as fish were found plentifully in all parts, particularly at Sandy Bay Point. Cucumber fish, or mullet, were very numerous at New Norfolk one year, and pleasure parties made trips to the township to enjoy the recreation of angling. After a flood in 1844 enormous quantities of fish were caught in the Tamar. The fisher-men estimated the number of fish brought into Launceston during a period of ten days at 3000 dozen.

A most beautiful specimen of sea leopard was caught at Kangaroo Point, measuring over three metres in length. Despite its beauty, it was killed and yielded twenty-seven litres of oil. They must have been short of oil in 1833.

In August 1844 a large seal measuring almost four metres long and weighing about 140 kilograms was caught in the Derwent, near Ralphs Bay. The schooner *Amphitrite* brought it alive to Hobart Town, where it was purchased by Mr Timothy Worster, 'a well-known peripatetic vendor of cabbages and cauliflowers'. Lashed to the back of Timothy's caravan and occasionally moistened with salt water and fed with fishes, the huge animal was carried about the town and exhibited to the gaping crowds for the small charge of one halfpenny, or 'any other small coin'. It was also taken to Government House to be seen and admired by His Excellency.

A caution was issued to bathers in January 1845 as the river was infested with 'ravenous monsters of the deep, sharks', more than had ever been known before. The almost tropical heat of the weather was supposed to have produced these visits.

The market for fish was not always lucrative, however, especially when matters such as this following one were brought to the public's notice. In May 1850 the *Courier* published a paragraph deploring the practice which prevailed on board a vessel then in port, the *Lady Montagu*. It was deemed 'extremely reprehensible' that the *Lady Montagu* committed the dead bodies of unfortunate passengers to the deep — in this case to the Derwent — one body having been washed ashore at Clarence Plains. The discovery of a 'half-devoured "coolie" operated most injuriously on our enterprising little band of fishermen — for on Saturday morning, not a purchaser could be found!'

16

Regattas and Recreations

A regatta, or a boat-race, was one of the first diversions offering to the people of the colony in the way of entertainment. As early as April 1824 there is mention of a regatta on the Derwent, although at that stage it was not an annual event.

Description of a boat-race was given in the *Colonial Times* in August 1829, a race which must have caused quite a lot of excitement. It took place 'across our river from the Jetty, to Kangaroo Point'. The distance was about six kilometres there and back, and the boats were manned by two native youths, with bets being placed at £5 each. Three other aquatic events were held in 1831, the first being a boat-race manned by 'regulars', starting from the Clyde at six o'clock one evening in January. Spectators waited at Battery Point to see the finish, and although it was rowed over a considerable distance it was later reported as being 'nothing of a race', despite the high stakes of £100 a side.

A regatta was next, taking place at the end of February, when it gave excellent entertainment to most of the people of the town. The boats entered for the match got ready early; the band of the 63rd Regiment started about noon and played popular airs during most of the afternoon. His Excellency and Mrs Arthur and their family watched the race from the terrace walk in Lieutenant Hill's garden.

The birthday of the reigning monarch was the reason for the next regatta in August, not normally a suitable month for such an event. However, it was a beautiful day, ending with a sumptuous dinner at Government House. The prizes were valuable, the first being a handsomely built and finished boat valued at about £80.

It was not until February 1834 that another regatta was held, when sixteen or seventeen sailing boats were entered, eight or nine whalers, and four or five gigs.

The weather was particularly favourable, and during the whole day there was a steady breeze from the south-east, and the sky being overcast, the ladies were not incommoded by the heat of the sun. About ten o'clock, people were seen flocking towards the Battery, and soon after eleven, the whole point of land was crowded to excess. The two bands of the 21st Regiment enlivened the scene by performing in most exquisite style several favourite airs — the brass band was on board a schooner, placed off the Battery for its reception, whilst the other delighted crowds of spectators on shore.

There is a break in such entertainment until 1838, when Sir John Franklin gave his consent to a regatta open to all the populace, which has become an annual event ever since. This first official sanction of 'The People's Day' met with much opposition from the clergy and upper classes, but it went ahead nevertheless and 'passed by with a spirit of éclat, which even its warmest supporters could have hardly anticipated'. The next regatta 'passed off with an éclat exceeding, if possible, that of last year'. From then on preparations were usually started about November to organise the regatta, which was invariably held the first week in December.

Sir John, however, put a damper on the 1842 event, when it was stated that 'His Excellency is opposed to publicans' or even private booths being allowed at the Regatta. The idea is absurd; everyone cannot afford to take servants with them to carry their provisions, and it is no joke to be without a cover to resort to from the hot rays of a burning sun, or the soaking of a heavy shower'. The Governor made known his determination not to attend the regatta unless all booths were prohibited. Being strictly teetotal, he was probably horrified by the way liquor was consumed by a large percentage of the population, although another reason put forward for his non-attendance was that he considered his relative and protégé, the police magistrate of Hobart Town, had been insulted at the last regatta.

The fifth anniversary of the colonial regatta again passed off with 'very great éclat', the withdrawal of Sir John's august patronage seemingly not bothering the crowd, for they all came to the holiday, determined to participate in as much fun and amusement as possible, despite the weather. The 'fairer part of creation' was decked out in delicate muslin dresses and white satin bonnets. Lady

Franklin entertained a large party at Government House to commemorate the discovery of Van Diemens Land, and received her guests with her usual urbanity, even though feeling ill. It was Sir John's last regatta, for the following year there was a new Governor, Sir Eardley Wilmot, who consented to patronise the forthcoming regatta.

New Norfolk also turned on a regatta, and in February 1846 the *Hobart Town Courier* gave it full coverage:

At a very early hour on the morning of Thursday last, the road between Hobart Town and New Norfolk presented a very animated appearance, owing to the concourse of nearly every description of vehicle. The steamer *Thames* left the Company's Wharf a little after nine, so full that a party of ladies refused to go on board. It was a most beautiful day. The position of the Regatta Ground being very straggling, made the numbers of visitors appear less... There were only three matches, a considerable time elapsing between each to spin out what would otherwise have been a very dull affair... The boats started from that part of the river which was immediately opposite the Government Cottage, passed through the bridge, and returned to where they started from. Previous to the steamers returning to town, a large party sat down to a substantial dinner at The Bush, and it was the general opinion there that was the most amusing part of the whole day's proceedings.

Unhappily, on the return journey from New Norfolk there was a most appalling accident. A seaman on the steamer *Thomas* had mounted on the top of the paddle-box to close the opening, when he suddenly disappeared through it, falling on the paddles which were revolving rapidly. No blame, however, was attached to the captain.

The tenth anniversary regatta in December took place in fitful weather while Trinity bells rang merrily. Aquatic sports were all the rage. A race between two boats, *Creeping Jane* and the *Shamrock*, for a wager of £2 was won by *Shamrock*, and similar events were quite common. Sandy Bay was holding an annual regatta as well, the second one being held on New Year's Day, 1850, when the weather was beautifully clear and warm. 'The New Wharf watermen found plenty of employment in conveying visitors to the ground, and some of them were loaded with edibles and potables to such an extent as to lead the bystanders to fancy they had cleared out for California, and believed there was no friendly port on the way.' The gold rush had begun, of course, and California was very much in the news.

A live bear was exhibited on this occasion, to be seen for a trifling sum, and an itinerant 'nigger melodist' performed. The following year the Sandy Bay regatta was held at Dunkleys Point, where the casino stands today.

The *Launceston Examiner* sent a report of another regatta on the Tamar in 1853, 'when the attendance was very large and the day was unusually favourable to the sport. However, great inconvenience was occasioned by the falling of the tide, leaving a wide piece of mud between the people and their boats, and some amusing mishaps were witnessed'. It was suggested that it would be easy to have a sort of pontoon bridge carried out to deep water.

The last day of the year was fixed for the fourteenth anniversary of People's Day. On that occasion the public was told that the custom of holding an anniversary regatta in commemoration of the discovery of Van Diemens Land might have to be discontinued for a while. Owing to the 'auriferous discoveries in the neighbouring colonies', one of the chief resources of the colony, the whaling industry, had declined, and consequently aquatic sports had not found much favour with the inhabitants, although it was planned one day to re-introduce the custom when a general holiday would once again be observed. This did not seem to prevent three regattas taking place in January 1853: the usual one at Sandy Bay, one at Kangaroo Point and the other at Battery Point.

Another sport which quickly gained popularity in Van Diemens Land was horse-racing. It was a sport for the wealthy, of course, but it soon attracted a following from among the ordinary citizens. In 1826 the *Colonial Times* advertised the Jericho races, to be conducted upon perhaps the finest course in the world — the Fourteen Trees' Plain. Several matches were made, the first for fifty guineas, between a bay colt called Sorell and a chestnut horse named Arthur, and much sport was expected. By 1831 it was found necessary to publish the laws in existence for the regulation of this fashionable amusement, as racing seemed to be the order of the day in Van Diemens Land.

Those who object to the sports of the Turf, and who state that the Colony is not sufficiently advanced for the enjoyment of them, or that its circumstances and situation unfit it for them, were greatly disappointed last Thursday, Friday and Saturday, when the Races so long looked for took place, to the delight of the largest assemblage of people which ever was witnessed in Van Diemen's Land.

The *Colonial Times* obviously derived a certain amount of satisfaction in making that statement, and continued to make further reports on all the race meetings.

Races were being held at New Town in 1834, and by 1835 the people had become regular race-goers. This must have been a typical scene on those gala days:

Today the town is all bustle and confusion — the races and nothing but the races — the people are all run 'cranky' and are loading carts, coaches, and steam boats for the races; with all the eatables that can be had in town, and are themselves tumbling out to enjoy everything.

For some reason the crowds dropped off a little in 1836, although more carriages and equestrians were reported present than ever before witnessed on a Van Diemens Land course. Apparently some of the punters were becoming rather disgruntled, for in 1837 the race folks, returning to town after a Saturday meeting, were disgusted at the sight of a horse, named Colonel Crocker, lying on the roadside with his throat cut. 'If the Colonel's efforts were no good, nay if he was sure to die, a more fitting place might have been chosen for his slaughter. The sight could not be agreeable to any, but to females in particular, it was to say the least extremely disagreeable,' complained the racing correspondent.

Sandy Bay was also conducting races, and at the first spring meeting in 1842 upwards of 1500 persons assembled to watch the sports, but it was remarked that 'they must have been all teetotallers, as no beverage but milk and water was drank on the course'. A steeple chase, regarded as a somewhat novel affair in the colony, was held in the same year, near the Berriedale Inn, Glenorchy. A delay of two hours caused great grumbling among a crowd of visitors who had come to watch the proceedings.

Launceston was also well up with the sport, and races that were held for the first time near Longford in 1846 'were rather numerously attended'. By now it was evident that undesirables were beginning to frequent the racecourses, and in a report on the New Norfolk races it was mentioned that the 'day wound up with a portion of drunkenness and squabbling'.

After the races had ended one Saturday, one of the spectators, perhaps to celebrate a winning streak, undertook to leap over a fence 1·7 metres in height. Considerable interest was aroused by this extraordinary feat in gymnastics, and many bets were laid. After several trials, in all of which the man was nearly successful, he gave up. The crowd had pressed round and caused much confusion, and the general opinion was that had there been less excitement the result would have been different.

A sign of the times was the announcement in 1850 by the secretary of the Tasmanian Turf Club that a cup manufactured in Californian gold was to be run for at the ensuing New Town races.

In 1853 the *Colonial Times* gave a good account of what often happened on the ride from the races:

> Several spills occurred on the way home from the races on Thursday. A four-wheeled cart capsized near the New Town watch-house, and six ladies and gentlemen turned unwilling summersets in the air. More from luck than good management they managed to pitch on a soft part of the road, and escaped without any further injury than rumpled feathers and fright. A little child was knocked down in Elizabeth Street by a gig, but fortunately escaped with a few bruises. Two or three spills occurred on the course, but the fates were propitious and bones remained unbroken.

Cricket, naturally, was played in Van Diemens Land at an early period. A grand cricket match took place in the paddock on 28 February 1833 to celebrate the birthday of Queen Adelaide. And in 1837 a match, described as the 'best ever', was played at Paddock Point between native youths, that is, colonially born youths, and the Derwent Club. The natives won and were delighted with their victory.

The game flourished, and a defiant newspaper reporter published these comments in 1840:

> In spite of our most miserable mis-governed Colony, we rejoice to find that the spirit of the people is not quite cowed, not quite extinguished. In proof of this we have only to adduce the manly and meritorious amusements which the people have recently encouraged and so manfully supported. The Cricket Match, played on the Domain, is a prominent example of their energy in this respect . . .

The match in question, with a subscription purse of one hundred guineas, was played for in the paddock on 1 February. Wickets were pitched precisely at ten o'clock, no person was allowed to enter without making a deposit of ten shillings, which was returned after the conclusion of the match, and the team had to be punctual in attendance. The first clubs formed were the Sorell and Derwent, who competed regularly, not only against each other but with the garrison. By 1850 the Vandemonian players had accepted a challenge by the Melbourne eleven, the match to be held at Launceston.

Blood sports were essential to the upper class, and mention was made occasionally of a run with the hounds. This enthusiastic account was given in 1835:

There have been some excellent runs within the last weeks. Mr Gregson's hounds have offered amusement to many, who, till within the last few months, never imagined there could be any sport in kangaroo hunting. The old foxhunters in England will tell you there is nothing like old Renard for sport; but foxhunting is as far inferior to following the hounds after a boomer, as sparrow hunting is to that of snipe...

A similar report in 1837 informed the devotees that the hounds had met at the log fence at Launceston the previous Saturday, when eighteen horsemen had soon found a forester near Muddy Plains. A hunt in 1841 afforded excellent sport to upwards of 500 people who chased a buck, according to the *Launceston Courier*. Perhaps the sport was more popular in the northern part of the island.

In 1840 the people of Hobart Town had their attention drawn to the benefits of bathing. One citizen believed that if a kind of framework were constructed at small expense, about £20, it would afford an effectual screen to anybody who wished to take a dip. The Derwent was very useful for this purpose, even in the Government Domain, 'while the uses and advantages of a Cold Bath, with a swim to boot, was certainly most desirable'.

A year later, public baths, called the Victoria Baths, were fitted up by a Mr Wise at considerable expense. They must have proved popular, for baths for sea bathing were also opened at Sandy Bay in 1847, while a bathing society was thriving rapidly by 1848. Women were not even considered to have a place in this recreation. Very likely they were regarded as being among the 'pedestrian itinerants' who were recommended to take a stroll to Sandy Bay, as far as Derwent Water and back again.

Another recreation provided for the citizens began in 1846 when a bowling green was opened by Mr Turner. Great credit was given to him for his enterprise and spirit. 'His excellent inn, the level and extensive "green", combined with the adjuncts of retirement and every possible accommodation for players and spectators are incentives to the sport,' it was said.

There were other activities which did not always meet with the approval of the respectable members of society, such as cock-fighting, prize-fighting and duelling. A 'bruising extraordinary' was described in the *Gazette* in 1818:

Several grand milling matches took place in a private field about a mile from the mill, now called the Waterloo of the fisty-cuffs. The first battle was between two of the cross-legged gentlemen, named Lyons and Williams; the former we stated in a later report of this nature to have had his seams flattened, but on this occasion he was more fortunate; for after a long contest, in which there were many rounds fought with the most determined bravery, and great doubts as to who would be champion, Lyons beat his antagonist; and to the no-small gratification of the spectators present, they both retired from the shipboard of action with their faces well plastered.

Another 'pugislistic exhibition' was given publicity in 1850. It was held near Browns River, when the candidates were London and Brummagen men, the latter being the victor. 'Aristocrats and sans culottes were mingled among the spectators, one or two of the former in blue shirts.' A few years later there is a record of a dog-fight and prize-fight, when a 'congregation of blackguards' assembled at Glenorchy near the Traveller's Rest to witness them. 'A week on the treadmill would very materially contribute to put a stop to these barbarous brutalities,' was the remedy suggested by the reporter of the incident.

Duelling can hardly be regarded as a recreation, but it was practised widely in those early times, mainly between 'the honourable fraternity of the highly aristocratic and pure merino class' of Hobart Town. 'Duels! Duels! Duels!!! — Nothing but duels and no fighting,' exclaimed the *Colonial Times*. 'How much would the Colony be benefited by a pair of these fools killing each other; at present we are stunned with "affairs of honor" where there is no "honor in the affair".'

That was in 1835, but duelling was still current in 1851, when an item in the *Irish Exile* told of 'two persons being engaged in a duel; after the first fire, one of the seconds proposed that they should shake hands and make it up. The other second said he saw no particular necessity for that, for their hands had been shaking ever since they began!'

Fortunately this occupation lost favour as time went on, but most of the other recreations — notably horse-racing, cricket, swimming and lawn bowls continue to attract adherents in ever-increasing numbers up to the present time.

Among the indoor recreations, skittles or bowls was very popular. An 'American Bowling Saloon' was in operation in Hobart Town, although business could not have been too brisk in 1854 as in an apparent effort to attract more customers it reduced the price of bowling to one half — one shilling during the day, and eighteen pence in the evening.

Individual oddities also occurred. A young man, well-known for his sporting propensities, undertook to lap up a saucer of milk in less time than a cat! However, his progress was slowed by a violent fit of laughing, which let the cat take the lead. But the gentleman managed to recover himself and soon caught up, and to the surprise of all present, won cleverly by two tablespoonfuls. At the start of this novel event, the odds were three to one on the cat, but they were soon changed to evens!

17

Religion and Education

The Reverend Robert Knopwood was synonymous with the Christian church in the early days of the colony. His retirement was announced in April 1823 after twenty years of duty which had begun with the formation of the settlement in 1803. He had been superseded by another chaplain, the Reverend William Bedford, stern and unbending; his dignity, however, was somewhat undermined by the sinful inhabitants, who called him Holy Willie!

Knopwood, who was credited in 1806 with adding a new word to the English language when he spoke of 'bushrangers', did not apparently go into complete retirement as letters were addressed to him in the *Gazette* in 1825 and 1826. The first letter enquired why he had ceased to preach on Thursday evenings, and the second demanded to know when 'you purpose to attend to the exercise of your Holy Office by baptizing, marrying and burying. This is a subject of general enquiry; numberless persons are waiting for the two first duties, and it is generally understood that a great relief to many persons' minds will be experienced by your publicly announcing your intentions. The reasons for this are public and notorious'. It was signed by 'Hater of Pride and Hypocrisy'.

Other members of the clergy were scattered throughout the colony and were called upon often to perform duties beyond the saving of souls, although many were hypocritical and lacking in faith. A letter in the *Gazette* in April 1825 gave a revealing glimpse of the conditions under which people were forced to live in those days:

Some time ago, you and I and everybody in Van Diemen's Land must with a sigh remember numerous condemned delinquents

160

pined through many a dreary week in the Hobart Town Gaol, alternately crying for provisions and for death.

It happened that a certain stout, tall, dark-visaged, surly-spoken person, whose profession no man more deeply than myself can venerate, heard those cries, and immediately afterwards said to the gaoler, who by the bye, is a very good sort of man — 'Mr B., procure from your baker a daily supply of sufficient bread (beyond Government allowance) for those poor men; and when the bill amounts to a few pounds, let me know the sum total, and I will discharge it!' So far so good. Well, the bread was consumed and the bill delivered, and — what do you think the aforesaid stout, tall, dark-visaged surly-spoken person did, in defiance of his aforesaid profession, which as aforesaid no man more deeply than myself can venerate? Why, he broke his promise! He refused to pay for the bread so ordered on his account! And because economy is the order of other persons, that bread has been since extra-officially paid for out of the public funds... (Sir, There is an old true saying, viz., 'Promises and pie-crust are made to be broken'.)

Another clergyman living at Pittwater, was approached by a Crown prisoner, who confessed that he had taken a false oath and was troubled by this. The Reverend Mr Garrard, in order to bring him relief, applied a 'blister' to his head, which was where he seemed most affected. The man returned home, but later, after undressing himself completely, ran furiously out of the front door, throwing himself into the nearby creek. His body was not discovered until nine days afterwards, 'which circumstance occasioned much unpleasantness amongst the Settlers, owing to their having during that time used the water'.

On one occasion a minister in a chapel noticed one of his congregation with spectacles on the end of his nose reading the Bible. This did not meet with the approbation of the Reverend Divine, for he immediately ordered the false eyes to be removed, for he felt sure they were not required to read the Bible! It was acknowledged by the reporter of the incident that the Bible ought to be perused with a 'single eye'.

It was not usual for any words of praise to be penned in favour of Colonel Arthur, but one obviously pious subject did just that, having been particularly struck at the marked improvement in the morals of the people in the town since the arrival of the Governor a few years previously. Prior to that period 'the church had been very thinly attended, as were all the other places of worship; children were to be found playing at games, while cursing, swearing and drunken-

The first appearance of the steamer *Tasmania* inspired a specially written poem, of which the first verse was:

The wished-for day has dawned at last.
And now the ocean bears
The expected treasure on its breast;
The Steamer now appears.
Swiftly it glides across the wave,
And hark the cannons roar;
While hundreds rush to hail a sight
They ne'er beheld before.

The early settlers, the pioneers, however, made their long journey to their new homes by sail, when shipwrecks were all too common. Statistics made public in 1834 gave nine vessels lost within twelve months while voyaging between the colonies and England, three of which were destroyed by fire. Of those lost at sea, 'the greater portion have been attended with most melancholy sacrifice of human life'.

Many who made a safe crossing down to the southern ocean faced the horror of being shipwrecked at their journey's end on the rugged coastline of Van Diemens Land. The ill-fated *George the Third* met its doom on a reef near the *Actaeon* in April 1835. Prayers were said for the unfortunates in the wrecked vessel, although the cynical voiced the opinion that it 'was too late for prayers, as all the lives were probably lost before the news reached Headquarters'.

Fears were always held for the safety of ships which had left the harbour; all too often they were never heard of again. The erection of a lighthouse off South Bruni in 1836 was of vital importance and undoubtedly saved many lives. At the end of 1848 there were six lighthouses situated on the coast of Van Diemens Land: at Low Head, Kents Group, Swan, Goose, Bruni and Iron Pot Island. Three had revolving lights, two had fixed lights, and one had a revolving flash.

Two French whaling ships were in port at Hobart Town in January 1838, with more ships expected. This gave the inhabitants much to speculate about, and the *Colonial Times* took the opportunity to further the rumours going around:

It appears that the French Government is now turning its attention to the whale fishing, and is offering large bounties to encourage the trade. It is understood that a French corvette will almost immediately be stationed here, and another at Sydney, in order to protect their commerce, and supply the whaling vessels

ness was the occupation of the Sabbath day'. At night no one could lie down without expecting an attack being made upon his premises. All that was now changed. Three Sunday schools had been opened, united in the common cause of training the children in the way they should go, and it was surmised that more marriages had probably taken place during the present administration than at any other time. This was all attributed to the example set by those in power, and it was felt that 'happy ought that people to be who have a Governor who cheerfully promotes every religious and moral institution laid before him, and who himself seeks out opportunities of benefiting the immortal souls of poor wretched men'.

In 1829 a new clock was erected on St David's Church, one which struck much louder than the previous one and faced two ways — to the east and to the west. Six large clocks for the different churches in the colony had just arrived among the stores in the last prison ship. Two years later the church clock had another face added to it, which it was hoped would be a 'truer time-keeper than the second one proved to be'.

A long-legged stranger who attended a service at St David's Church complained about the confined quarters of the pews, and apologised for not being able to stand during the creed and other parts of the church service, because he had become wedged in a small space and could not move his 'cumbersome members'. However, he had been amused by the ingenuity displayed by the pew-opener, a short person in black, who had shown the congregation to their seats. First of all he walked one person into a pew in a very orderly fashion, and then in a very orderly fashion walked him out again, putting him into another pew, to make room for the owners of the seats who had just arrived! Divisions of families were accommodated to a 'mathematical nicety', and as many as eight people could be squeezed into one pew.

There was always gossip going on about the clergy, and it was rumoured that a certain Reverend Divine took his duties in such a casual way that he sat down 'quite at home' during the time he was preaching the sermon. One Sunday the Venerable the Archdeacon preached at New Norfolk, where it was later reported that 'the A.D. is far from having anything in his mode of delivery at all approaching eloquence. It is one continued vibration of the same note — a dull, monotonous, sleep-rending sound, calculated to destroy much of the effects of the particular expressions which thus find utterance...' The Archdeacon was far from popular, for it was mentioned in the *Colonial Times* in May 1833 that 'the most gratifying intelligence of the week is that the Venerable the Archdeacon departs from these shores for Sydney in the *Lotus*'.

St David's tower, which was blown down in a gale, was replaced by another in 1835. This new structure, slightingly referred to while under construction as St David's Pepper Box, was said on completion, 'considering all things, not to look quite as ugly as might have been expected'. The three church clocks in Hobart Town — St David's, St Andrew's and the Trinity — kept anything but correct time. This was because the management of the clocks was under the supervision of three opposition clock-makers, who all had a time of their own! 'There was no mean time in Hobart Town, the ordinary difference between the faces of the clocks varying according to whether it was a fine or a wet day, and seldom exceeded more than forty, and never less than twenty minutes.'

If that was not bad enough, animals were prowling in the churchyards and desecrating the graves. An eye-witness told how he had seen a dog in the churchyard carrying away a human head, which the dog had scratched out of the ground. The mention of this, it was hoped, would be sufficient to make the authorities build a wall or a fence around the 'receptacale for the dead'.

Later on it was the question of the 'parson's cow'. This fine fat milch cow was damaging the grasses and tombs in St David's burying-ground, in some instances exposing the coffins and disturbing the headstones. However, the people were sure the colonial chaplain was unaware of the misconduct of the cow and hoped that he would soon give directions that she should not be allowed to feed and fatten among the tombs and graves of the metropolitan cemetery.

News of the death of the Reverend Robert Knopwood came in September 1838. He was in his seventy-sixth year. It was felt that great disrespect was shown to that deceased gentleman at his funeral as only three clergymen were present.

The foundation stone of the new Presbyterian Church at Kensington, O'Briens Bridge, was laid by His Excellency in December 1839, while the following July the first stone of the Catholic Church in Macquarie Street was laid by the Reverend Mr Therry. By 1843 a new cathedral on Trinity Hill was proceeding at such a rate that its beauty could be appreciated by the public. The same year, however, the Queen made St David's Church the cathedral of the colony, the chaplain officiating under the auspices of the Bishop. A Jewish Rabbi had also come to the colony, so the various denominations were well represented by this time.

Meanwhile, the Director of Public Works was anxious to meet the wishes of the public for the immediate erection of a bridge over the rivulet, 'so that the good Catholic townsfolk who reside northwood of the creek may be enabled to find safe and easy mode of transport to their place of worship, while the more humble, but equally worthy Baptists, who dwell in the south, may be enabled to pass to and fro to their unpretending temple'. The people had already subscribed £130, and it was felt that it would be a simple job for the working prisoners to perform. The site for this particular bridge in Harrington Street was at that time 'occupied by a precipice'.

Apparently acting on the principle that 'God helps those who help themselves', the inhabitants were at this time making an all-out effort to provide their own places of worship and instruction. The Jewish community, 'these industrious and persevering people', were to provide themselves with a synagogue, a piece of land having been given by Mr Judah Solomon. The dedication of this 'beautiful little edifice' was performed in July 1845, and it opened for the usual ceremonies the following March. A subscription had been opened by those of the Catholic faith to collect enough money to erect a cathedral and school, a project which apparently had the enthusiastic support, not only of those intimately involved, but outsiders as well.

Evidently the Bishop was a strict dogmatist, for in September 1844 a short, pungent paragraph appeared in the *Colonial Times:* 'We regret to learn that Bishop Nixon during his lecture and exposition of the Church of Rome last Sunday evening, got into purgatory so deep, that it is uncertain when he will be able to get out again.' As well, there must have been a number of red faces at Eastertime in 1845, when Good Friday was observed on the wrong Friday, the full moon occurring the following week. 'What have the Bishop and the Church of England been about?' was the question on everyone's lips. What with church bazaars, ordinations, sermons on the Queen's birthday, and other religious activities, the churches of all denominations were well to the forefront in the 1850s.

A handful of people, the congregation and supporters of the Wesleyan cause in the New Norfolk district, subscribed over a period of three years 'for the promotion of the work of God in its various departments, upwards of £800 — all this from a country congregation which has been despised for its very smallness and insignificance'. Not everything went along so smoothly, unfortunately, for the newly erected Roman Catholic Church of St Paul at Oatlands fell down one afternoon in August 1850, and a man named Flannagan was killed. The contractor, a Mr Stuart, narrowly missed the same fate. The luck of the Irish did not hold out on that occasion.

A very odd advertisement appeared in the *Hobarton Guardian* in 1854, which apparently had everyone baffled:

TO DYERS ... Wanted, about half-a-gill of hair-dye, to finish
off the hair and whiskers of an elderly Presbyterian clergyman.
N.B. As the purpose for which the dying liquid is requested is
important, none but the best quality will be taken.

'Give us light!' appealed the printer of this advertisement, but no
explanation was ever given, so it still remains a mystery.

Education of the young usually depended upon the clergy and also
upon the circumstances of the parents, so that all too often the
children of the poor were forced to remain illiterate. The Establishment for the King's Schools at Hobart Town began in March 1828
when a Government notice in the *Gazette* called for applications
for admission. These became known as the orphan schools, although
a child did not necessarily have to be deprived of both parents to
qualify for admission. The application form was a cold official
document, which read in part as follows:

... Your Petitioner therefore humbly prays that the said child
may be admitted into the King's School; and if this prayer be
granted your Petitioner hereby agrees that the said child shall
remain in the King's School so long as The Lieutenant-Governor
shall think fit, and that when of a proper age shall be disposed
of at His Excellency's discretion as an apprentice or servant.

'Disposed of.' What an ominous future for the luckless child.
However, it did offer a better chance in life for these children than if
the conditions had remained the same as they were in 1825. An
editorial in the *Hobart Town Gazette and Van Diemen's Land
Advertiser* in January of that year revealed the desperate plight of
these young people:

There is a subject which we long have considered with much
seriousness, and to which we most earnestly beg attention; we
mean the education of those abandoned children who prowl our
streets in shreds of wretchedness — without a mother to cherish
or a father to protect them; or who, if not indeed orphans, are
exposed to the contagion of their parents' example, and thrown
on the vile world without a guide, except depravity, or the least
adroitness, save in blasphemy! For such poor helpless ones, a
refuge is solemnly demanded. Nature weeps aloud in their
behalf ... Political economy would receive advantage from their
wellbeing; and we do most warmly entreat that 1825 may be the
honoured era in which judicious benevolence shall rescue them
from ignominy; How small a pittance from the opulent would

effect the blessing we aspire for! ... Alas, we know too many painful instances which, if publicly developed, would advocate the cause we are enforcing, far better than language can. In particular, one poor pennyless forlorn and nearly houseless widower has just craved bread for ten motherless children ... he must forage as others have been obliged to do before. But where we ask is the bread of tuition for them? What are they to do whilst their heart-broken father is earning with the sweat of his brow a dinner for them? O surely it is obvious that in such a station, unless public bounty aids them, they will reach maturity like pigs without discretion — like goats without chastity — and like savages without one social element.

Under such circumstances a great many of these children would not have reached maturity at all, but at least someone had cared enough to speak out on their behalf.

A day school for the more privileged was opened in 1827 by Mrs Gregory, in Brisbane Street, for children of both sexes, at £1 per quarter, or £25 per annum for boarders. Notice was given in July 1828 that a school to be called the King's Grammar School was to be founded in New Norfolk. An advertisement appeared in the *Colonial Times* in 1829, intimating that the 'young gentlemen' attending the Hobart Town Academy would be resuming their studies at the beginning of February. Other schools advertised in 1831 were the Richmond Hill Academy, Norfolk Plains Grammar School, and the Ladies' Seminary.

It was noted with unfeigned satisfaction by the *Colonial Times* in 1830 that rapid progress was being made in education among the lower orders, and that there were now no fewer than 194 children being regularly taught in the Sunday schools established by the Wesleyan congregation in the town. About the orphan schools it also had its say. The suggestion was made that instead of educating children to apprentice them to masters and mistresses as servants, they should be taught trades to 'prepare them for the occupations which await them in the world'. It went a little further: 'and although we fully go along with the teaching of every person both to read and write, we most decidedly think that among the lower classes whatever in the one goes beyond the being able to read the Bible, and in the other the writing one's own name, much more frequently produces harm than good...'

On the other side of the fence there was the prospect of an institution being established for the offspring of the gentry, who were often sent home to England for their education. Such an institution would no longer 'expose the children to the demoralizing

TOP: Kangaroo Bay, looking towards Hobart Town, with snow-capped Mount Wellington in the background. BOTTOM: A view of the township of New Norfolk, *c*. 1842. (*Both from the Allport Library*)

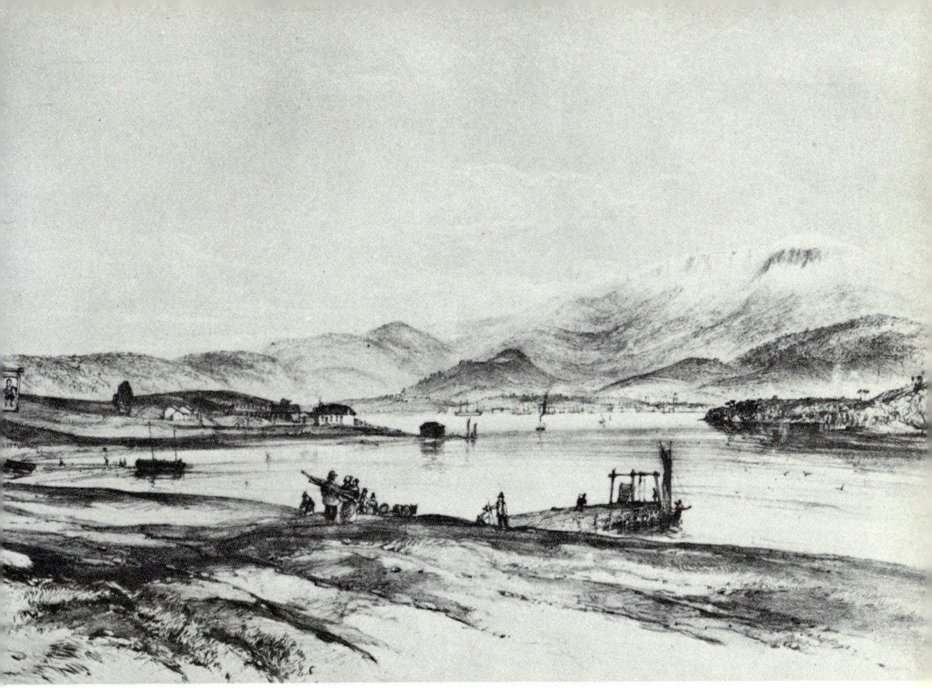

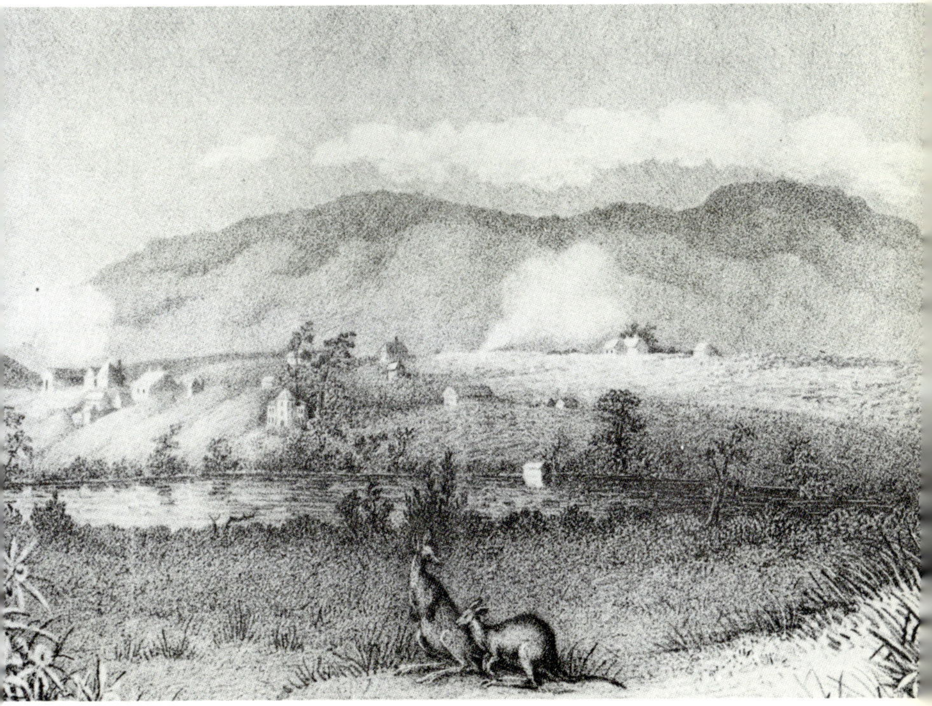

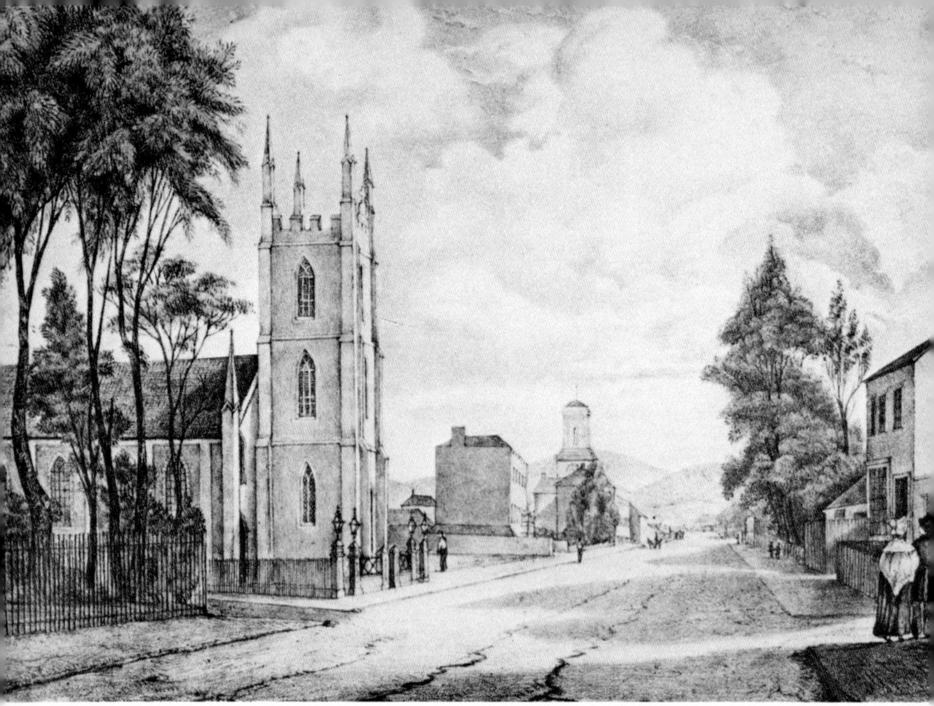

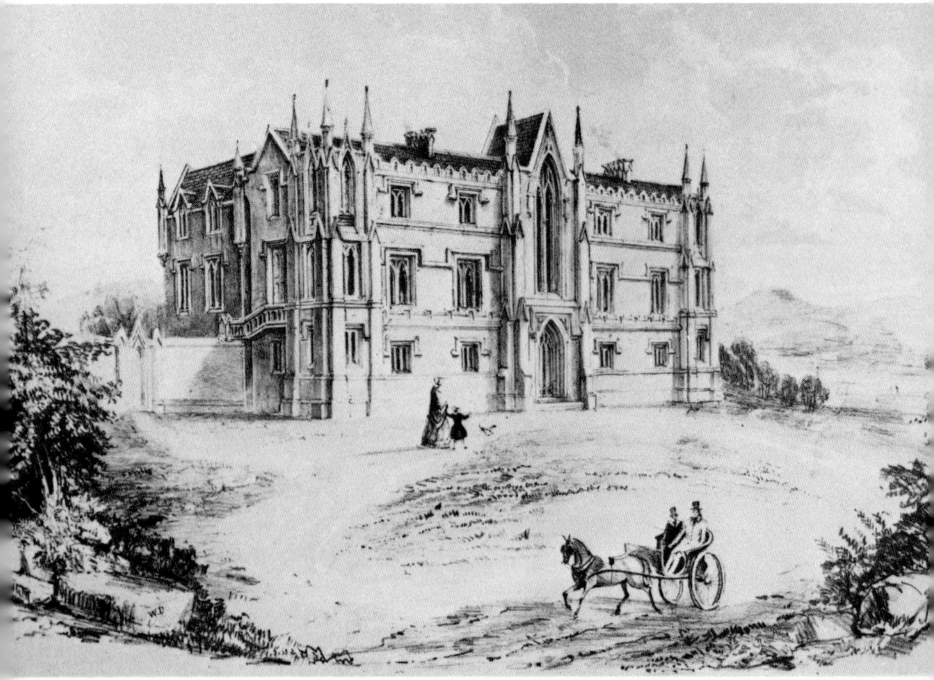

effects of a journey or a voyage, a separation from parental regard, and the suspension, if not annihilation, of all the social and affectionate feelings which ought to grow up and strengthen in a family as the children rise in years, and immerge into society'.

Class distinction was practised in many ways; one distasteful instance came to light in a letter to the editor of the *Colonial Times*, to the effect that the father of four young children, whose mother had died, placed two girls of the family in a respectable boarding school. But because the dead mother had been a prisoner, the wife of a high public officer threatened to take her own daughters away unless the motherless girls were instantly removed. The two girls were sent home to their father on the second day of school.

A general system of education for the colony was said to be occupying the attention of the local authorities in 1839, and there are indications that efforts were being made to advance education from that year onwards. However, the proposed college at New Norfolk, the idea and cherished plan of Sir John and Lady Franklin, received wide criticism, and it was suggested that a better place for such a project would be in the centre of the island at Campbell Town or Ross, or at Sandy Bay in Hobart Town, where an offer had been made of a hectare of land. The coins placed under the foundation stone of the college had been, colonially speaking, 'shook' on the day when the farce was performed. Even the stone itself went missing, and the plan never went any further than that.

The public school in Campbell Street was attended by seventy to eighty pupils in 1842, and was under the direction of the Reverend Mr Raven and his son, who acted as assistant. However, the house was too small, and due to the 'parsimony of the Government' not a single inkstand was provided. The orphan school was in a bad way too, and in April 1843 it was reported that the mortality among the children was alarmingly high. About twenty-seven of the girls alone 'had gone to their long home', and the death rate among the boys was nearly as high. A few months later the orphan school in Davey Street became a total ruin after a period of heavy rain. The school still continued, however, and was said to be 'still managed in a very superior manner, consistent with the means possessed to do so'.

There was a marked improvement in the situation by the next year, fortunately, the public being made aware of the 'fair and equitable manner in which the Home Government treats this Colony'. For each of the children of convicts in the asylum, £10 per annum was paid by the British Treasury. 'We have now no cheerless beings — children too — crawling along the roads and byeways, badly clothed, and idly rambling; they are now strictly kept to their proper avocation and studies, and properly furnished

Well-known Hobart Town buildings in the 1840s. TOP: St Joseph's Church, with St David's in the background. BOTTOM: The High School. *(Both from the Allport Library)*

with warm and comfortable clothing.' This warm tribute was given by the *Colonial Times*.

In 1846 it was announced that the medical profession, members of the Bar and the police magistrates intended to follow the example of the clergy by endowing scholarships for the children of their respective professions by means of subscriptions raised among themselves. The same year saw Hutchins School opened on 3 August at its premises in Macquarie Street for the use of the Hobart Town grammar schools.

In 1848 a parent wrote a letter to the *Courier* about the then current Education Act:

> May I request to know whether the parents in one district will have the option of sending their children to the school in a neighbouring district, supposing the new Education Act comes into force? Because I should imagine that many would prefer to support the best rather than the nearest school. Many children in this neighbourhood come several miles to school every day, and would come still further, if they thought by that to gain a better education...

This new Act was to the detriment of the schoolmasters, whose salaries were reduced to such an extent that one of them wrote to the newspaper asking whether it was the Governor's intention to drive every respectable schoolmaster to renouncing his occupation?

The Hobart Town High School came into operation in 1849, with its first Headmaster, James Ecclestone, his wife and children, arriving from England by the *Success* in November. Four months later he was dead, his sudden death attributed to brain fever, due 'perhaps to the anxieties of the office'. In 1851 the High School was hailed as the 'Athens of the Southern World', a sort of Tasmanian University, or the basis of one, being founded under the name of the High School. It was understood that 'the inhabitants of the Colony have contributed liberally, as regards the spirit of the contributions and their pecuniary amount'. Obviously it did not live up to its expectations, as three years later, according to the *Hobarton Guardian*, its position was this: 'At last the catastrophe has arrived... This educational establishment witnesses on its brow, the self-confessed testimony that its operations throughout have been as fruitless as its system has been thoroughly principleless...'

The Inspector of Schools, Mr Arnold, a nephew of the celebrated Dr Arnold of Rugby, had taken up his appointment in 1850. At

St George's School the children held their usual Christmas treat in Mr Butler's paddock near the church, where there was plenty of fun to be had, and in the evening for their special enjoyment 'dissolving views' were exhibited at the Mechanic's Institute.

Meanwhile, the clergy were experiencing a few difficulties, judging by this advertisement which appeared in the *Launceston Examiner* in 1854:

WANTED: A Church of England Clergyman — for the township of Westbury, to bury the dead, as the present incumbent has been missing about a fortnight. Two bodies are now awaiting burial.

18

Entertainments and Festivals

The following lively picture of 'lower-class pleasures' in Hobart Town was given in the *Colonial Times* in 1834.

'How delightful it is to hear the band on Sunday night!' This is in the mouth of every assigned servant in Hobart Town, male and female. 'I must have a new bonnet and a new gown, and I know, too, how to get them, even if I get the Factory next day,' say the women servants in every house in the town. It would be cruel to prevent such delightful assemblies, as are now collected every Sunday night. Besides, how could the 'Black Houses' and the other licensed houses get on, to say nothing of the 'unlicensed', with the little snug back parlours, which every Sunday night are now so fully occupied? Oh, it is a fine thing, the band on the Sunday nights — Hobart Town is then all alive!

However, it would never have done for the more respectable members of the community, whose tastes differed altogether. There was very little offering in the way of entertainment during the first twenty years of the settlement. The first public concert which the island had ever known took place in 1826. It was held at the Court House, a place not exactly conducive to joyous emotions, considering the great number of condemned criminals who had trembled there as the judge donned the familiar black cap. Despite this unsocial atmosphere, over 250 people attended, even though the weather was bad.

The band of the 40th Regiment played all the popular airs which set a few toes tapping, while the programme was made up of a number of songs. Three gentlemen sang the Glees, consisting of three songs: 'Glorious Apollo', 'Fair Flora' and the 'Witches'. A Mr Swan rendered 'The Sun that Lights the Roses' and 'In the Cottage', while the audience appreciated a recitative and air called 'Death of Nelson'.

In 1831 it was reported that a plan had been drawn up for the establishment of a new theatre, 'for the benefit of the community conferring amusement, certain pleasure regularly, in all parts of the Island, to the great relief of ennui and the prevention of rum drinking, which brings on inevitably a speedy and equal system of dying suddenly'.

A Christmas concert was held in 1832, which took place for some odd reason on 9 January. It was conducted by a Mr Deane, and once again the Court House was used for the event. Tickets were seven shillings, and five shillings for children. Another concert was presented the next year by Mr Deane, who played the violin, as well as a 'Duett' with one of his sons. Mr Peck's concert that same year went off uncommonly well. The room was crowded and the audience highly entertained. As a violin player Mr Peck was said to be 'the very best that ever set foot on this shore; and in addition to his splendid knowledge of music, he is master of the eccentricities of the celebrated Paganini'.

A favourite melodrama, *Clari*, was performed at the old theatre in January 1834. Considering the difficulty of the piece and small size of the stage, it went off remarkably well. 'Mrs Cameron appeared as Clari, but she did not please us so well in that character as she did in that of Mrs Haller, in the *Stranger*...Mrs Taylor is rapidly improving; indeed, her Vespina was excellent, and her little song of "Love Was A Mischievous Boy" was excellently well sung and performed.' The *Colonial Times* gave this critique, as well as the information that Mr Cameron had rented the Theatre Royal Argyle-Rooms.

The new theatre was to be fitted up with a gallery, which would seat 500 persons, with plenty of room for a large stage. The price of tickets would be reduced as they were too dear at the present confined theatre, which had the added disadvantage of being connected to a tavern. People did not like applying at the tap of a tavern to buy tickets.

There had been complaints about ladies at the theatre shutting out the view of those sitting behind them, as the custom was to wear enormous bonnets. However, at the performance following the complaints certain ladies 'whom it is common to class among the aristocrats or leading fashionables, very properly, most particularly, attended to the public request, and one and all wore little or no ornaments on their heads, by which those sitting behind were not at all inconvenienced'.

Unfortunately, not all the patrons were so considerate. 'We knew how it would be! When we heard that "Ginger-beer" was called for by the ultra elegants in the dress boxes at the Theatre, we expected that Gin itself could not be a long way off... There are many drawbacks attending upon a play-house at a tavern...' The peace and quiet of the town was now disturbed nightly by some noisy brawl or other at the play-house, which had been for families for amusement and recreation, but was now 'the ring for pugilistic rencountres!'

Theatrical entertainment was still very popular during 1834. *Black-Eyed Susan* was put on specially for the subscribers to the regatta, and soirées were commenced in the Argyle-Rooms. There was a full house at the first soirée, when a new musical instrument was introduced 'called the Accordion, which for sweetness and softness of tone cannot be excelled'. Mr MacKay's benefit concert took place in August, and the house was crowded. Mr Bedry danced a Calcutta hornpipe, much to the satisfaction of the audience who thoughtlessly encored him, forgetting that such performances required physical strength and could not be repeated without considerable inconvenience!

The ceremony of laying the foundation stone of the new theatre occurred in November, and at least 1000 people were there. All the vessels in the harbour had their colours flying in honour of the occasion. This was to be the Theatre Royal, which today 'still flourishes like a palm tree by the river side'.

A Theatre of Arts was opened by Mr George Peck in February 1835 in a large room in Elizabeth Street. A 'unique and highly mental amusement' was presented in the form of a mechanically operated device which apparently projected scenes in a very novel manner. 'The whole was accompanied with appropriate music; a young lady of surprising talent, only twelve years of age, presided at the piano-forte, and played solos occasionally. "Buonoparte Crossing the Alps" and the "Storm at Sea" were the opening numbers.'

In July the great star, Mrs Chester, performed at the Argyle Theatre, and the audience was not disappointed, this being the only occasion on which a first-rate singer had so far appeared in Van Diemens Land. Unfortunately, Mrs Chester was rather hoarse from the effects of a cold and not accustomed to the company or the theatre.

An occasional performance still took place at the barracks, but it was felt that now there was a well conducted theatre in town this should cease. By now the Royal Victoria Theatre, renamed in honour of the Queen, was well established. The last performance of the 1840 season was fairly attended, with the play, *Rory O'More*, being acted for the first time. The house was smothered in smoke from the cigars of gentlemen at the back of the boxes, and the saloon was little better. 'A respectable place of rational entertainment is much wanted,' was the opinion of the *Colonial Times*, and probably many other citizens as well. *Aladdin* was produced for the first time in the colony in November.

The South Polar Expedition, a new piece by an unknown author, filled the Royal Victoria Theatre to capacity in 1841. It was considered a shame that Sir John Franklin did not patronise the theatre, but his loss was amply made up by the consideration of Colonel Elliott and his wife. They always commanded a full house, 'and by their liberality, excite the kindest feelings towards them in the public mind'.

A good house witnessed the performance of the *Beggar's Opera*, and another piece entitled *Love's Livery* in 1842. The review stated: 'The performance was most respectable, and the latter piece kept the house in a roar of laughter throughout... Between the pieces, Miss Young danced in excellent style what is here designated the "Highland Fling", she looked well in the kilt, but her upper costume was not at all appropriate. It was too bad to encore her in this dance, the fatigue was too much for her.'

A real treat in 1843 was the second appearance of Mr Lee and his 'sagacious dog Bruin'! Also being presented for the first time in the colony was a new historical drama called *The Woodman's Dog*, or *The Fiery Ordeal*. Mr Lee and his dogs were of course the grand attraction of the night. A good pantomime performer, Mr Lee appeared to have complete command over his 'four-footed companions'; the mere lifting of a finger, or just a look or a sigh, controlling them 'more completely than the cudgel or the blow'.

Captain Blackwood and the officers of H.M.S. *Fly* gave a performance of what was technically called a 'bespeak', the play being Colman's musical drama *The Mountaineers*. This took place in January 1844, while in the same month Shakespeare's tragedy of *Macbeth* was played to the best houses of the season.

For those who could not afford such highbrow entertainment there were always the Sunday amusements. Boys and young men were said to congregate together on the Government Domain for the purpose of playing cricket, leap-frog and 'perchance a spell at pitch and toss, with other gambling pastimes'. This caused great annoyance to the respectable inhabitants, who very likely enjoyed a stroll on the Domain on Sunday. However, the police finally caught up with these 'disreputable characters' when a 'smash' was made on their hideout, a retired nook of the paddock, with scouts placed at certain distances to give an alarm should the 'traps' be on the look-out. They were sentenced to two months' hard labour, and three months for a second offence.

A pantomime was given in January 1845 at the Royal Victoria, with a very genteel audience in the boxes, and the pit nearly full. There were many 'fine and interesting children present, having come for the purpose — to see and enjoy the Pantomine'. Mention is made in September 1846 of a 'neat little theatre', the Pantheon, gaining ground in public favour.

Meanwhile, the Royal Victoria Theatre in Campbell Street had been the scene of an accident. Mrs Young fell through the floor while dancing the concluding act of *The Bronze Horse*. Some time previously a hole had been formed in the stage to take a large pole for a performance; the covering gave way under the pressure of Mrs Young's foot, and one of her legs went completely through. It was some time before she was extricated from her unpleasant situation! She had severe contusions from her knee downwards which prevented her from resuming her role in the piece.

A new pantomime was well attended on Boxing Night in December 1847. The Lieutenant-Governor's box was occupied by the Aborigines from Oyster Cove, there under the care of Dr Milligan and Mr Prout. The theatre was then under new management. However, by August a small item in the *Courier* said that 'efforts are about to be made to re-open the Victoria Theatre', so it appears likely the theatre was forced to close down from time to time due to the bad name it had acquired. It did re-open, as there was a performance there in December on regatta night when it was well filled.

Herr Imberg's miscellaneous concert was held there in January 1849, and at the end of the month a really novel event was in store for the people of Hobart Town. At a benefit for Mr Newland, of the Daguerrean Gallery, an apparatus was fitted up for illuminating the theatre with gas during the whole of the performances of *The Flying Dutchman*, or *The Phantom Ship*. Several songs, dances, and the interesting afterpiece of *Catching an Heiress* were included in the bill. The appearance of the ghostly ship was supernaturally heightened by the effect of the gas.

The sub-committee of the Amateur Dramatic Club waited upon Sir William Denison in January 1850 to request his patronage at their forthcoming amateur performance. Meanwhile, there was an unfortunate 'fall of the Drama' in Launceston, when about half-a-dozen ticket-of-leave men who had been performing on the stage were sentenced to two months' hard labour for a breach of the convict regulations.

Minstrel shows really caught on, and in March 1851 the New York Serenaders gave their first public concert at the Royal Victoria Theatre. The house was crowded, and every private box was taken, with the music lovers well pleased with the whole performance. They were not so well pleased when a band of female serenaders arrived the following December, however, and it was remarked that apart from the novelty there was nothing particularly extraordinary in their presentation.

By 1852, apparently, after all this stimulation, there was a falling off in entertainment, as there was general lamentation that Hobart Town was never so dull as far as public amusements were concerned. 'No soirées musicales, no soirée dansante, no "nigger" melodies, no theatre, not even a fantoccine show for the amusement of the young.' 'Beyond an occasional performance of the military band, no enlivening strains are heard except at a public dinner or a public-house singing saloon, where newly inspired artists grind the air . . .'

It must have been a relief to hear that the Ethiopian Serenaders intended paying Hobart Town another visit, their first having been in 1850, and by March 1854 this inimitable company of 'care-killing "darkies"' was attracting crowded audiences. 'It is no small proof of the excellence of their entertainment that a visit to one of them only begets a desire to be present at another.' A new piece introduced was *Ben Bolt* which was rapturously encored every night. The *Colonial Times* must have been their greatest fan!

Ali-Ben-Sou-Alle, the famous performer on the turkophone, also arrived in October. A band of itinerant musicians had arrived earlier by the steamer *Tasmania*. These were a German family who had come to travel through the various towns in the colony, 'to test the liberality of the inhabitants'. On a Saturday evening they performed several popular airs in the market place, and were evidently pleased at the 'substantial marks of approbation showered upon them'.

More intellectual pursuits were usually held at the Mechanic's Institute, and there is record of such a meeting held in 1831 at the Court of Request's room. The lecturer was Dr Ross on the subject of 'Pneumatics'. Some machinery from England, consisting of air pumps, was demonstrated. It was hoped that this 'slumbering Institution', now that means were within its power, would prove a monthly entertaining evening relaxation, from the dullness of Hobart Town life. It was a false hope, however, as even two years later the *Colonial Times* mentioned that the Mechanic's Institute 'is said to have awoke from the repose in which it has long indulged, under auspices highly favourable to its future success'.

It was reported that a reading-room and small library were to be established at New Norfolk, when it was expected that the settlers would support such an institution. It was hoped that similar establishments would be formed in every township in the interior. A year later, in 1836, Mr Davis opened his extensive Reading Rooms in Hobart Town, when the newest London publications were offered to the public. This was progress indeed, and an enthusiastic account was to follow:

> What with the Circulating Library, the extensive Reading Rooms, the fancy goods, the splendid shew of first-rate piano-fortes and other musical instruments, Mr Davis's rooms are now made to resemble the first descriptions of Libraries that are so frequented at the British watering places. We believe, within a few weeks, he will be regularly supplied with several files of the London, Scotch and Irish Journals — as, also, with the most popular magazines.

By now Queen Victoria was on the throne, but her birthday celebrations in May 1839 went off 'in a manner most stale, flat and unprofitable in the Colony', which did not indicate much loyalty on the part of her far-flung empire. People evidently got more enjoyment out of such festivities as Twelfth Night, when a good display of variegated lamps were placed over the doors of the confectioners, and a lot of fun went on in raffling for cakes at Hedges and Marshalls. At one confectioner's shop, about fifty splendid cakes were raffled one year, and many ingenious devices of confectionery were displayed for sale. Tables were spread with 'luxurious viands'. A monster cake, about twenty centimetres thick, and about one metre in circumference, was raffled on one occasion and must have caused a lot of excitement among the people.

In 1842, for the lovers of art, attention was called to a sale of some splendid oil paints by celebrated masters, brought out to the colony by Mr Turner, who had just returned from Britain after an absence of three years. Exertions were made the following year to establish a School of Painting under the direction of Mr Munday, an artist of Hobart Town. A Mr Prout delivered a lecture at the Mechanic's Institute in 1844 upon 'drawing and perspective'.

Mr Prout was to make his mark in the colony. A couple of years later he and a party of gentlemen returned from a sketching tour on the other side of the island. Nearly a hundred of Mr Prout's drawings of well-known spots between Hobart Town and Launceston were shown, and they were considered equal, if not superior, to any already known to the public. A notice publicising a portfolio of Mr Prout's sketches was given in the *Courier*, describing them as the most beautiful sketches in watercolours, surpassing anything yet seen in the colony. The views were principally of the Break-o'-Day district, Tullochgorum, Killymoon, Fingal and St Marys Pass.

The lovers of painting, of course, had flocked to view Mr Duterrau's collection in Campbell Street and had been most impressed by the two paintings he had done of two Aboriginal chiefs, Timmy and Jack. These portraits, on a gigantic scale, were exhibited in 1839. As well, the public was favoured by an exhibition of another novelty, dissolving views, at the Mechanic's Institute in 1853. The splendid new apparatus used had been recently imported. It was manufactured by the famous opticians Horne and Thornewite. The lanterns were described as remarkably good, furnished with lime burners; the brilliant oxy-hydrogen light, combined with powerful lenses, produced a fine effect. The painting on the slides was 'admirably executed', and the scenes from the 'State funeral of the great Duke' were acclaimed as 'perfect gems'. The only complaint was about the light, which was said not to be strong enough. It was hoped that the gas (which was used only for entertainment purposes then), would be of better quality for the next performance.

'The Campbell Town Waltzes', published by Mr Henslowe in 1850, must have been appreciated by those who loved music. These waltzes were dedicated to the ladies of that district, and lithographed by the artist Mr Thomas Brown, of Macquarie Street. The title page was embellished by a view of Campbell Town. Mr Henslowe later wrote the Louis Napoleon polka and often provided musical novelties for Christmas parties.

Christmas was regarded as the season of congratulations and reunions, with Boxing Day meant for the amusement and entertainment of the public, with events such as greasy pole climbing, and a Fancy Ball at the Royal Albert. In honour of Christmas many shops were gaily decorated with evergreens, tastefully arranged in bower-like fashion, others contenting themselves with a simple bunch of green holly over their doors. A description of the Christmas festivities for 1847 said that 'arrangements for keeping up the Christmas holidays in the city have been very complete, and nothing but hilarity has prevailed. The busy hum of the populace, so thickly thronging our principal streets on Christmas Eve, augured extensive sales by our shop-keepers. It is some time since such crowds were seen together'.

The annual festival of the Teetotal Society was usually held in the Government Domain on New Year's Day, when the members walked from Scotch Church in procession, accompanied by a band of music and with appropriate banners displayed. A tea party was given at the society's hall in Bathurst Street in the evening.

May Day festivities were always observed in Hobart Town, as well as All-Fools Day. This account was given of the April 1850 festivity:

Monday last was 'All-Fools Day', and the commencement of our shooting season. After despatching young urchins on mysterious messages to shoemakers and druggists' shops, Cockney sportsmen turned out for the day. Many hair-breadth escapes occurred, and the greatest consternation prevailed upon the proprietors of rural hen-roosts and dilapidated piggeries in the interior.

19

The Weather
and Natural Phenomena

The weather affected the lives and well-being of the early settlers perhaps more than any other factor. On it depended the harvest, the state of the roads and transport, health and husbandry. Tasmanians of today will recognise the variableness and moods of their climate, which has seen little change since the first settlement.

'Salubrious' was the word the settlers usually chose to describe the climate of Van Diemens Land, although at times they appeared amazed and awestricken at the variety of weather which Nature often served up to them. Newspapers of the era usually commented on such an important subject and often published letters from settlers describing any extraordinary weather pattern which had occurred, so that it is possible to follow the meteorology from the first published reports.

The winter of 1816 was of 'unexampled severity'.

[It was] much to the dissatisfaction of the Settlers, [and] impeded their generality from bringing their Subscriptions, which consist in Grain, to Hobart Town; and their anxiety on this account is highly praiseworthy; some Settlers have in the course of last week, absolutely waded for miles through Water and Mire with a Load generally of Two Bushels of Wheat on their backs to lodge in His Majesty's Stores, for the Relief of the heroic Sufferers by the memorable Battle; a Proof of generosity, and likewise of their Zeal (whatever may be their distance from their Native Country) in support of the British Character. If the weather should become in any degree favourable, it is expected that the whole of the Subscriptions will be collected on Saturday next, when a general List of their Names and Benefactions will be published.

The *Hobart Town Gazette* was responsible for this piece of intelligence, at a time when Napoleon and Waterloo were still very much in the news and the settlers' hearts and sentiment still with Home and England.

Conditions were better in 1818 when a very favourable season, warm with occasional rains, was enjoyed. 1820 was a good year also, and in February many of the settlers had already finished harvest, owing to the long spell of fine weather. In April, after a wet evening, the first fall of snow for the season was experienced on Table Mountain, which soon assumed a very wintery appearance, and the weather was unusually cold.

The inhabitants of Van Diemens Land took great interest in natural phenomena, and duly observed any astronomical events. The comet which appeared in October 1825 was commented upon in the *Colonial Times*: 'One of these beautiful heavenly bodies has again appeared. It may be seen every evening blazing with the most vivid brilliancy in the regions of the heavens, between the north and east. It appears in magnitude very much to resemble that of the year 1810.' It was later remarked by an old woman that the appearance of the comet in the hemisphere was a token of some awful calamity in Tasmania. 'Good God deliver us from all our enemies,' was the earnest desire of the reporter of this prophecy which, considering the fact that the colony was then under the leadership of Colonel Arthur, was not without implications.

A letter written by a settler at Big River, High Plains, dated 8 February 1826 told of the most 'tremendous storms of thunder, lightning and hail', which he had ever known. Hailstones as large as hens' eggs lay deeply on the ground and could have been collected by bushels. They came with such tremendous force that the fowls in front of his hut were 'struck dead' with them. His sheep dog was believed to have met the same fate as it had not been seen since. The poor sheep were driven in all directions for shelter and the next morning were 'whiter than hands could make them'. A quantity of Virginia plant under cultivation was totally destroyed.

A tremendous hailstorm took place at Green Ponds in 1827.

The curious and minute observers of nature noticed a most singular confliction of the elements. The sea in the harbour rose to an unprecedented height. The swell was excessive, and all nature seemed to labour with some internal irruption. The sky presented a crazed and fantastical appearance; and the wind was suddenly violent and irregular — one moment blowing a gale, and the next a dead calm. We cannot account for this in any other way than by attributing it to the effect of some subterraneous fire, which as yet has found no vent which we know of in this Island.

An earthquake, suggested by De la Perouse's voyages of discovery, was another explanation put forward, although an earthquake had never been heard of since the colonisation of the place.

A journey by Lieutenant-Governor Arthur into the interior in 1829 resulted in another interesting theory being made public. It had been proved beyond all question that some of the best and most valuable soil and pasture in the world remained undiscovered in the colony. This point was of itself sufficient encouragement for emigration, but the fact that part of this hitherto unexplored territory was so elevated that it had an atmosphere capable of freezing water in the middle of summer was considered of greater importance in view of the warm climate. These regions would make it possible to cure provisions there for shipping to New Holland, the East Indies, and all the adjacent islands in the great Pacific Ocean, as well as being much cheaper than any coming from Europe, goods not being subject to deterioration. This would hold out a certain market for all the beef and pork which the fertile colony could rear. It is doubtful whether this scheme was ever put into practice, however.

Another tremendous hail and thunder storm took place near New Norfolk, in March 1829. It came on suddenly and seemed to take a particular direction and spend all its fury 'in a small stripe of the bush', tearing up several trees by the roots. Once again the hailstones appeared as large as hens' eggs, and all the birds flying about at the time were turned upside down in the air as if shot. It raged for about an hour, then suddenly subsided into perfect calm.

In July 1830 it was being said that never, at any period since the year 1814, had the winter been more severe than that then being experienced. It was recollected that during the 1814 great fall of snow, the first fall ever known in the island by the European inhabitants, thousands of parrots and other birds had continually hovered about the houses and gardens for warmth. During 1830 it was believed that not so much rain had fallen within the last ten years, but that it was evident that the winter had become considerably colder than formerly. Notwithstanding the wet winter, the lambing season had turned out favourably, with little loss among the lambs, although good fat sheep and beasts were scarce and commanded high prices.

What a topsy-turvy climate! The next year the winter experienced by the inhabitants was the finest ever known; the nights were frosty, but the air was free from those fogs and damps usually prevalent at that season. Come December and summer the oldest settlers were asserting that since they could remember, 'there never was such a season as the present'. For three weeks they had been visited with one continual hurricane — sometimes the winds were of so parching and sultry a nature that scarcely any vegetation could exist, and in a few minutes these were followed by such a change of cold winds that fires were required 'to keep one from trembling'.

Floods were experienced in 1832. Long stretches of wet weather made most of the roads in the colony impassable, and complaints were received from all quarters of bridges being swept away, with holes in the road large enough to entomb a cart, and other such grievances. The men of the chain gang were obliged to leave the hulk at the New Jetty and retire to the prisoners' barracks. Owing to the stress of the weather the hulk laboured so much that there was over a metre of water in the hold.

A remarkably wet spring was the cause of many rejected ascents of Mount Wellington. However, in December the first actual visit of the season was accomplished by a party of merchants of Hobart Town. They arrived at the flagstaff in two hours and fifty minutes exactly from the time of leaving the factory; and after taking a small meal, and moving through a few waltzes to the tune of their musical snuffboxes, they descended before half-past six in the evening. The reason for their odd behaviour was not given, but perhaps they had been affected by the high altitude.

The greatest floods on record for some time were suffered in March 1836. A report of the devastation went as follows:

The Hobart Town Creek began to rise on Saturday morning, and by the evening it became a complete torrent, carrying away houses and out-buildings which had been erected on its banks. At the Old Market Place the rush of water broke the wall, and a stream as large as the creek itself found its old channel, and rushed with violence by the store of Mr Stokell. The brick bridge in Argyle Street was undermined, and must be rebuilt, which, when done, we trust will be made as wide as the street itself. Among the greatest sufferers by the flood are Mr Kemp, whose valuable stone and brick wall was washed from the side of the creek into the sea; Mr Brobribb, some of whose family had a narrow escape for their lives, when the back part of his house

TOP: The Orphan Schools at New Town, 1841 *(Allport Library)*. BOTTOM: The store of Nathan, Moses & Co. at the corner of Liverpool Street and Murray Street, *c.* 1843 *(Archives Office of Tasmania)*

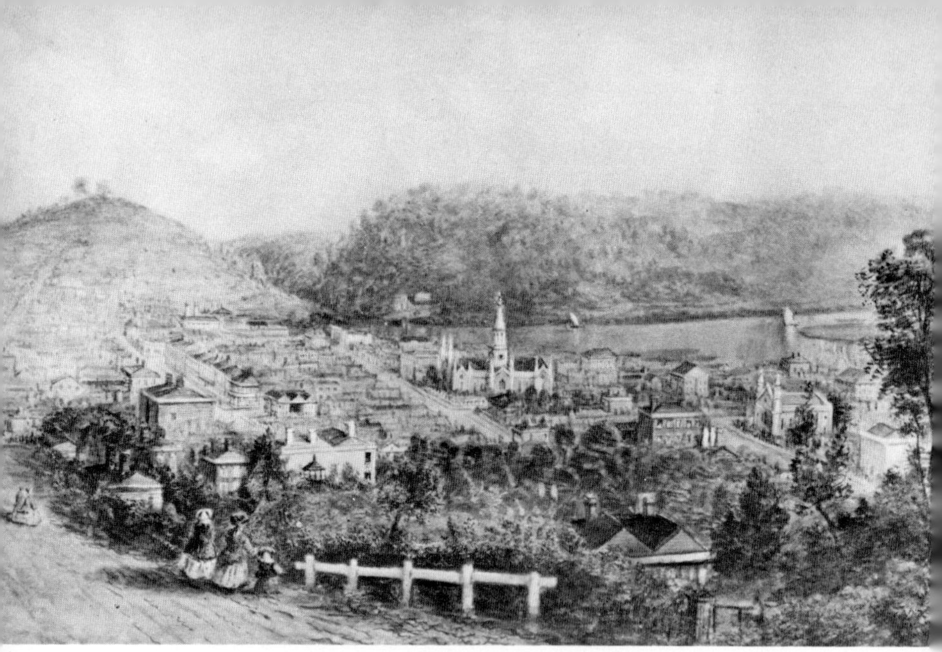

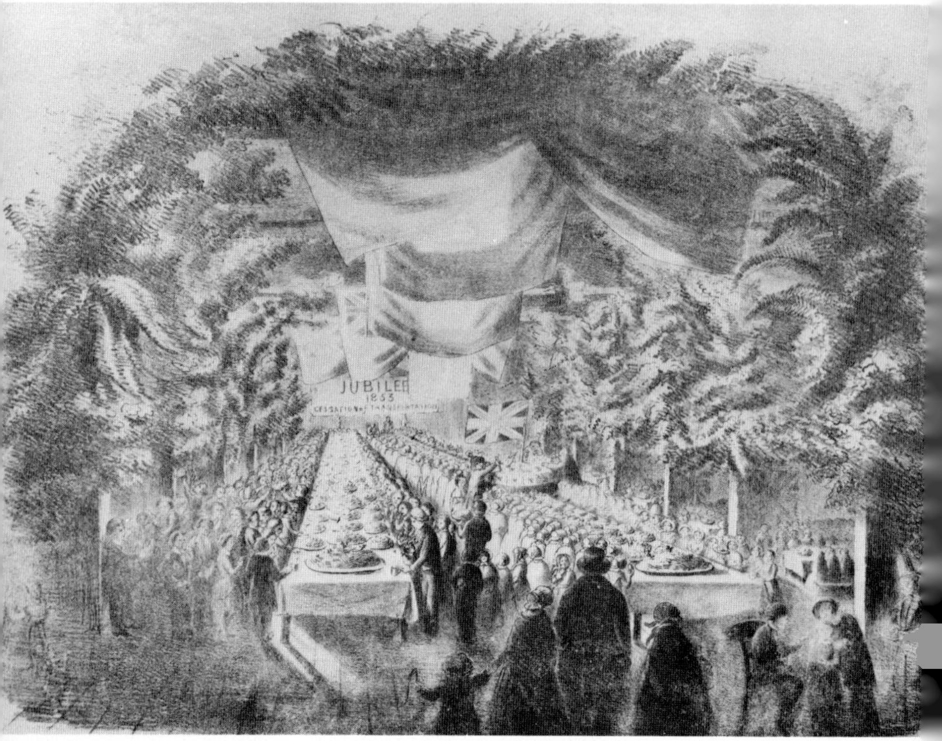
JUBILEE
1853
CESSATION

was carried away, and another individual had a horse and cart washed away, and the cart shattered to pieces. Almost every individual living on the edge of the creek has suffered more or less severely. Among other remarkable and fortunate escapes may be instanced that of a man falling into the creek near the bridge in Campbell Street — he was turned over and over again, like a tub by the force of the water, till he came to the rock under the slaughterhouse, against which his head struck violently; as an apparent last effort, the man stretched out his hand, and fortunately caught the gunwale of a boat, in which were some men picking up the property the flood was carrying to the sea. The man was saved, and is doing well. Particulars from the country have not yet been received, and we are led to believe the flood to have been only partial. O'Brien's Bridge, among others, is carried away, and now we trust a substantial one will be built.

By June the weather was severely cold, the chilliest the oldest inhabitants had ever experienced. The River Derwent, about Hobart Town, was frozen over in most of the bays, and the creeks were clogged with ice. At New Norfolk the ice was over two centimetres thick. As was always the case in the colony the frost was followed with rain which fell in torrents for a couple of days.

One evening in May the south-western hemisphere was brilliantly illuminated by the *aurora australis*, which extended from above the Cascade far beyond Mount Nelson and was extremely vivid and beautiful. The eclipse of the moon early in October presented an interesting sight to the spectator, while the spring weather was truly delightful, 'and Nature in all its charming departments, responds to the genial call'.

Constant heavy rain occurred in November 1842 and caused a sudden and very heavy flood which did considerable damage in many places. The body of a private in the 51st Regiment was found floating in the town river. The force of the rivulet had swept the paltry wooden bridge at Harrington Street clean away and also carried away the outside bearer and railing on one side of the Barrack Street bridge. The poor man was reported to have walked upon this trap, and so met his death in the boiling flood.

Terrific gales and wet weather beset the settlers in 1844, the creeks and rivers becoming so swollen in October that an end was put to stage coach travelling for a while. Bushfires and the sirocco took precedence the next year, with the weather so hot in October that the bush in the neighbourhood of the town was on fire, burning fiercely on the Dynnyrne Hills and Clarence Plains.

TOP: A watercolour by Frederick Strange depicting Launceston and the River Tamar *c.* 1855–60. BOTTOM: The children's Jubilee Festival 'on the occasion of the Cessation of Transportation', Hobart Town, 10 August 1853. (*Both from the Allport Library*)

In contrast, Launceston in May had such a dense fog that the mail team was led through the town preceded by two men with lanthorns; even with this assistance it was impossible to see the houses on either side of the street.

'The climate of the Island has certainly the last few years undergone a serious change for the worse. A falling barometer no longer indicates rain, but heavy hot winds.' This was the conclusion reached by the *Colonial Times* at the end of 1846, while the *Hobart Town Courier* said a few months later: 'Extreme heat to cold is more sudden in Van Diemen's Land than perhaps no other country in the world.'

February undoubtedly was the month for bushfires in Van Diemens Land, and the year 1847 was no exception, with alarming bushfires visible on the mountain tops and other elevated grounds. Late in the evening, after the moon went down, the spectacle from the city of bushfires in every direction was one of 'awful grandeur'. Bushfires were also raging extensively around Launceston.

A long drought then ensued, and by October vegetable life was pining away, with the market scantily supplied. The fires were just as bad the next year when much fencing was destroyed, and much pasture was burned up. The drought continued, but apparently broke when a remarkable storm passed near Launceston. Pieces of ice the size and double the thickness of a halfpenny descended in showers, with a violence that brought about much destruction. Whole bunches of grapes were cut off as by a knife.

Diversions for the inhabitants were in a number of interesting natural occurrences during 1849. The first was a meteor, much larger in appearance than any of the planets, which was observed on New Year's night in the town. It arose in the north, about ten minutes before ten o'clock, at the feet of Auriga, and, crossing the milky way, it set in the south, near the right hand of Centaur, after being seen for about seven minutes. It had a fiery glare, and to an observer who stood in the middle of Macquarie Street, it appeared in the direction of Grass Tree Hill on the Richmond Road and vanished down the Derwent.

Later in the month a lunar rainbow was seen at Hobart Town, a happening regarded as quite a novelty, and in August a total eclipse of the sun occurred. An occultation of the planet Saturn took place the first week in September, which was described as 'perfect at three o'clock in the morning'. Another phenomenon seldom witnessed in Hobart Town occurred as well in September, and that was a snowstorm.

The 'sirocco' was to cause great havoc again in February 1851 'when the city and suburbs were visited by a scorching wind and overflow of dust for several hours, obscuring the atmosphere and exhibiting an unusual lurid glare. The temperature was exceedingly high. The storm left behind it traces of the devastating effects; fruit in the gardens being materially injured, and trees blown down in all directions'. To the succeeding generations of Hobartians this has been a very familiar story.

'Bountiful libations from the sky have poured through the veins of the earth, and in the "golden age" have revived the hopes of the farmer.' This was the weather report published in June. In other words it rained, and apparently kept on raining, for by the end of November floods were general throughout the country.

In 1854 there occurred the greatest flood for twenty-five years. The *Advertiser* gave this vivid account of the terrific storm floods and loss of life:

For the last two days our city has been visited with one of the most terrific storms, attended with loss of life, that has been known for a quarter of a century. The rain commenced about eight o'clock on Sunday morning, and continued incessantly up to the time of our going to press last evening, the town creek rising some eight feet above its usual height, and sweeping all before it. Mills, houses, barns, stables, bridges and piggeries might be seen floating down to the sea, piece by piece, and in fact everything that came within reach of this devastating element ...the stream at one time threatened to undermine many of the dwelling houses... At Wellington Bridge two prisoners of the Crown, in attempting to rescue some property that was being washed down the creek, were carried down by the current, and their bodies have not as yet been picked up. A man named Rush, an old pieman, who expired on Friday last, was also carried off in his coffin, and a woman and child were found drowned in Wapping. Rumours are abroad that several other persons are missing. A building belonging to Mr Hood, at the back of Dr Crooke's, being undermined by the current, fell and dammed up the creek for some time, causing it to overflow very considerably, but through the exertions of Messrs Hedberg and Chandler, assisted by a gang of prisoners and other parties, having removed some of the timber the rest was carried away with a rush. We are sorry to add that this was not the only damage sustained, the shipping in the harbour having suffered very severely.

Another flood was feared the following month, but the rain ceased in time, although damage was done in various parts of the city. An aftermath of the big flood was the unearthing of a small coffin found at the upper end of Warwick Street. In it were the remains of an infant a few weeks old; a coffin plate, supposed to be from the Catholic burying ground, was found at the lower end of Macquarie Street.

At the end of this eventful year, the oldest colonists were complaining that they had never known so peculiar a season as the present one — snow on the mountain from the base to the summit, when normally in December they experienced hot winds and great drought. At least it gave them one topic which could be safely discussed at all times. That, of course, was the weather!

20

Colonial Newspapers, Humour and Poetry

The 'Times' are bad — 'tis thus they boast
Of being independent:—
'The freedom of our Press is lost,
'And Trial by Jury is a ghost;
'The Officers who rule the roost,
'Will quickly make an end on 't.'

This dirge, written by the *Gazette* after it had been taken over by the Government, was directed at the *Colonial Times*, which had been forced to relinquish the title of the first regular newspaper published in the colony.

Attempts had been made prior to 1816 to start a newspaper for the benefit of the people, but the *Derwent Star* and the *Van Diemen's Land Intelligencer* were little more than gossip sheets and only ran a few months. The *Hobart Town Gazette* was a weekly half-sheet, the property of Andrew Bent and published by him. It progressed without any major setbacks until the arrival of Colonel Arthur in 1824. Shortly after his arrival the *Gazette* was declared to be Government property, and Bent was compelled to assume a new title for his newspaper, which he styled the *Colonial Times*. This change-over culminated in the trial of Andrew Bent, the first action being taken in March 1826. He was found guilty of printing and publishing three libels upon the Government in the *Hobart Town Gazette*.

Again in May 1827, in the Criminal Court, Andrew Bent was found guilty of 'two scandalous and malicious libels in the *Colonial Times* on 2 February 1826'. These libels were attributed to the pen of the editor, Mr Lathrop Murray, but as Bent was the proprietor he suffered the penalty. An Act of Council in October 1827 imposed a stamp duty of tuppence on every newspaper, and required that a licence be taken out by every publisher. Bent was the only printer denied a licence, which resulted in the *Colonial Times* being published with blank columns in a heavy mourning border on the day the Act came into operation. Bent then began issuing a monthly journal named the *Colonial Advocate*. As soon as the Newspaper Act became known in England it was ordered to be withdrawn by the then Secretary of State for the Colonies.

The first volume of the *Hobart Town Gazette* was dated Saturday, 8 June 1816. The main news was the printing of Government and official notices. An issue in January 1819 has the title of the *Hobart Town Gazette and Southern Reporter*, but the story behind the early newspapers confuses the 'issue' somewhat, so it is better simply to recount the names of the various newspapers as they come to notice.

The *Hobart Town Gazette*, 29 December 1819, made the announcement: 'The fifth Volume of the *Hobart Town Gazette* commences this day; the settlement having been founded near seventeen years, and we return our best thanks to the Public for past favors, and solicit their continuance.' The commencement of the eighth volume in January 1823 mentions the hope of the *Gazette* to enter upon the year with a paper of four pages, but owing to the non-arrival of type from England this was not possible. In May there came the report: 'By the *Thalia*, a New Patent Printing Press for *Hobart Town Gazette*, imported to Van Diemen's Land, but not long expected new Types.'

Then, on 8 November, the readers learned that the new printing office in Elizabeth Street, 'on the right side going from Wellington Bridge to the New Road', had been completed. 'This is the first complete Printing Office that has yet been built in Van Diemen's Land,' it was proudly pointed out.

The tenth volume of the *Gazette*, which started in January 1825, lists the names of two new weekly newspapers, the *Tasmanian*, and the *Australian*. In its editorial it gave an account of the problems which beset the printer of a colonial newspaper:

Few except ourselves can comprehend even a tithe of the difficulties which ten years ago we had to grapple with; our type was so limited that we could not compose, at once, more than is contained in one of our present sized columns!...Two sheets of Common Chinese paper cost two guineas sterling per ream ... Was it likely that a Paper could flourish where the only intelligence bore reference to crime, and the usual records were of infamy! It was not...

The editor went on to extol the virtues and progress of the *Gazette*, which even had to manufacture its own printing ink, as there was none available in the colony.

Its difficulties with the authorities were also becoming very obvious. On 7 January 1825 an issue was put out with the title *Hobart Town Gazette and Van Diemen's Land Advertiser*, with an editorial giving a very highly coloured account of the changes which had taken place in Van Diemens Land, apparently as a result of having the stimulus of a weekly newspaper in its midst:

> ...and, to sum up all in a few words, without us what would it have still been? Why merely a foreign gaol of immense extent, surrounded by the sea instead of walls. But now let the contrast be well observed; it is beloved as the emigrants' *dulce domum*; as the peerless spot to live and expire on which thousands elect to bid their native land 'good night!' and mount the barque doomed never to return. Now its inhabitants, when mentally and morally classified, rank high... And now instead of being as it once was, dreaded by guilt as a desolate coast, where Hope, sweet lingering solace of the wretched, never cometh — where nought but a flash of desperation lights the gloom; and no sound, save the wild shriek of agony, invades sepulchral silence — it swells the matin lay of many an enamoured minstrel, and the vesper theme of many an enlightened senator, as a Southern Paradise, which might almost tempt Monarchs to make it their retreat, and virtue to offend for the bonus of transportation!

On 20 May the *Gazette* announced 'with considerable pleasure' that another press was to be established within a few weeks, with a Mr Ross as its editor. Then later came the astounding news that Ross and Howe, the newly appointed Government printers, had published a journal not only with the title, but also the number of the *Hobart Town Gazette*.

The original *Gazette* then changed its name to the *Colonial Times*, and from then on a newspaper war of words existed between the two rivals. The motto of the *Colonial Times* was 'Not Names, But Things — Not Persons, But Principles'. It was not until January 1829 that the *Times* was able to report:

> [We] hail with the most unfeigned satisfaction the restoration of one of the most valuable privileges claimed by Englishmen —

a free and unrestricted Press... We may venture to say, where books are very scarce, and the inhabitants live far apart, the people must by this time have sunk almost into total ignorance and barbarism, had no newspapers appeared, detailing the principal occurrences of the world, and furnishing a correct view of the true state of the Colony...

The 'free press' was still very much in question, although the people of the colony felt that they had obtained a 'most glorious triumph, in the Freedom of the Press being again restored to them, by command of His Majesty, King George the Fourth'. It was rumoured that the town was quite alive in anticipation of a splendid dinner at the Dallas Arms in commemoration of this event.

A new Cornwall paper was published in Launceston in 1829, along with the *Tasmanian*, which made its appearance in 1825. The *Hobart Town Courier* first began publication in 1827, while a new publication, *Hobart Town Anniversary*, was said to be starting in 1831. The *Times* commented in 1833 that there were nine newspapers in Van Diemens Land; the population amounted in round numbers to 30 000 souls, while at the Cape of Good Hope the population was upwards of 120 000 souls, but two newspapers sufficed for that colony!

The *Colonial Times*, which had begun printing its journal twice weekly from 1831, became angry in 1833 with the *Colonist* for dubbing itself the 'paper of the people', and accused it of plagiary. Then Henry Melville, the proprietor of the *Colonial Times*, was gaoled in November 1835 for having been in contempt of court. In an impassioned appeal in his newspaper, he said:

Mr Pedder sat, as Judge and Jury in the case, and his mild sentence is — that I am to be enprisoned in gaol for Twelve Calendar Months!! — then to pay a fine of £200 to the King!! and then to be bound £300 myself, and two Sureties of £150 each, for my good behaviour for Two Years!!!

Fellow Colonists! My pride is that I have assisted in saving the life of an innocent man — that I have done my duty as a Colonist; power may incarcerate me in gaol, but in these times of terror the safest place is the gaol! I call upon the Colonists for support — for assistance during my incarceration; but a day of retribution may and will come, when I will again say — 'I tremble for those who have thus acted!'

Henry Melville sent a petition to the House of Commons in England by the *Grecian*; copies were also sent to the Governor

190

and Chief Justice Pedder. He was released from his 'unwholesome dungeon' in January 1836. A free pardon was sent by the next prison ship to Mr Robert Bryan, whose life had been saved by the intervention of this courageous gentleman.

The Captain of an American vessel which left Hobart Town about that time shook his head in bewilderment, and said as he took his leave that 'in all America, there was only one Editor of a newspaper incarcerated in gaol, and he was there for telling "a parcel of lies"'. To this the *Times* countered: 'How different are things managed in Van Diemen's Land; here there are two Editors, two Publishers, and two Printers in gaol for telling the truth!'

After the departure of Henry Melville the *Times* fell into new hands, and in 1838 it was published by John Campbell MacDougall. In 1841 it appeared in a new and enlarged form, with its weekly circulation above 8000 impressions.

Some other newspapers were the *Trumpeter*, *Tribune*, *Weekly Advertiser*, *Hobart Town Advertiser*, and the *Guardian*. The last named made its appearance in 1847, with its professed object being to support the continuance of transportation of convicts to the colony, according to the accusations of the *Courier*. As well there was the *Tasmanian Weekly Despatch*, and a few other papers which did not last very long. The *Irish Exile and Freedom's Advocate* ceased publication early in 1851. In the north of the island, the *Examiner*, *Cornwall Chronicle* and the *Launceston Advertiser* seemed to hold sway, with the *Examiner* eventually emerging as the leading newspaper there.

In 1849 the *Colonial Times* took over the *Tasmanian*, while the *Hobarton Guardian* or *True Friend of Tasmania* later incorporated the *Mercury*. On 6 May 1854 it announced in an editorial that it was closing its 'literary career'. The new paper was the *Hobarton Mercury*, incorporating the *Hobarton Guardian*; it became simply the *Hobarton Mercury* by 1855. The *Colonial Times* and the *Courier* were still in circulation in the 1850s, although the *Mercury* was eventually to become Tasmania's biggest newspaper.

Despite the persecution of the press by the Government and the feuding which went on between the respective papers, the public were kept supplied with news as it came to hand. English news, of course, was what the people were particularly interested in, and they were kept remarkably well-informed on what was taking place 'at home' and in the rest of the civilised world, even if the news was often five or six months behind the times. The papers depended on the speed of the ships for their information, and in the very early days it was the passengers who brought the news with them. In the 'Ship News' section in the *Gazette*, January 1818, there was a typical announcement: 'By a gentleman who arrived in the *Derwent*, we are in hopes of being favoured with the loan of a few late India papers. Should any information appear in them worthy of attention, we shall give it insertion in our next.' In December 1821 they told their readers: 'We have been favoured by a Gentleman with the perusal of late Calcutta Journals.'

With a large proportion of the population being ex-convicts, a significant feature of the advertisements in the 'Situations Vacant' column was quite often the proviso: 'None need apply whose character will not admit of the strictest examination.' A hard-working, industrious widower, who advertised for a respectable, elderly female to take entire charge of his domestic concerns, 'and to instruct his two daughters in the common and useful branches of female education', added the postscript: 'None need apply who are not truly respectable as to character for decency and sobriety.' Others stressed 'a good address' as an advantage.

The *Times* announced in 1832 that a new club was being established in Hobart Town, to be an entirely literary club, and no member was to be admitted except those who were, had been, or intended to become editors of colonial journals. It was presumed that it would be scientific, and that no personal abuse would be permitted in the clubroom. In another number a handsome reward was jokingly offered to any individual 'who will form the Printers of this Establishment into a regular Temperance Society'.

The people liked to be kept informed about what was taking place in royal circles. In one instance, in 1831 they were told that 'the King is in good health, and still popular. The Ministers are also popular, but...' With the accession to the throne of Queen Victoria in 1837 a 'splendid and gorgeous description' of her coronation was published in the colonial papers. In 1840 the principal topic was the approaching marriage of 'Queen Victoria and Albert, the German, who is three months younger than the Queen'. An editorial in the *Times* two years later made scathing reference to the 'outrageous demonstrations of joy and congratulation which Her Majesty's most loyal subjects displayed in honour of the birth of the Prince of Wales!' From then on the remark 'The Queen is again in an interesting situation' appeared quite frequently, along with the news of the poor in Ireland, revolutions and European wars, which were all duly recorded.

Serialised versions of popular works were also published by the press, and in January 1838 the *Times* presented *Pickwick Papers*, edited by 'that facetious fellow Boz'. Other novels by Charles Dickens later became the favourite reading of the people in the colony. The first number of a publication by Boz of *Nicholas*

Nickleby was believed to be the only copy then in Van Diemens Land.

Naturally, births, deaths and marriages occupied space in the papers much as they do today. One birth notice, a little irregular perhaps, read: 'On the 23rd instant, very unexpectedly in Macquarie Street, the Lady of Mr J., of a daughter. (Stillborn).'

Although death overshadowed the colony, and accounts of violent deaths and executions were written up as a matter of course, the deaths of respectable citizens were treated in a different vein altogether. They were accorded extravagant obituaries, which often bordered on the maudlin. The distressing details of the last illness of the deceased were usually given as well, which added to the pathos, and very likely reduced the readers to a flood of tears. There was great suffering among the people, which was borne with resignation and stoicism.

> Died at River Plenty, Anne B., aged forty-eight, after a lingering illness of the dropsy, with which she was affected for more than two years, which she had borne with the most Christian fortitude, having undergone the operation of being tapped eight different times, and the amazing quantity of more than sixty gallons of water having been taken from her.

It may have been just a coincidence, but under this notice there was a recipe for a cure for hydrophobia! In the case of the tragic death of a young wife and mother in her twenty-first year, the obituary concluded with the words:

> We have not much occasion to say that the deceased is deservedly lamented; the many mental adornments and attractive virtues with which she was gifted, will long remain cherished in the bosom of her numerous relatives, and host of surviving friends. To delineate the grief of the astonished widower, and young father, is a task to which our pen is quite incompetent.

In several instances where the deceased happened to be particularly well-known and distinguished, black banners were ruled down the sides of the paper. Sometimes, sudden deaths were reported in rather a ludicrous fashion, as in this case: 'A poor woman dropped down dead the other day, in perfect health.'

Courtship and marriage, colonial style, was usually treated in a rather facetious manner by the press, although the following announcement of a marriage in 1816 could be regarded as quite conventional: 'On Thursday last, by Special Licence, was married by the Reverend Robert Knopwood at the Derwent Hotel, Thomas William Stocker, to Mary Hayes, Widow, of the Derwent Hotel, Elizabeth Street, after a tedious courtship of two years.'

It was reported in the same year that the practice of beating wives had become so general that the assistance of the police was often needed.

One young man was so anxious to be wed that despite being lame from an accident he insisted upon being carried in a cart to the home of the clergyman. On the other hand, a 'Hibernian whose finances were rather low, brought his wife to the hammer', and sold her for one gallon of rum and twenty ewes. She was described as 'not prepossessing in appearance'.

With a shortage of women in the colony the ladies often took advantage of the situation, and knowing they could pick and choose, did not hesitate to leave home when something better turned up. This type of notice, inserted by exasperated husbands, was very common in the papers:

Whereas my wife Jane M., is again walked away with herself without any Provocation whatever, and I hear, has taken with a Fellow who looked after Cattle in the neighbourhood of the Macquarie River — this is to give Notice that I will not pay for bite or sup, or for any other things she may contract on my Account to man or mortal; and that I am determined to prosecute with the utmost Rigour the Law will allow, on any Person or Persons who may harbour, conceal, or maintain the said Runaway, Jane M.

An Irishman who had not long arrived in the colony offered himself as a candidate for marriage, provided that any 'Widow Virgin or other Lady' had sufficient unincumbered property to support him as an independent gentleman, 'or in other words to pamper him with the best wines, and the richest meats of every description, to put up with his doing nothing, except shooting, riding, billiard-playing, getting frizy-topsy every morning before breakfast, and condescendingly giving her a drubbing only when he may perchance elect to feel himself offended'.

Marriage was not all bliss, and a correspondent of the *Cornwall Chronicle*, having had reason to complain of the incontinence of his wife, generously offered, if any person would consent to take her and keep her by honest industry, to resign his right, title, and interest in her to any person of good character! On the other hand, a woman who was a bonnetmaker, taking on female apprentices, found that, despite the care she took to guard their virtue, could not prevent them from being exposed to 'the libertine propensities of her husband; and this man — if man he be — had boasted that a large number had fallen victim to his brutal lusts'!

There is no doubt about whom this young man wished to marry. He declared his intentions in a very forthright manner in this 'Ode to Miss Annie Bread', which was printed in the *Courier* in 1851:

While belles their lovely graces spread
And fops around them flutter,
I'll be content with Annie Bread,
And won't have any but her!

The following explanation of the expression, 'rum 'un', believed to be peculiar to Tasmanians, was given by the *Colonial Times* in 1833:

The expression is not yet forty years old; and though it was nursed in London, and served its apprenticeship in Gloucestershire, where it was born, it has long worked journey-work in Staffordshire. Jonas Bell, a country schoolmaster...had a pupil so remarkably stupid, that on one occasion, when he found it necessary to exhibit his abilities before the lady patroness at a fixed examination, he selected the most familiar words to commence his analysis upon; the first was M-I-L-K. 'And what does that spell?' said Jonas. 'Don't know,' said the lad. 'What does your mother put in her tea?' said Jonas, quite cock-sure of his answer. 'RUM, Sir,' replied the promising youth. The lady patroness vanished, Jonas Bell was bothered and the boy was pleased with his own sharpness; but it soon became a matter among the sports of Gloucestershire when recommended to the favour of a young lady, first of all to enquire if she was a 'rum-un'.

Present-day Tasmanians use the expression in a different form, it all depending on the tone of the voice used when a person is referred to as a 'rum 'un' whether he is laughably funny or oddly peculiar. The gentleman in the next story definitely belongs to the latter category:

A certain old bachelor was very particular in having his egg boiled three minutes and twelve seconds, and in order to have the eggs properly cooked, the following was the means resorted to. On the gentleman leaving the bedroom, a servant, who always stood at the breakfast-room door, in an audible voice said, 'Prepare.' 'Prepare,' said a man on the landing. 'Prepare,' said another at the top of the kitchen flight. 'Prepare,' said another at the bottom. A pause followed, when the cook had the egg in the spoon, and the water was bubbling hot with impatience. 'Ready,' cried she. 'Ready,' said the man at the bottom of the kitchen stairs. 'Ready,' cried the fellow at the top. 'Ready,' echoed he at the landing. 'Ready,' said the servant-in-waiting with a very low bow. The gentleman then took out his watch, and as the moment hand covered the sixty, 'In,' he cried. 'In,' 'In,' 'In,' when the cook in a shrill voice cried 'In,' and the egg splashed the foaming billows in the egg saucepan. When the prescribed second arrived, 'Out,' cried the gentleman. 'Out,' 'Out,' Out,' 'Out,' re-echoed to the lower regions, when there was a pause of half a second, and 'Out it is,' cried the cook. The egg was then pitched from one to the other and the servant-in-waiting popping it into a silver egg-cup brought it into the egg amateur. The whole process, all included, only took three minutes and fourteen seconds.

The *Colonial Times* was responsible for that 'true' story.

Poetry, undoubtedly, was appreciated by all classes of people in Van Diemens Land, and the first issues of the *Gazette* contained poems by homesick soldiers and sailors, who found this method of expressing their emotions by far the most satisfying. Much of the poetry written in the beginning of the nineteenth century conformed to the high literary style, and could only have been understood by those with a classical education, but later on it became diffused by Victorian sentimentality and melancholia.

One poem, 'The Cicad', published in 1819, has a certain charm that is due to the shortage of type then being experienced by the *Gazette*. The first stanza was printed as follows:

> *The Cicad when the noontide ray*
> *Of fummer giles the fhade*
> *In frolick chirrups life away*
> *And fkips from blade to blade.*

Although the editor welcomed contributions of verse from the readers, some of it was obviously too poor for publication, and that meant that tactful answers had to be given in the columns explaining why some poetry was not published. 'Miranda's poetry is too good for vulgar eyes to gaze upon'; 'Dorothy's Disclosure must be kept a secret'; 'The Captive's Lament is indeed lamentable'; and 'The Angler would fish in troubled waters, but we will not let him' were some of the replies.

The pseudonyms given included such names as 'A Breaker of Stones', 'Gingerbread', 'Old Groggy Himself', and 'Another Subscriber', which shows that the appropriate muse was not class-conscious. An extremely long poem, written by a gentleman during the passage out from England in 1823, proved what a tedious journey it must have been, as the one canto published took up an entire column in the *Gazette*.

Although the verse written by the early settlers now appears overdone and melodramatic, the subjects which had led to the writing were genuine. The high child mortality, poverty, sad partings, sorrow, care and woe were frequent themes.

And must the sad sound — fare thee well!
Escape from my half-breaking heart?
What words can express — or what language can tell!
My grief when I say, that we part — For Ever!

'Hidden Grief', 'The Exile's Wife', 'Death', 'The Lamented One', 'Melancholy Thoughts'; the titles alone show that morbidity and death preoccupied the thoughts and feelings of the people, though now and again a little humour crept in. The following poem, published in 1825, was called 'The Gay Deceiver', and was the kind the people liked:

Joan, a maid of fifty-five,
Was at her toilet dressing;
Her waiting maid, with iron hot,
Each paper'd curl was pressing.
The looking-glass her eyes engrossed,
While Betty humm'd a ditty;
In fact, she gaz'd so on her face,
She really thought it pretty.
Her painted cheeks and pencill'd brows
She could not but approve;
Her thoughts on varied subjects turn'd,
At length they dwelt on love.
And shall, said she, a virgin's life
Await these pleasing charms;
And shall no sighing, blooming youth
Receive me to his arms?
Forbid it love! she scarce had spoke,
When Cupid laid a trap;
For at the chamber door was heard
A soft and gentle rap.

Cried Betty, 'Who the deuce is that,'
'Aye, tell,' said Joan true.
When straight a tender voice replied,
'Dear Madam, I dye for you!'
'What's that,' she said, 'O Betty say;
A man — and die for me!
And can I see the youth expire;
O no, it cannot be.
Haste, Betty, open quick the door.'
'Tis done — and lo, to view,
A little man with bundle stood,
In sleeves and apron, blue.
'Ye Gods,' cried Joan, 'what is this;
What vision do I see;
Is this the man, O mighty love,
The man that dies for me.'
'Yes, Ma'am, your ladyship is right,'
The figure straight replied;
'And hard for me it would have been
If I had never dyed.
'La Ma'am, you must have heard of me
Altho' I'm no high flyer;
I live just by at Number One,
I'm Billy Dip, the dyer.
'Twas me, Ma'am Betty, you employ'd
To dye your lustring gown;
And I not only die for you,
But, dye for half the town.'

Another poem, obviously written long before Women's Liberation
was even thought of, was called 'What a Wife Should be Like':

A wife, domestic, good, and pure,
Like snail should keep within her door;
But not like snail, in silver tract,
Place all her wealth upon her back.

A wife should be like echo true —
Not speak, but when she's spoken to;
But not like echo still be heard
Contending for the final word.

Like a town clock a wife should be,
Keep time and regularity;
But not like clock harangue so clear,
That all the town her voice may hear.

Young man, if these allusions strike
She whom as bride you'd wish to hail,
Must just be like — and just unlike
Three things — ye echo, clock and snail.

The first stanza of a long poem 'The Native's Lament' showed that a compassionate attitude towards the Aborigines was felt by some:

Oh, where are the wilds I once sported among,
When as free as my clime through its forest I sprung,
When no track but the few which our fires had made,
Had tarnished the carpet that nature had laid.
When the lone waters dashed down the darksome ravine
O'er hung by the shade of the Huon's dark green,
When the broad morning sun o'er our mountain could roam,
And see not a slave in our bright Island home.

The names of the poets were rarely given, usually initials or a pen-name sufficing.

The Launceston *Cornwall Chronicle* in 1836 began a 'Gallery of Comicalities', which gave a very clear idea of the people that figured largely in the lives of the poorer inhabitants of the colony. The court house was a familiar place for most, either as the defendant, as in the following poem, or as the plaintiff.

THE DEFENDANT
Heaven bless us: When my copper's hot,
I feel as brave as Julius Caesar;
And in this precious mess I've got,
For hitting Muggins on the sneezer.

As to my temper, in the town
Some swear you cannot find a worse 'un,
And, as in cash I can't come down,
That old Giles must pay in person.

Ere long to prison, with a sigh,
And empty pockets, I must journey,
The devil take the law, say I,
And every mischievous attorney.

And, neighbours all, observe this rule —
When of strong beer, you've had your dose,
Be sure to keep your temper cool,
Nor give your friend a bloody nose.

THE PLAINTIFF
By Goles it is a foolish plan,
In Court to settle a dispute;
And I, alack! am like the man
Wot gain'd his cause but lost his suit.

Don't marvel that my face is long
Nor quiz me for my shoulder shruggins;
If I've one copper left I'm wrong,
And law has done for poor Mat Muggins.

With extra costs and extra fees,
These vile attorneys always cook you;
Your last remaining coin they squeeze,
And then for Whitecross Prison book you.

Better to let our quarrels die,
Then sink to poverty and tatters;
Better if neighbour Giles and I
Over a pot had settled matters.

All glory to our code of laws!
Of right or wrong a sad confuser!
And if I'm floored, who gained the cause,
May Lord have mercy on the loser.

And finally:

THE JUDGE
Thou sage expounder of the 'Law'!
And blest with skill to lay it down,
We gaze upon thy wig with awe,
And bow with reverence to thy gown.

Upon thy tongue CONVICTION dwells;
The wrong from right 'tis thine to wrench;
And every bright decision tells
A second Blackstone on the Bench.

Other verses were entitled 'The Sheriff's Officer's Dog', 'The Barrister', 'The Briefless Case', 'The Attorney' and 'The Never Failing Undertaker', all of which were strongly part of life in the nineteenth century.

21

Acts, Petitions and the Jubilee

Long enough we've borne our troubles,
We must act now bold and brave;
England cannot taunt us longer,
Tasmania will not be her slave.

'The Colonies — what are they worth? Prejudices break down slowly, and the question: "What are the Colonies good for?" will be discussed but not settled, in the next Parliament.' This discussion took place in 1850, when the fate of the colonies could no longer be easily pushed into the background and conveniently ignored. However, thirty odd years before this, the answer to the question, as far as Van Diemens Land was concerned, was that the colonies made good penal settlements.

The settlers who chose to live in the southern hemisphere in the first quarter of the nineteenth century had to accept this fact and were made very aware that they were living under military rule. In Van Diemens Land, proclamations were issued from time to time informing the inhabitants of any changes in the administration. There were proclamations against hawkers and pedlars, against working on the Lord's Day, as well as concerning rates and duties to be imposed and levied upon spirits made or distilled from malt or grain in the colony of New South Wales or its dependencies (Van Diemens Land was then a dependency) and about the granting and settling of land.

One proclamation which gave satisfaction to the people was made public in the *Gazette* on 5 December 1825. Van Diemens Land had been made independent of the Government of New South Wales.

'The erection of this Colony into a distinct and separate Independency, which was solemnized on Saturday, is a glorious and an important era in the annals of history.' At least it, together with an Act which had been announced the year before, that Supreme Courts were to be established in New South Wales and Van Diemens Land, each to be beholden to a Chief Justice, was a step forward.

The death of George the Fourth in 1830, and the accession of William the Fourth, brought about another proclamation and also reduced the colony to a state of uncertainty: '. . . the whole soil of this Island continues vested in the King at the present moment, not one particle of it having yet been legally parted with.' This disturbing news was passed on to the settlers by the *Times* in 1831. Public-spirited men had been anxiously calling meetings over a period of years to try to improve the lot of the people. A meeting was convened in 1827, at the Royal Oak Inn, Cross Marsh, 'for the purpose of taking into consideration the best means of forming an Association for the prevention of sheep-stealing'. The aim was to do away with a repetition of 'the melancholy executions' which had taken place during the previous year. In 1830, as a result of a petition on the matter, the *Times* was able to report that trial by jury had been successfully obtained.

A cause of great joy was the news from England concerning the abolition of the death penalty in certain cases. This was recorded in the *Colonial Times* on 8 January 1833:

We rejoice to state, that by the Law of England, the punishment of death in all cases is now repealed, where property alone is affected. Murder, and other injury to the person remains, as it very properly ought, a capital offence. After this, we trust we may never again witness in this Colony the cruel mockery of justice of hanging a man for endeavouring to recover his liberty when sentenced to a place of punishment.

In matters concerning progress the colony seemed to take one step forward and two backwards, and the few gains which were made never brought the benefits the people expected. Dissatisfaction was expressed by the *Times* in 1834 at the proposed Jury Bill, as 'it was to be a cripple, or lopsided one'.

We are to have a jury for pounds, shillings and pence, but not for our liberties. The Grand Jury is to be done away with... this is good; but as to the Petty Jury, we shall be as badly off as ever. The reservation clause states that all issues between the King and the people are to be tried by Assessors. Let another meeting be called, and let us be determined to have the Bill, the whole Bill, and nothing but the Bill!!! and if we cannot obtain it otherwise, let us petition our good King Bill to grant it us.

Four years later the *Times* was telling its readers that 'among the first boons that may be expected from the present enlightened administration, we believe we may reckon "Trial by Jury" as it obtains in the Sister Colony'. It took justice quite a while to catch up in Van Diemens Land, and it still tended to be a mockery on many occasions.

In June 1841 the Legislative Council met for the first time in the Long Room of the New Custom House. A small crib was parted off for the press, which those gentlemen considered should have been twice the length. They greeted the news in January 1843 that Hobart Town was to become the City of Hobart with cynicism:

The *Morning Herald* of the 1st October announces the immediate establishment and conversion of Hobart Town into a City, with all the usual corporate authorities of Mayor, Aldermen, Councillors, etcetera, by which we shall have the honour and pleasure of taxing ourselves. This is the true cause for conferring privileges upon us, which the Home Government has at length discovered to be a measure of considerable economy to the British Treasury.

The outcome of this move was the Lighting and Paving Bill, which threw the colonists into a 'perfect fever'. The *True Colonist* considered it 'reasonable and just that proprietors of tenements in Hobart Town should pay for making lighting, and paving their streets...and paying for the water, which they have so long been calling out'. However, the spirit of the people was aroused through the length and breadth of the land and they refused to be taxed, even if it was supposed to be for their own benefit. A meeting was held at New Norfolk to petition against this 'odious means', while an editorial in the *Times* of 1 March 1845 announced with satisfaction that 'we are gratified at the effect of our recommendation to abstinence from all taxed articles for one year'.

The Municipal Bill was thrown overboard by the Council, which meant that water could not be brought to the city by the Government that year. For lighting in Hobart Town the streets still used the only means available then, which was oil and candles. Gaslight was known in the colony, but only as a novelty. However, as early as 1825 the *Gazette* stated that 'an ingenious mechanic at Pitt-water has been enabled to construct an Oil-Gas Apparatus in miniature'. It was hoped that this beautiful and cheap light, so generally in use in England, would soon be illuminating the shops and private homes of Tasmania.

This was wishful thinking, as the next mention of gas was not until February 1843, when another 'very ingenious mechanic [Mr Custance] commenced manufacturing gas in his back premises at Roxboro' House in Elizabeth Street, with the intention of arranging that he can make it transportable in iron cases, for the use of shops in any part of town. The brilliancy of this splendid light was beautifully displayed one evening in one pipe to many respectable gentlemen'. Mr Custance was advised to form a company. Six years later, in November 1849, the preliminary meeting for the formation of a Gas Company was held. Although an Act was passed in 1854 decreeing the use of gaslight in the streets of Hobart and for domestic purposes, the Gas Company did not start actual operations until 1857. The difficulty of getting a suitable site, and the need to wait for the essential equipment to be sent from England, contributed to the long delay. Launceston was to follow Hobart in 1860.

Great public interest continued to be felt upon the subject of the formation of the Legislative Council, and the position of the 'six gentlemen' who had tendered their resignation of their seats in November 1845, as well as the six members who had replaced them upon the nomination of the Lieutenant-Governor. But another matter, the transportation question, was rapidly coming to a head, and in May 1847 a great public meeting was held in favour of abolition of transportation, the number of people present being not less than 1500. As well, a public meeting at the theatre in October was against the transfer of Sydney convicts to Van Diemens Land.

A new crisis arose in January 1848 when the Government tried to remove Mr Justice Montagu from the Bench, which the *Courier* felt was 'under colour of a regard for the administration of the law to the end and the profit of the Government itself'. This led to a public meeting in support of the independence of the judges, which resulted in a petition to the Queen, praying that Her Majesty would secure for the future the independent administration of Justice in Van Diemens Land. This was signed by 1570 inhabitants of Hobart Town.

On the day of the public meeting for free institutions and against transportation, early in 1850, the whole city was in motion, with many old colonists coming from the country to countenance 'the cause of liberty and morality involved in this movement'. The hall of the Mechanic's Institute was filled to suffocation. The petitions to Parliament were placed for signature in Elizabeth Street, near Mr Stump's premises, so that all who were interested in freedom could sign their names. A second public meeting against transportation was held in September. A public breakfast was held at Launceston in 1851 to give the colonists an opportunity of meeting the delegates of the Association for Promoting Cessation of Transportation to Van Diemen's Land, before they left for Melbourne.

In February the long-awaited Act came at last, when it was felt that 'one step has been taken to grant the people their acknowledged rights, and to give them a place among the free communities of the Empire'. It was not entirely good news, although the people knew they were expected to be grateful, but after being petitioners for between twenty and thirty years they had been favoured with only the smallest concession of legislative power.

A poem was written by a New Norfolk resident especially for a demonstration against transportation. It was called 'Tasmania Will Not Be Her Slave', one of its eight verses insisting:

> *We are infants now no longer,*
> *Brighter prospects glimmer faint;*
> *'Tis not parental to inflict us*
> *With the loathed fettered taint.*

Electioneering movements were also under way for a new Assembly. The draft of a bill to provide for the establishment of a Legislative Council for the division of Van Diemens Land into electoral districts was published in a supplement to the *Courier* in April 1851. However, in an editorial in July it announced: 'The Legislative Council has died, and made no sign. It has gone out, not in the best humour possible, as became a body which perished on inanition...'

Meanwhile, a 'household movement in the Anti-Transportation Cause' was taking place, and in July a public meeting was convened by the executive board of the League, which was to be held at an early date in Sydney. In August came the news of the 'Temporary suspension of transportation of male convicts' for a period of two years. 'We have scotched the snake — not killed it,' was the reaction of the Council. However, a little premature celebration was caused by a placard posted about the city: 'Fellow Colonists Rejoice. Transportation to this Colony Has Ceased. The Aurora has brought the glad tidings... Henceforth we can be Free, United and Happy. Honour to our Gracious Queen.' It evidently spurred the 'native born' to gather in the old market square in an open demonstration of their continued repugnance to the system of transportation to Van Diemens Land. There was also a triumph at the end of the year, as the members who were returned to serve in the first session of the first elective Legislative Council of Van Diemens Land were all anti-transportationists!

Another event of historical significance was the invitation of the colonists to meet in the hall of the Mechanic's Institute on 18 November 1852 to consider and adopt a petition to the Queen and both houses of Parliament, as follows:

That the Order in Council constituting this Island a Penal Colony may be rescinded, and that Van Diemen's Land may henceforth be called Tasmania. That all persons not under punishment for offences committed in the Colony, or whose confinement may not be absolutely necessary in the public safety, be liberated from all disabilities consequent on their transportation, so as to be placed in the position of free subjects. That Her Majesty will be pleased to withhold her assent from 'The Convicts' Prevention Bill' lately passed at Victoria, and from any similar measures which may be adopted by any of the neighbouring Colonies; and that the Land Fund and the moneys granted by the Imperial Parliament and promised by Earl Grey, the late Secretary of State, for the purposes of Free Immigration to this Colony, be immediately thus appreciated.

A caution to the Campbelltonians was issued, stating that a clandestine petition asking for the introduction of 12 000 more prisoners was being hawked around the district of Campbelltown for signature. This would have been given scant support by the public at that period.

When the public opened the *Colonial Times* on 10 February 1853 the details of the Queen's speech were read, the most significant part being:

Her Majesty never shed a brighter light over the Australian Empire than when she announced the cessation of transportation ... Such her speech means; scarcely disguised by wary forms. Let the eleventh day of November, 1852, and the first day of February, 1851, go down to posterity... The Queen's Speech does not promise the instant stoppage, but it does not say a word of 'gradual'...

Later English news brought the wonderful news by the *Harbinger*, the first of the line of steamers, and it was published on 28 April in the *Times:*

THE CESSATION OF TRANSPORTATION...thus on the 12th February, the words were spoken; and by the close of April they will be read in every village of the southern world. Hurrah for the Australasian League! Hurrah for the Legislative Councils! Hurrah for the Queen! The glorious tidings of release from the greatest curse and disgrace which ever rested on the people, will be welcome to every class of the community, save a few official men... The Colonists owe to their children a day to be remembered, a day of rejoicing; they owe it that loyalty shall be avowed, when it is not disgraceful or servile. We heard remonstrances against transportation intimidated by imputations of treason. Our best, our noblest citizens have been so stigmatized by the enemies of the good cause...

The *Times* spoke of transportation and executions in a later editorial, saying that the frequently recurring executions both in Hobart and Launceston proved that, although small offences decreased, the character of the population was degraded. Many thousands still assembled at the scaffold to see the sight, with as little feeling as spectators at a cattle show. If the question of abolition of punishment by death had ever been put to the mob, the paper doubted if they would have answered in the affirmative. They would have liked to have the exhibition made a little more ostentatious, with the hero of the piece allowed more time to deliver his 'last dying speech'. When the penalty was almost abolished elsewhere, the colony of Van Diemens Land was still able to show the last agonies of the guilty to the admiring population. All the same, every effort to hasten the removal of every relic of the convict system was urged to take place immediately.

One excellent result of the cessation of transportation was the decision to pull down the gallows at Launceston. Facing the river, the first object which met the stranger's eye was the permanent gallows, which was a substantial affair built up with bricks and stone, with a huge beam securely let into the walls. It had been designed for any amount of service.

The children at Launceston were given a holiday in celebration of the wonderful news of the cessation, while a meeting of the 'native born' to consider a coming demonstration took place in July in the Temperance Hall. August 10 was to be a public holiday for the Jubilee celebrating the foundation of the colony and in commemoration of the cessation of transportation.

In Hobart Town the Governor, Sir William Denison, had refused to declare this special day a general holiday, but the citizens took the matter into their own hands. All places of business, including the banks, closed, no ships landed goods, while the church bells rang at break of day, and then at a later hour to summon Christians to church to thank God for rescuing the colony from degradation.

Services were held at St David's, at the Free Church, at the Independent Chapel in Collins Street, and at the Baptist Chapel. The children went at one o'clock to the New Wharf 'to partake of the ample refreshments provided for them', the day closing with a splendid display of fireworks on the Domain. No newspaper was issued on 10 August.

The account of the demonstration was reported in the *Times* on the day following. Such an event could not be glossed over in a few terse words, but had to be savoured, with a suitable prologue leading up to the great, never-to-be-forgotten day. This is a sample:

A thick fog partially enveloped the city — Aurora was roused from her lengthened slumbers by the pealing of Trinity Bells, but as the morning advanced, it climbed up the rocky steeps of Mount Wellington, and speedily concealed itself at the behest of the great monarch of the day. And then what a lovely prospect was presented! The sun shone in its full strength — the very clouds had taken a holiday, for not one was visible. The bosom of the placid Derwent reflected back the unsullied azure of the heavens, and boats glided gracefully across its surface, leaving lines of glittering silver behind. Nearly all the shops were closed, and many of those that were open are accessible more than six days in the week. The ships were decorated with colours, and flags were flying from several private residences. In fact, business was suspended; and in the early part of the morning, the quiet of the Sabbath prevailed. Numberless groups with happy faces wended their way to the Store lent by Isaac Wright Esq., for the entertainment of the young folks; and at about half-past ten the arrival of the monster 'Demonstration Cake' was greeted with three tremendous huzzas. At noon several rounds were fired from the vessels in harbour.

A public thanksgiving was then held. The celebrations concluded with a display of fireworks in the open space fronting the High School in the presence of thousands of inhabitants. At the same time bonfires announced to all the country around that convictism was dead, 'and that the loyal and respectable portion of the Colonists were rejoicing that their beloved Queen had spoken the word of liberation which again binds the Colony to her throne'. The only mourner was Sir William Denison, described as 'the mis-representative of his Sovereign's feelings'. He had issued a circular the previous day, ordering all Government officers and clerks not to be seen out of their offices on the day of triumph.

At Launceston, at the close of an oration delivered in St John's

Square by the Speaker of the Legislative Assembly, an anthem was sung by the people to the tune of 'God Save the Queen':

Sing! for the hour is come!
Sing! for our happy home!
Our land is free!
Broken Tasmania's chain,
Wash'd out the hated stain;
Ended the strife and pain!
Blest Jubilee!

Sons of Tasmania, sing!
Daughters, sweet garlands bring;
All joyful be!
Raise, raise our banner high;
Star of the Southern sky!
Banner of Victory!
Cross of the Free!

God bless our Fatherland!
God bless our patriot band!
Staunch have they been.
Truth has confounded spite,
Justice has conquered might;
Heav'n has maintain'd the right,
God Save the Queen!

Back in Hobart Town, a Jubilee Ball was held in a large room, again lent by Isaac Wright, while at Richmond the rejoicings went on for three days. At New Norfolk, it was due to the 'personal exertions' of Mr Richard Thompson of the Union Inn that the rejoicing went off so well, as he provided the buns, biscuits, beer, and other dainties, as well as the wood for the bonfire.

After existing in such a state of euphoria for several days, the people must have come down to earth again with quite a bump. When the celebrations finally ceased they would have found that conditions had changed very little, although now there was hope for a happy future, instead of frustration and despair. All the same, their immediate surroundings remained as they had been before the Jubilee — the scotch thistles were spreading even further in the rural districts, the town creek was still offensive, and petty bickerings had not ceased.

Earlier in the year it had been reported that the aldermen had voted the mayor a salary of £600 per annum, which if true, meant that the 'enormous sum of £1300' was swallowed up in paying the salaries of three officers! It was hoped, however, that as one of the aldermen had declared himself opposed to taxation, that perhaps the amount would be made up among themselves. As well, the Corporation and aldermen were not popular with the press as they tried to exclude reporters from their meetings. Various reports of their intentions listed the rumour that they intended to apply for convict labour to carry out the city works.

Another movement gaining ground was for the confederation of the colonies, which, according to the *Times*, was a fact which had to be accepted whatever might have been the objections against it. This was a prophetic statement, but it belonged to the new era — held in abeyance for a future date.

At that particular time the colony was in a 'transition state', just emerging from 'bondage to freedom'; but an announcement which put the final seal on its new status was given in the *Mercury*, on 21 December 1855: 'Young Tasmania has just purchased a New Constitution, and our Gracious Queen has legalized our more euphonious name, TASMANIA.'

The people who lived in those early times and participated in the great struggle have long passed away, but in keeping with their period, it is fitting to remember the sentiments of an unknown philosopher whose words were quoted in the *Colonial Times* in 1841: 'In a single century four thousand millions of human beings appear on the face of the earth, act their busy parts, and sink into its peaceful bosom.'

Bibliography

Burn, D. *A Picture of Van Diemen's Land*. (A facsimile of a work published in the *Colonial Magazine* 1840–41.)

'The Captain' (Ford, T. G.) *The History of Van Diemen's Land*.

Melville, H. *The History of Van Diemen's Land*.

Von Stieglitz, K. *The Pioneer Church in Van Diemen's Land*.

West, J. *The History of Tasmania*, vol. 1.

NEWSPAPERS
(From the collection in the Archives Office of Tasmania)

Colonial Times (1825–46).

Colonial Times incorporating *The Tasmanian* (1847, 1849, 1853, 1855).

Cornwall Chronicle (1836–37).

Guardian or *True Friend of Tasmania* (1847).

Hobart Guardian (later incorporating the *Mercury*) (1854).

Hobarton Guardian or *True Friend of Tasmania* (1854).

Hobarton Mercury (1854–55).

Hobart Town Advertiser (1847).

Hobart Town Courier (1827–28, 1833, 1846–53).

Hobart Town Courier and Van Diemen's Land Gazette (1843–44).

Hobart Town Gazette (1816–33, 1853).

Hobart Town Gazette and Southern Reporter (1819).

Hobart Town Gazette and Van Diemen's Land Advertiser (1825).

Irish Exile and Freedom's Advocate (1851).

Launceston Examiner (1842).

True Colonist (1836, 1844).

Index

Aborigines, 2, 49–58, 59, 174, 177, 199
—*named:* Black Tom, 50–1; Dempsy, Mary, 50; Derwent, William Thomas, 50; Dick, 70; Jack, 70, 177; Mary Ann, 57–8; Musquito, 50; Timmy, 177; Truganini, 58
Absentee landlords, 3
Adelaide, 67, 88, 100, 112, 116
Adelaide, Queen, 156
Adventure Bay, 1
Agriculture, 105–10, 115–22, 179–84
Albert, Prince, 192
Allenvale, 50
Alumy Creek, 138
Animals, 115–22
Anson, Lord George, 12
Antill Ponds, 43
Argyle Street, 102, 116, 138, 141, 182
Arnold, Mr, 168
Arthur: *see* Governors
Arthur Jetty, 15
Auckland, 90
Austin's Ferry, 60

Bagdad, 64, 111
Baker, Mr, 141
Bakers, 96–7

Barclay and Kershaw, 5
Barnes Bay, 144
Barrack Street, 183
Bass Strait, 56, 107, 144
Bateman, Mr, 60
Bathurst Street, 19, 103, 128, 178
Batman, John, 51
Battery Point, 42, 48, 131, 143, 147, 151, 152, 154
Bedford, Dr, 129
Bedford, Rev. William, 79, 140, 160
Bedry, Mr, 172
Ben Lomond, 51
Bent, Andrew, 187, 188
Benwell, Charles, 75
Benwell, Eliza, 74
Berriedale, 155
Bicheno, Mr, 36
Big River, 180
Black Brush, 66
Black Snake, 110, 135, 136, 143
Black War, 50–5
Blackwood, Captain, 173
Bligh, Captain William, 1
Blood sports, 157–8
Blue Hills, 117
Bluff, The, 135

212

Blundell family, 12
Bock, Mr, 9
Bostock's store, 130
Bothwell, 91
Bournbank, 120
Bowen, Lt John, 1
Boxing, 157–8
Brady, Matthew, 60, 61
Bread, Annie, 195
Brickfields, 83, 140
'Bricks' gang, 140
Bridges, 134–40
Bridgewater, 126, 136, 137, 138, 144
Brighton, 66
Brisbane Street, 76, 99, 138, 166
Broadmarsh, 64
Brock, Dr, 129
Brodribb, Mr, 182
Brothels, 103–4
Broughton, Mr, 71, 103
Brown, Rev. Dr, 70
Brown, Thomas, 177
Brown's River, 131, 158
Bruni Island, 145
Bryan, Robert, 191
Buenos Aires, 87
Burton, Mr, 104
Bushrangers, 2, 14, 17, 24, 26, 43, 59–67, 68, 71, 160
—named: Armitage, 63; Beard, 63; Bird, 62; Brady, 60, 61; Britton, 62, 66; Bryant, 61; Cash (& Co.), 43, 64–6; Conway, 65; Dalton, 67; Dunne, 62; Fisher, 63; Hogan, 63; Howe, 60; Jacky Jacky, 67; Jeffries, 61; Jeffs, 65; Jones, 64–6; Kavanagh, 64–6; Kelly, 67; McCabe, 60–1; Perry, 61; Platt, 66; Priest, 67; Smith, 67; Thomson, 61; Tilly, 62; Westwood, 63
Butchers, 96–7
Butler's Paddock, 104, 169
Byron, Admiral John, 12

California, 20, 93, 94, 111–13, 146, 147, 153

Cameron, Mr & Mrs, 171
Campbell, Isabella, 89
Campbell Street, 33, 167, 174, 177, 183
Campbell Town, 63, 91, 167, 177, 206
Canada, 34, 89, 90
Cannibalism, 71
Cape Colony, 91, 190
Cape Grim, 56
Capon, Mr, 65
Carroll, Sir William, 30
Cascade brewery, 102
Cascade Road, 130
Cascades, 102, 110, 183
Cash & Co., 43, 64–6
Cattle, 22, 116–17
Cawthorne, Mr, 64, 110
Champion, Mr, 100
Chandler, Mr, 185
Chelsea Pensioners, 86, 89
Chester, Mrs, 172
Chisholm, Mrs, 88
Churches: Baptist, 162, 208; Catholic, 163, 164; Church of England, 15, 20, 27, 38, 70, 75, 79, 80, 152, 160–5, 169, 208; Congregational, 208; Free, 208; Independent, 208; Methodist, 164, 166; Presbyterian, 163, 165, 178; Wesleyan, 164, 166
—St Andrew's, 163; St David's, 15, 27, 38, 88, 147, 162, 163, 208; St Matthew's, 99; St Paul's, 164; Trinity, 153, 163, 208
Clarence Plains, 150, 183
Clarke's Island, 147
Clergy, 10, 11, 15, 20, 70, 75, 79, 140, 152, 160–5, 167, 169
Clinch, Captain, 111
Clyde, River, 65, 151
Coach Act, 141
Coal, 7, 110
Coal River, 63, 108, 110, 120
Cocked Hat Hill, 141
Collins: see Governors
Collins Street, 5, 96, 102, 109, 116, 138, 208
Concerts, 170–5
Constitution Dock, 111

Convicts, 13–25; church parades, 15; escaped, 13, 14, 15, 19, 20, 46, 47, 49, 62, 67, 71, 72, 90, 147; female, 7, 78–84; numbers, 1, 7, 16
—*named:* 'Boxer', 18; Broughton, 71; Greenwood, 46–7, 72; Macavoy, 71
Cook, Captain James, 1
Cook, Mr, 64
Cornelian Bay, 66
Cove Point, 135
Cox, J. E., 141
Crayfish Point, 143
Cricket, 156, 158, 173
Crime and punishment, 13–25, 59–67, 68–77; drunkenness, 16, 21, 22, 102–3, 171; executions, 63, 66, 67, 68–77, 202, 207; fines, 8, 22; flogging, 2, 14, 16, 20, 24, 46–7, 71, 72; sheep-stealing, 3, 4, 22, 69, 91, 202
Crooke, Dr, 185
Crooked Billet, 138
Cross Marsh, 202
Crowder, E., 135
Curramore, 110
Custance, Mr, 204
Cygnet, 114

Darlington, 90
Davey: *see* Governors
Davey Street, 102, 137, 167
Davis, Mr, 176
Deane, Mr, 171
Dee, River, 56, 65
Deep Gully, 15
Defence, 24–5
Degraves, Mr, 120, 132, 133
Delamere, 121
Denison, Lady, 38
Denison, Sir William: *see* Governors
D'Entrecasteaux Channel, 57
Derwent, River, 60, 110, 135, 136, 142, 143, 144, 147, 148, 150, 151, 157, 183, 208
Derwent, William Thomas, 50
Dickens, Charles, 192–3
Disease, 123–30

Doctors, 11, 20, 123–30
Dog Act, 119
Dogs, 118–19, 129, 163, 173
Domain, 116, 137, 139, 156, 157, 173, 178, 208
Drunkenness, 16, 21, 22, 102–3, 171
Dry, Mr, 60
Duelling, 158
Dunkley's Point, 154
Duterrau, Mr, 177
Dynnyrne, 183

Eardley-Wilmot: *see* Governors
Eastern Tiers, 62
Ecclestone, James, 168
Education, 162, 164, 165–9
Education Act, 168
Edwards, Ann, 71
Elizabeth Street, 33, 70, 96, 99, 104, 137, 141, 156, 172, 188, 194, 204
Elliott, Colonel, 173
Elliston, Mr, 112
Emmett, Mr, 47
Escaped convicts, 13, 14, 15, 19, 20, 46, 47, 49, 62, 67, 71, 72, 90, 147
Esdaile, D. C., 89
Esk, River, 62

Fagan, Mr, 71
Farming, 105–10, 115–22, 179–84
Fauna, 115–22
Female Factory, 78–84
Fenton, Captain, 87
Fergusson, Joshua, 102, 107
Ferrari, Signor, 9
Ferries, 134–40
Fingal, 67, 113, 114, 177
Fishing, 149–50
Fitzhardinge, F., 46
Flannagan, Mr, 164
Flinders Island, 34, 47, 56, 146
Flogging, 2, 14, 16, 20, 24, 46–7, 71, 72
Forster, Captain, 140
Forth, Captain, 138
Forth, River, 90
Franklin, Lady Jane, 33–5, 83, 153, 167
Franklin, Sir John: *see* Governors

French, 1, 145–6
Furneaux, Captain Tobias, 1

Garrard, Rev., 161
Gatehouse, G., 102
George IV, King, 190, 202
George Town, 45, 61, 63, 99, 121
Germans, 88, 174, 175
Gilbert, Mr, 9
Gladstone, William Ewart, 36, 37
Glenorchy, 110, 111, 155, 158
Gold, 111–14
Goose Island, 145
Gorringe, T., 102
Goulburn Street, 104
Government Cottage, 28, 153
Government garden, New Town, 44–5, 111
Government House, 24, 33, 34, 36, 38, 104, 116, 119, 133, 138, 150, 151, 153
Governors, 26–40
—Collins, Colonel David, Lieutenant-Governor 1804–10, 26
—Davey, Colonel Thomas, Lieutenant-Governor 1813–17, 26, 27
—Sorell, Colonel William, Lieutenant-Governor 1817–24, 3, 27, 28
—Arthur, Colonel George, Lieutenant-Governor 1824–36, 6, 14, 27–32, 33, 34, 45, 50–5, 79, 80, 81, 98, 151, 161, 180, 181, 187, 190
—Franklin, Sir John, Lieutenant-Governor 1837–43, 32–6, 38, 56, 64, 132, 133, 152, 153, 163, 167, 173
—Eardley-Wilmot, Sir John Eardley, Baronet, Lieutenant-Governor 1843–46, 23, 36–8, 43, 150, 153, 204
—La Trobe, Charles Joseph, Administrator 1846–47, 38
—Denison, Sir William Thomas, Lieutenant-Governor 1847–55, 38–40, 90, 91, 92, 93, 99, 136, 168, 174, 207, 208
—Young, Sir Henry Edward Fox, Governor-in-Chief 1855–61, 40
Grant, James, 113
Grass Tree Hill, 184

Green Point, 64
Green Ponds, 60, 66, 102, 180
Greenwood, Joseph, 46–7, 72
Gregory, Mrs, 166
Gregson, Mr, 157
Grey, Earl, 39, 206
Guillem, Samuel, 73
Gunning, G. W., 120

Haig, Captain, 112
Halfway House, 110
Hamilton, 138
Harrington Street, 133, 137, 164, 183
Hawke, Admiral Sir Edward, 12
Hayes, Mary, 194
Haynes, Mr, 144
Hedgberg, Mr, 185
Hedger, Mr, 96
Henslowe, Mr, 177
High Plains, 180
Hill, Lieutenant, 151
Hiring Act, 84
Holy Trinity Church, 153, 163, 208
Hood, Mr, 185
Horne, Judge, 76
Horses, 117–18, 139, 154–6
Horticulture, 105–10
Hospitals, 123–30
Hotels, 171, 172
—named: Berriedale Inn, 155; Britannia, 102; Bush, 94, 153; Cornish Mount, 18; Dallas Arms, 190; Derwent, 194; Freemasons, 94; Golden Lion, 76; Old Commodore, 76; Royal Oak, 202; Ship Inn, 23, 129, 141; Star and Garter, 76; Travellers Rest, 63, 158; Turf, 76; Union Inn, 209; Woolpack Inn, 64
Howe, George Terry, 100, 189
Howe, Michael, 60
Hunter's Island, 27
Huon River, 35
Hutchins School, 168
Hyrons, Ben, 141

Imberg, Herr, 174
Impounding Act, 22, 98

Impression Bay, 75
India, 3, 87, 95, 109, 117, 142, 143, 192
Irish exiles, 39, 89–95
Iron Pot light, 145
Irvine, Captain, 148
Isis, River, 66

Jarvis, William, 73
Jeffrey, Mr, 120
Jemmy the Rover, 83
Jericho, 63, 154
Jerusalem, 32, 65, 138
Jewish community, 163, 164

Kangaroo Bottom, 35
Kangaroo Point, 4, 135, 143, 144, 149, 151, 154
Kangaroos, 119, 157
Kelly, James, 147
Kelly Street murder, 75
Kemp, Mr, 182
Kensington, 163
Kent Islands, 145
Kermode, Mr, 50
Kershaw, Mr, 5
Killymoon, 177
King, Mr, 56
King George's Sound, 25
King's Grammar School, 166
Kirkby, Mr, 98
Knopwood, Rev. Robert, 160, 163, 194

Lachlan River, 132, 139
Lagoon Bay, 36
Lake Plains, 11
Lake River, 66
Lake Sorell, 63
Lamb, Captain, 117
Lambe, Mr, 73
Land grants, 1, 2, 3
Language, 2, 11, 160, 195
La Pérouse, Jean-Francois de, 181
Lascelles, T. A., 47
La Trobe, Charles Joseph, 38
Lauderdale, 120
Launceston, 7, 24, 25, 30, 35, 38, 41, 42,

43, 44, 45, 53, 61, 62, 65, 67, 70, 75, 76, 90, 92, 93, 94, 98, 107, 113, 117, 129, 138, 141, 149, 154, 155, 156, 157, 174, 176, 184, 190, 191, 204, 205, 208
Laurenny, 60
Lee, Mr, 173
Lemprière, General, 91
Lightfoot, Theophilus, 101
Lighthouses, 145
Lipscombe, Mr, 109
Liverpool Street, 18, 98, 100, 102, 116, 119, 137
Loane, R. W., 101
Loftus, Mr, 25
Longford, 104, 155
Lord, Edward, 60
Low Head, 145
Lyons, Mr, 73, 158

MacDougall, John Campbell, 191
MacKay/McKay/M'Kay, Mr, 65, 73, 172
Mackenzie, William Lyon, 90
MacLachlan, Mary, 70–1
Macquarie District, 50; Harbour, 13, 14, 35, 71, 111, 138; Plains, 64; River, 3, 55, 115, 194
Macquarie Street, 5, 92, 99, 101, 131, 132, 133, 137, 163, 168, 177, 184, 186, 193
Mail, 41–4, 65, 141
Malays, 87
Maoris, 90
Maria Island, 13, 90, 91
Marlborough, 114
Martin, Mr, 91, 94, 104, 141
Mason, Thomas, 23, 45–8, 72
Mather, Mr, 119
Mc Manus, Pellew, 90–4
Meagher, T. M., 90–1
Mechanics Institute, 57, 169, 175–6, 177, 204, 205
Melbourne, 94, 111, 156
Melville, Henry, 46, 190–1
Melville Street, 100, 141

Meredith, Mr, 60
Military establishment, 2, 6, 23, 24, 25, 35, 38
—regiments: 21st, 24, 152; 39th, 136; 40th, 170; 51st, 109, 183; 63rd, 23, 71, 151; 96th, 24, 35, 116; 99th, 25, 38
Millbank, 78
Milligan, Dr J., 174
Mills, Mary Ann, 73
Mister Muster Master Mason, 23, 45–8, 72
Mitchell, John, 91, 94
Montagu, Algernon, 19, 204
Montagu, John, 29, 131
Moore, John, 92
Morton, Constable, 66
Mount Direction, 120
Mount Dromedary, 64
Mount Nelson, 183
Mount Wellington, 4, 113, 132, 182, 208
Muddy Plains, 120, 157
Munday, Mr, 176
Munro, Duncan, 89
Murdoch, Dr, 124
Murray, Lathrop, 188
Murray Street, 5, 76, 101, 133, 138, 139, 140, 141, 147
Muster, 14, 17, 23, 45–6
Muster Day, 14

Naire, Mr, 90
Nairn, Captain, 27
Newland, Mr, 174
New Jetty, 48, 182
New Norfolk, 7, 20, 22, 28, 33, 34, 43, 45, 47, 48, 50, 62, 73, 74, 76, 91, 92, 94, 99, 106, 110, 113, 119, 120, 126, 127, 129, 132, 136, 138, 139, 140, 141, 143, 144, 147, 149, 153, 155, 162, 164, 166, 167, 176, 181, 183, 203, 205, 209
Newspaper Act, 188
Newspapers and journals, 187–200
—Australian, 188
—Colonial Advocate, 188

—Colonial Times, 6, 7, 8, 9, 10, 13, 14, 20, 22, 23, 25, 28, 29, 30, 31, 33, 34, 36, 37, 39, 41, 42, 44, 45, 46, 47, 51, 52, 53, 57, 62, 63, 64, 66, 72, 73, 77, 79, 85, 88, 94, 96, 103, 108, 113, 118, 119, 126, 127, 133, 138, 139, 140, 143, 147, 149, 151, 154, 156, 158, 162, 164, 166, 167, 170, 175, 180, 184, 187–92, 195, 196, 202, 203, 206, 210
—Colonist, 190
—Cornwall Chronicle, 32, 73, 113, 191, 194, 199
—Cornwall Press, 190
—Derwent Star, 187
—Government Gazette, 14, 30, 77, 92, 94
—Government Gazette (NSW), 93
—Hobarton Mercury, 39, 40, 58, 67, 94, 140, 191, 210
—Hobart Town Advertiser, 113, 185, 191
—Hobart Town Anniversary, 190
—Hobart Town Courier, 11, 19, 30, 37, 39, 48, 91, 112, 135, 144, 148, 150, 153, 168, 174, 177, 184, 190, 191, 195, 204
—Hobart Town Gazette, 2, 4, 8, 14, 20, 26, 28, 41, 49, 50, 51, 60, 85, 99, 102, 105, 117, 120, 130, 135, 157, 160, 165, 180, 187–9, 191, 196, 197, 201, 203
—Hobart Town Guardian, 12, 56, 76, 89, 93, 94, 164, 168, 191
—Irish Exile and Freedom's Advocate, 92, 93, 158, 191
—Launceston Advertiser, 191
—Launceston Courier, 90, 157
—Launceston Examiner, 109, 111, 123, 154, 169, 191
—Morning Herald, 203
—Southern Reporter, 188
—Spectator, 37
—Sydney Herald, 90
—Tasmanian, 188, 190, 191
—Tasmanian Weekly Despatch, 74, 191
—Tribune, 191

— *True Friend of Tasmania*, 191
— *Trumpeter*, 11, 191
— *Van Diemen's Land Advertiser*, 189
— *Van Diemen's Land Intelligencer*, 187
— *Weekly Advertiser*, 191
New Town, 4, 18, 44, 45, 46, 89, 102, 103, 106, 111, 155, 156
New Town Road, 9, 109
New Wharf, 33, 138, 144, 147, 153, 208
New Zealand, 88, 90, 108, 113
Nixon, Bishop Francis Russell, 164
Norfolk Island, 1, 17, 66
Norfolk Plains, 166

Oatlands, 62, 67, 74, 91, 164
O'Brien, W. Smith, 90–5
O'Brien's Rivulet, 137, 163, 183
O'Connor, Roderic, 66
O'Doherty, Mr, 91, 92, 94
O'Donohoe, Patrick, 90–4
Old Wharf, 15, 27, 99, 138
Ouse, River, 108
Oyster Bay, 60
Oyster Cove, 57, 174

Paddock Point, 156
Page, Sam, 141
Palmer, Mr, 89
Paupers, 85–8
Pavilion Point, 34
Peck, George, 171, 172
Pedder, Sir John, 38, 42, 69, 70, 73, 74, 190, 191
Pennyroyal Creek, 51
Perth, 42, 73
Perth (WA), 86
Pittwater, 51, 106, 161, 203
Platypus, 120
Plenty, River, 120, 193
Police Office, 7, 16, 17, 68, 119
Political prisoners, 89–95
Polyglot Academy, 9
Population, 1, 7, 16, 81, 85, 88
Port Arthur, 14, 17, 19, 30, 62, 63, 64, 66, 67, 74, 75, 91, 92, 93, 111
Port Dalrymple, 27, 107

Port Davey, 114
Portland Bay, 148
Port Phillip, 88, 89, 98, 116
Port Sorell, 55, 63
Postmaster-General, 43
Post Office, 2, 41–4
Poverty, 85–8
Proctor's quarry, 110
Prosser's Plains, 117
Prout, J. S., 174, 176, 177
Public executions, 63, 66, 67, 68–77, 202, 207
Public health, 123–33
Public service, 41–8, 208
Pudney, William, 100

Quebec, 90
Queenborough, 27

Rabbits, 122
Ralph's Bay, 149
Raven, Rev., 167
Raycroft, Mr, 120
Recherche Bay, 148
Regattas, 151–4, 172
Religion, 160–5 — *see also* Churches, Clergy
Richmond, 43, 62, 94, 110, 184, 209
Richmond Hill, 166
Rio de Janeiro, 19
Risdon Cove, 1, 26, 144
Roads, 134–41
Roberts, J. L., 102
Robinson, George Augustus, 55, 56
Rocky Cape, 56
Rodney, Lord George, 12
Roseneath, 121
Ross, 121, 137, 167
Ross, Dr James, 42, 175, 189
Rowe's Emporium, 138
Rowles, James, 70
Roxboro House, 204
Rush, Mr, 185
Russell, Lord John, 89
Russians, 25

Safety Cove, 111

St Andrew's, 163
St David's, 15, 27, 38, 88, 147, 162, 163, 208
St George's School, 169
St John's Square, 208
St Mary's Hospital, 129
St Mary's Pass, 177
St Matthew's, 99
St Paul's, 164
Sandy Bay, 90, 134, 138, 139, 149, 153, 154, 155, 157, 167
San Francisco, 93, 111, 146, 147
Sanitation, 123–33
Saunders, Eliza, 74
Schools, 164, 165–9
Scott, Dr James, 61, 128
Scott, Mr, 55
Scottish immigrants, 89
Sealers, 49
Sheep, 3, 4, 7, 22, 69, 91, 115, 202
Ships, 142–50
— named: Actaeon, 145; Amethyst, 19; Amphitrite, 149; Antipodes, 40; Barclay, 67; Boadicea, 82, 109; Bolivar, 142; Buffalo, 90; Calcutta, 146; Camilla, 148; Candia, 95; Castor, 90; Channing, 147; Cheviot, 148; Comet, 102; Creeping Jane, 153; Cressy, 36; Culloden, 57, 144; David Lyon, 14; Derwent, 144, 146, 147, 192; Deveron, 19; Duke of Richmond, 17; Eagle, 143; Earl Grey, 83; Edward Coulson, 81; Eliza, 29, 146; Elizabeth, 143; Elphonstone, 31; Emma, 94; Eudora, 36; Fairlee, 33; Fly, 173; Flying Fish, 111; George the Third, 145; Grecian, 190; Harbinger, 206; Henry, 67; Hope, 142; Imogene, 10; Kinnear, 147; Lady Bird, 94; Lady Denison, 90; Lady Montagu, 150; Lindsays, 87; Lotus, 162; Majestic, 82; Manlius, 143; Martha and Elizabeth, 148; Mary Ann, 40; Mary Sharp, 90; Monarch, 40, 144; Muffat, 47; Nancy, 143; Native Youth, 144; Neptune, 91; Newtons, 146; Ocean Queen, 88; Orleana, 87; Petrel, 146; Prince Leopold, 99; Prince of Denmark, 148; Princess Charlotte, 78; Providence, 78; Resolution, 1; Resource, 143; Roman, 19; Sally, 142; Sarah, 81; Sea Horse, 144; Shamrock, 153; Sir Allan McNab, 89; Sir Charles Forbes, 71; Spring, 41; Strathfieldsaye, 81; Success, 168; Surprise, 143; Swift, 90; Tamar, 14; Tasmania, 144, 145, 175; Thalia, 188; Thames, 87, 144, 153; Thomas, 153; Tybee, 143; Union, 19; Vansittart, 56; Victoria, 91; Waterlily, 18; Water Witch, 63, 90
— Russian warship at Launceston, 25
— Ships seized by convicts, 19, 20, 90, 147
Shipwrecks, 142, 145, 146
Shoobridge, Mr, 76, 106
Simpson, George, 51
Single Hill, 120
Smith, Mr, 9, 76
Snakes, 120–1, 129
Solomon, Judah, 100, 164
Sorell, Lake, 63; Port, 55, 63; River, 110; Town, 51, 60, 156
Sorell, William: see Governors
South Australia, 40, 67, 88, 100, 101, 112
Spring Bay, 111
Spring Hill, 65
Stafford, Constable, 89
Stage coaches, 140–1
Stocker, T. W., 194
Stoddart, Mr, 64
Stokell, Mr, 182
Stuart, Mr, 164
Stump, Mr, 204
Sudds, Joseph, 72
Sullivan, Mary, 76
Sullivan's Cove, 1, 26
Sunday schools, 162, 166
Sutton, 'Little Master', 46
Swan, Mr, 171
Swan Island, 145
Swan Port, 67
Swan River settlement, 86, 143
Sydney, 17, 18, 63, 69, 79, 88, 90, 93,

108, 142, 143, 145, 148, 162
Table Mountain, 51, 180
Tamar, River, 111, 149, 154
Tamar Bank, 7
Tasman, Abel, 1
Tasmania, name changed from Van Diemens Land, 107, 206, 210
Tasmanian tiger, 119–20
Tasmanian Turf Club, 156
Tasman's Stingo, 102
Taylor, Mrs, 171
Terry, Mr, 73, 99
Theatre, 171–5
Theatres: Argyle, 171–2; Pantheon, 174; Royal Albert, 177; Royal Victoria, 173, 174, 175; Theatre Royal, 171–2
Therry, Rev. John Joseph, 163
Thompson, Patrick, 72
Thompson, Richard, 209
Tibbs, Mr and Mrs, 61
Tinderbox Bay, 107
'Tom and Jerry' gang, 139–40
Tooth, Mr, 111
Tower Hill, 113
Town Crier, 48
Tradesmen, 96–104
Transportation, 13–25; agitation against, 19, 204, 205, 206; cessation, 19, 205–7; 'rattlesnake cargoes', 2; retransportation from NSW, 1, 17, 66, 204
Trinity Hill, 163
Truganini, 58
Tucker, Dan, 39
Tullochgorum, 177
Turnbull, Mr, 99
Turner, Mr, 157, 176
Turriff Lodge, 34

Uncle Tom's Cabin, 57
Usury, 6, 98

Van Diemen, Anthony, 1
Van Diemen, George, 49–50
Van Diemen's Land: name changed to Tasmania, 107, 206, 210; origin of

name, 1; separation from NSW, 201–2; settlement, 1–12
Veranda Stores, 100
Victoria, 25, 76, 88, 89, 94, 98, 111, 113, 116, 206
Victoria, Queen, 33, 34, 163, 176, 192, 206
Victoria Baths, 157
Victoria Theatre, 173, 174, 175
Vinegar Cottage, 102

Wages, 7
Walker, Mr, 99, 102, 109
Walker, Hookey, 43
Walters, John, 12
Wanstead Park, 117
Wapping, 116, 185
Warwick Street, 186
Watchorn's Emporium, 100
Water, 90, 124–6, 130–3, 161
Water Act, 132
Watson, Mr, 148
Webb, Mr, 101
Wellington Bridge, 131, 137, 185, 188
Wellington, Mount, 4, 113, 132, 182, 208
Westbury, 63, 111, 121, 169
Western Australia, 86, 143
Weston, Dr, 129
Whaling and whalers, 7, 19, 23, 54, 103, 142, 145–50, 154
William IV, King, 192, 202, 203
Williams, Mr, 76, 158
Willis, Mr, 117
Wilmot, Judge, 48
Wilmot, Sir Eardley: see Governors
Wilson, Mr, 73, 96
Winstanley, Peter, 65
Wise, Mr, 100, 157
Woodcutters Hill, 67
Worster, Timothy, 149
Wrest Point, 90
Wright, Isaac, 208, 209

York Plains, 117
Young, Miss, 173, 174
Young, Sir Henry: see Governors